Indonesian Polit

NORDIC INSTITUTE OF ASIAN STUDIES
Studies in Contemporary Asian History
(series editor: Robert Cribb, Australian National University)

Stefan Eklöf
Indonesian Politics in Crisis

Sukardi Rinakit
The Indonesian Military after the New Order

Stefan Eklöf
Power and Political Culture in Suharto's Indonesia

Duncan McCargo and Ukrist Pathmanand
The Thaksinization of Thailand

INDONESIAN POLITICS IN CRISIS

The Long Fall of Suharto 1996–98

Stefan Eklöf

Nordic Institute of Asian Studies
Studies in Contemporary Asian History, no. 1

First published 1999
Reprinted in 2004 by NIAS Press
Nordic Institute of Asian Studies (NIAS)
Leifsgade 33, 2300 Copenhagen S, Denmark
Tel: (+45) 3532 9501• Fax: (+45) 3532 9549
E-mail: books@nias.ku.dk
Online: http://www.niaspress.dk

Typesetting by the Nordic Institute of Asian Studies
Printed and bound in Great Britain
Production by Bookchase

© Stefan Eklöf 1999

British Library Catalogue in Publication Data
Eklof, Stefan
　　Indonesian politics in crisis
　　1.Indonesia - Politics and government - 1966-
　　2.Indonesia - Economic conditions - 1945-
　　I.Title
　　959.8'039

ISBN 87–87062–69–0 (paperback)

Contents

Preface	vii
Acknowledgements	viii
Note on Spelling and Translation	ix
List of Abbreviations and Acronyms	x
Map of Indonesia and environs	xii
1 Suharto's New Order	1
2 Dealing with the Opposition	23
3 Riots and Conspiracies	50
4 A Festival of Democracy?	75
5 Economic Crisis	96
6 Towards a Seventh Term for Suharto	122
7 Student Opposition and Regime Repression	154
8 The End of Suharto	175
9 Conclusion	220
Bibliography	238
Index	261

Preface

In July 1996 the international news magazine *Asiaweek* dubbed Indonesia's President Suharto the most powerful man in Asia.[1] After having ruled his country for three decades, the president indeed seemed all-powerful and his authority virtually unchallengeable. He had six times been unanimously elected president and he presided over a political system which had repeatedly proven its capacity to suppress or sideline any challenges to his leadership. As the 'Father of Development' he had led Indonesia in an unsurpassed economic success story that in less than a generation lifted the country from an economic basket case to an aspiring newly industrialising economy.

Two years later, in the first months of 1998, it seemed that all the achievements of the previous three decades lay in ruins. Economic crisis had struck much of Asia and Indonesia was the country worst hit. Observers increasingly saw Suharto himself as at the heart of the problem. As the effects of the crisis began to be felt by millions of Indonesians in the forms of unemployment and food shortages, social tensions and unrest escalated and exploded in large-scale violent riots around the country. In the universities, students demonstrated for political reform and burnt effigies of the president. Eventually, on 21 May 1998, President Suharto was forced to resign, putting an end to his reign as Asia's longest serving leader.

This book sets out to explore the two-year political crisis in Indonesia which led to the fall of Suharto. His fall was precipitated by the economic crisis and the dynamics of international market mechanisms. However, the Asian economic crisis was not the beginning of the story. Economic collapse provided the

---

1. *Asiaweek* (5 July 1996).

impetus for the political crisis to evolve in full, but Indonesia was already in the midst of a political legitimacy crisis when the economic crisis struck in mid-1997. This political crisis, its background and development, is the theme for this book.

Acknowledgements

Research for this book was carried out in Indonesia, mainly Jakarta, on four separate occasions, in March 1997, September–October 1997, June 1998 and September–December 1998. In addition, library research was undertaken in Leiden in July 1998 and in Canberra in September 1998. The research trips were made possible through generous grants from the Bokelund Geographic Fund, the Swedish Institute, the Craaford Foundation and the Centre for East and Southeast Asian Studies at Lund University, for all of which I am most indebted.

In Indonesia, my greatest gratitude is to all the people who took the time and patience, both in formal interviews and in informal discussions, to explain to me the intricacies and workings of Indonesian politics in the late Suharto era. A list of all these people would be too extensive to include here, but I want to mention my special gratitude to Purwani Diyah Prabandari. I am also grateful to the Centre for Strategic and International Studies (CSIS) in Jakarta, for helping me in my work and for providing a stimulating intellectual environment during my most recent stay in Jakarta. Special thanks go to Clara Joewono, J. Kristiadi, Tommy Legowo and Marcellianus Djadijono at the CSIS.

My single greatest gratitude is to the series editor (and my assistant thesis supervisor) Professor Robert Cribb, who has put great effort and patience into reading and commenting on the drafts at various stages of the writing process. His well-informed suggestions and analytical sharpness have contributed immensely to the shape of the present text. In addition, I wish to thank my thesis supervisor Professor Eva Österberg for reading and commenting on the text, as well as my wife, Anna-Karin Eklöf, both for her comments and suggestions and for her support throughout the entire research process. Any mistakes or shortcomings in the text, however, are entirely my own responsibility.

Note on Spelling and Translation

In 1947, the official Indonesian spelling conventions were changed so that 'u' replaced 'oe', and in 1972 further changes were made so that 'c' replaced the former 'tj', 'j' replaced 'dj', 'kh' replaced 'ch' and 'y' replaced 'j'. However, many people continued to use the old, unofficial spelling of their names, causing two (or sometimes more) spellings of their names to be used. For the sake of simplicity, the new official spelling convention has been consequently employed throughout the text, except for the replacement of 'kh' in the place of 'ch', since this has been the least respected and least widely used of the spelling changes. In cases where the old spelling differs from the new and the old spelling is still in frequent use, the latter will be given in square brackets the first time a name is mentioned in the text. The original spellings have been retained in citations and in the bibliographical information.

All translations from Indonesian are, unless otherwise stated, by the author.

List of Abbreviations and Acronyms

ABRI	*Angkatan Bersenjata Republik Indonesia* (Armed Forces of the Republic of Indonesia)
ASEAN	Association of Southeast Asian Nations
CSIS	Centre for Strategic and International Studies
Forkot	*Forum Komunikasi Mahasiswa se-Jabotabek* (Greater Jakarta Students' Communication Forum)
GDP	Gross Domestic Product
Golkar	*Golongan Karya* (Functional Groups)
Golput	*Golongan Putih* (White Group)
ICMI	*Ikatan Cendekiawan Muslim se-Indonesia* (Association of Indonesian Muslim Intellectuals)
ILO	International Labour Organisation
IMF	International Monetary Fund
IPTN	*Industri Pesawat Terbang Nusantara* (Aircraft Industry of the Indonesian Archipelago)
Kadin	*Kamar Dagang dan Industri* (Indonesian Chamber of Commerce and Industry)
KISDI	*Komite Indonesia untuk Solidaritas Dunia Islam* (Indonesian Committee for Solidarity with the Islamic World)
KKN	*Korupsi, Kolusi dan Nepotisme* (Corruption, Collusion and Nepotism)
Kodim	*Komando Distrik Militer* (Military District Command)
Komnas HAM	*Komite Nasional Hak Asasi Manusia* (National Commission for Human Rights)
Kontras	*Komisi untuk Orang Hilang dan Tindak Kekerasan* (Commission for the Disappeared and Victims of Violence)

Kopassus	*Komando Pasukan Khusus* (Special Forces Command)
Kostrad	*Komando Strategis Angkatan Darat* (Army's Strategic Reserve)
LIPI	*Lembaga Ilmu Pengetahuan Indonesia* (Indonesian Academy of Sciences)
MARI	*Majelis Rakyat Indonesia* (Indonesian People's Assembly)
MPR	*Majelis Permusyawaratan Rakyat* (People's Consultative Assembly)
NGO	Non-Government Organisation
NU	*Nahdlatul Ulama* (Rise of the Islamic Scholars)
PDI	*Partai Demokrasi Indonesia* (Indonesian Democratic Party)
PKI	*Partai Komunis Indonesia* (Indonesian Communist Party)
PPP	*Partai Persatuan Pembangunan* (United Development Party)
PRD	*Partai Rakyat Demokrat* (Democratic People's Party)
SIAGA	*Solidaritas Indonesia untuk Amien dan Mega* (Indonesian Solidarity for Amien and Mega)
SMID	*Solidaritas Mahasiswa Indonesia untuk Demokrasi* (Indonesian Students' Solidarity for Democracy)
TGPF	*Tim Gabungan Pencari Fakta* (Joint Fact-Finding Team)
TRuK	*Tim Relawan untuk Kemanusian* (Volunteers for Humanity)
TVRI	*Televisi Republik Indonesia* (Television of the Republic of Indonesia)
UI	*Universitas Indonesia* (University of Indonesia)

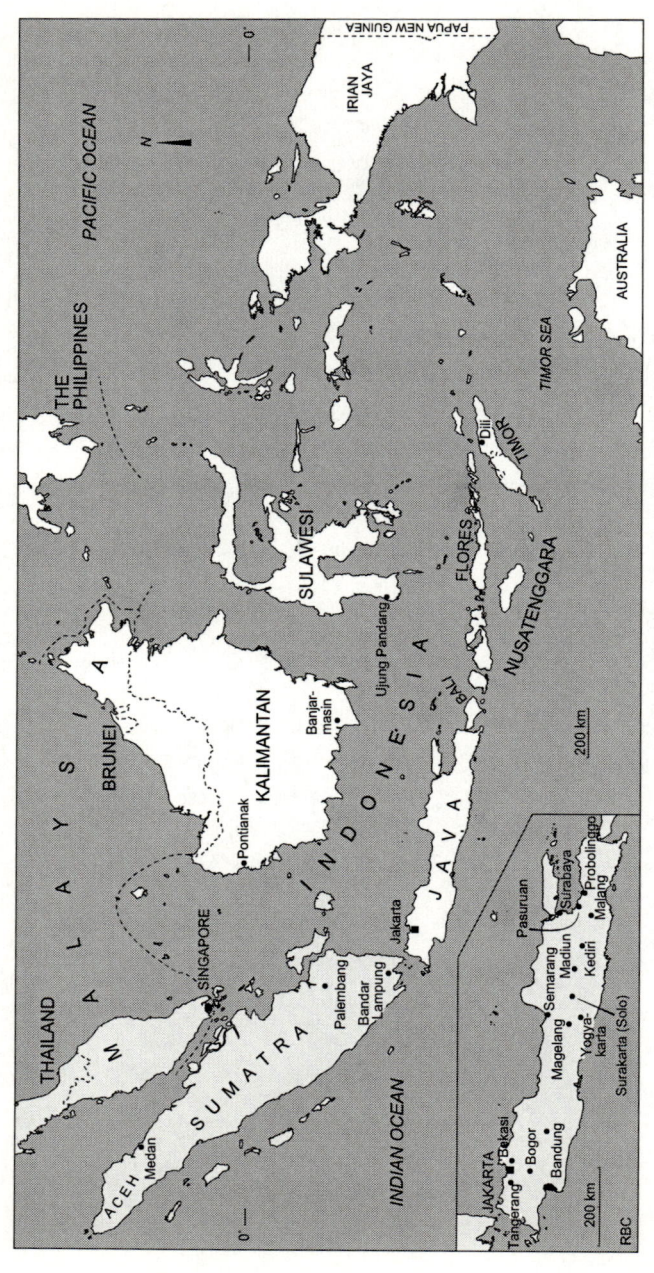

Indonesia and environs (© Robert Cribb 1999)

CHAPTER 1

Suharto's New Order

With over 200 million people, Indonesia is the world's fourth most populous country, and one of the most diverse in terms of human and natural geography. Hundreds of different ethnic groups are spread around the archipelago, each with its own history and traditions, and most with their own language as well. Islam is the religion of close to 90 per cent of the population, but Protestantism, Catholicism, Hinduism and Buddhism are also official religions, each counting millions of followers.

Throughout the twentieth century this diversity has given rise to a wide range of political aspirations, often providing challenges and threats to the central government. Consequently, since Indonesia proclaimed independence in 1945, maintaining the national unity has been one of the main preoccupations of the central government. In this respect, President Suharto [Soeharto] and his so-called New Order regime was very successful for most of more than three decades in power, and few serious threats to the regime emerged. Invoking the need to maintain national unity and stability, the regime circumscribed or repressed all political activity that was not approved by the government, a policy which largely managed to keep sectarian and separatist aspirations at bay.

Up to mid-1997, the regime was also successful in engineering economic growth and development which brought about increased standards of living for the majority of the Indonesian people, as well as extensive and sometimes traumatic social change. As these unprecedented developments occurred, however, the regime did not envision any fundamental political change for the country. Instead the regime continued to rely on its ruling formula of combining authoritarian controls and repression with a degree of popular legitimacy mainly derived from its success in delivering economic benefits to the vast majority of Indonesians.

For over two decades this formula had proved remarkably successful, but by the mid-1990s, with President Suharto already over 70 years old, it became increasingly clear that the static political and social outlook of the regime was causing much resentment among large and increasingly vocal groups in society. By this time, however, the personal power of President Suharto had become so deeply entrenched that no one seemed to know quite how to bring about even moderate political change.

A Military Dictatorship?

Few of the world's major countries have been so completely dominated by one person as Indonesia was by Suharto from the mid-1970s to 1998. When he was forced to step down in May 1998 he had already by far surpassed his predecessor and Indonesia's first president Sukarno [Soekarno], as the country's longest serving head of state. As Suharto had led Indonesia for 32 years, few other world leaders had led their countries for longer than the Indonesian president.

Suharto and his New Order regime came to power in 1966 in the wake of an abortive coup attempt the year before in which six top army generals were murdered. The circumstances around the coup are still unclear, but the event provided a pretext for the military to move against its main political adversary, the Indonesian Communist Party, PKI (*Partai Komunis Indonesia*). In a nation-wide purge from October 1965 to March 1966, an estimated 500,000 real and imagined Communists were killed as long-standing social and political tensions exploded, fuelled by the army's organised campaign against the PKI. Although discussion of these killings was silenced by the regime, their memory was still very much alive in the minds of politicians and power-brokers as the Suharto era neared its end 30 years later. Paired with the apparent unshakability of President Suharto's rule right up to his very last days, these memories gave rise to concerns among the political elite that the succession from Suharto might see a repetition of the horrors in 1965–66.[1]

During his 32 years in power, Suharto presided over tremendous changes in the social and economic spheres. Enormous progress was made in health, education, agriculture and poverty eradication to mention a few of the most important fields. From 1969 to 1994 GDP (Gross Domestic Product) growth averaged 6.8 per cent and real GDP per capita increased more than threefold. From the early 1970s up to 1997 this economic development formed the basis for the regime's main claims to legitimacy. Suharto personally could claim a large share of the credit as being the leading proponent for development and economic modernisation. The fruits of the development also trickled down to Indonesia's thousands of villages and urban neighbourhoods in the forms of new schools, roads, health-care centres and irrigation plants. On large billboards along the roads and in the towns the president oversaw the country's prosperity and progress. This was at the heart of Suharto's and the New Order's legitimacy.[2]

Critics of the New Order have often tended to characterise the regime as a military dictatorship.[3] However, although the

---

1. For the coup event and the transfer of power from Sukarno to Suharto, see Hughes (1968), McVey and Anderson (1971) and Andersson *et al.* (1977). On the massacre, see Cribb (ed.) (1990).
2. On the New Order's economic success, including the macroeconomic indicators of economic development, see Booth (1994) and Hill (1996: 1–29). For a discussion of the public billboards depicting Indonesia's development success, see Maurer (1997: 221–223), with accompanying illustrations.
3. For example, Caldwell (ed.) (1975), Southwood and Flanagan (1983) and Wertheim (1989).

military, ABRI (*Angkatan Bersenjata Republik Indonesia*, Armed Forces of the Republic of Indonesia), held significant political influence it never completely dominated the government or the administration under Suharto. The New Order's rise to power in the mid-1960s was supported by an alliance of various groups in opposition to President Sukarno and the PKI, including the military as well as student groups and Muslims. Civilian bureaucrats and professionals at different times exercised considerable influence over politics and decision-making under the New Order, and one of Suharto's closest aides and the man who eventually would succeed him as president was a civilian, Bacharuddin Yusuf [Jusuf] Habibie.

The relationship between ABRI and the civilian politicians was always uneasy, as was at times the relationship between ABRI and the president. The military vigorously defended its prominence in politics, enshrined in the doctrine of the dual function (*dwifungsi*) of the military. The doctrine stipulated that ABRI, because of its historical role in the struggle for national independence, had two roles, one in defence and security, and the other in social and political management. ABRI also saw itself as the essential vanguard for national stability and unity. Most evidently, the dual function meant that ABRI was represented by an appointed faction in parliament, and that active and retired officers held key posts in the government and throughout the bureaucracy. Besides the presidency, ABRI clearly was Indonesia's most politically influential institution under the New Order.[4]

A more crude side to ABRI's political role was its repressive functions, the scope for which, however, narrowed considerably in the later years of the regime. As mentioned, the New Order came to power in 1966 in the wake of a Communist massacre which left an estimated 500,000 people dead, much of the

---

4. For dual function of ABRI, see Jenkins (1983) and MacFarling (1996).

responsibility for which lay with the army. In the heyday of the cold war these atrocities gained almost no international attention. In the 1980s some 3,000–4,000 alleged criminals were extra-judicially executed by military death squads, and in 1984 troops opened fire on demonstrators in the Tanjung Priok area of Jakarta, killing up to 200 people, with fire brigades reportedly washing the blood off the streets. Neither of these events gained very much attention internationally. By contrast, the end of the cold war and the spread of global communication technology from the late 1980s brought about changes both in the accessibility of information and in attitude from the international community. Consequently, when the military in 1991 shot dead probably 100–200 demonstrators in the Vera Cruz cemetery in Dili, East Timor, they were harshly criticised both internationally and domestically. The criticism led President Suharto to establish a National Commission for Human Rights, Komnas HAM (*Komite Nasional Hak Asasi Manusia*) in order to improve the regime's human rights image.[5]

Politics in the New Order

The early years of the New Order saw a thorough restructuring of the political system in which the independence and influence of the political parties were severely circumscribed. Several of the parties experienced pressure and manipulation from the government and the military in their internal affairs, and those parties which were not banned were pressed to merge to form two non-government parties. Consequently in 1973, four Muslim parties merged to form the United Development Party, PPP (*Partai Persatuan Pembangunan*) and three Nationalist and

---

5. For the extra-judicial killings in the 1980s, see Bourchier (1990); for the Tanjung Priok massacre, see Bresnan (1993: 219–244); for the Dili massacre and its aftermath, see Feith (1992), and for a discussion of the establishment and early activity of the Komnas HAM, see Human Rights Watch /Asia (1994: 122–135).

two Christian parties merged to form the Indonesian Democratic Party, PDI (*Partai Demokrasi Indonesia*). Both parties had to adhere to the state ideology *Pancasila* and were formally not supposed to be opposition parties.[6] Rather, their function was to demonstrate a broad consensus around the government's national leadership and to enhance the democratic credentials of the regime. Due to these constraints and to internal factionalism neither party could exercise any significant influence over central policy formulation or decision-making.[7]

Parliamentary elections under the New Order were heavily rigged affairs. The military as well as the bureaucracy more or less overtly supported the government's electoral vehicle, Golkar (*Golongan Karya*, Functional Groups, formally not a political party) which always won an absolute majority of the votes in the quinquennial elections. After the party mergers in 1973, there were only three election contestants, Golkar, the PDI and the PPP, and the scope for campaigns and debates was severely circumscribed by government restrictions, ostensibly in the interest of national stability. Up to the 1997 election, 400 out of the 500 seats in the national parliament, the DPR (*Dewan Perwakilan Rakyat*, the People's Representative Council), were contested in the elections. The remaining 100 seats were reserved for the military and were filled by military appointees of the president. All candidates for parliament were screened

---

6. *Pancasila* was originally formulated by Sukarno in 1945 and consisted of five principles designed to be broad enough to be acceptable as a national ideology to all of Indonesia's many ethnic and religious groups, as well as to a broad stratum of political aspirations. The five principles were: belief in one God, a just and civilised humanity, the unity of Indonesia, democracy through deliberation, and social justice for the Indonesian people. The New Order advocated an authoritarian interpretation of *Pancasila*, emphasising aspects of social and political control, and on several occasions the regime used the state ideology to persecute dissidents; see Morfit (1986).
7. A summary of the New Order's formal political structure can be found in Thoolen (ed.) (1987: 35–55).

beforehand by both military and civil authorities for formal qualifications and ideological correctness. The more outspoken parliamentarians were generally removed from the candidate list for the next election. As a consequence, the parliament was a very weak institution, and the gravity of power clearly lay with the executive branch of the government.

In accordance with Indonesia's 1945 constitution, the president and vice-president were elected by the country's highest legislative body, the People's Consultative Assembly, MPR *(Majelis Permusyawaratan Rakya*t). This 1,000-member body consisted of the 500 members of parliament and another 500 representatives of different functional groups and of Indonesia's 27 provinces. The appointment of these 500 delegates, together with the 100 appointed members of the military faction of parliament, was in the hands of the president. In practice thus, Suharto controlled the appointment of 60 per cent of the delegates in the assembly which elected him. Every fifth year between 1973 and 1998, the MPR unanimously re-elected Suharto for the presidency.

Besides this waterproof system of political representation, the government undertook to organise much of the rest of society in functional groups in order to control the social and political aspirations of the people. The government tried, with varying success, to monopolise the representation of major interest groups, such as workers, students, peasants, women and religious congregations through control over their respective interest organisations. These included, for example, trade unions, student associations, various women's organisations and organisations for all of Indonesia's five officially recognised religions. The government both initiated the formation of new organisations and sponsored those already existing, providing them with official recognition and funding. In exchange the organisations were obliged to channel the government's policies and political aspirations to their members, and to give electoral support to Golkar. The reorganisation of the political system and of society at large reflected a corporatist ambition on behalf of the government, aspiring to monopolise most forms of collective representation on the national as well as regional and local levels. This structure, combined with the all-pervasive state bureaucracy and widespread military presence in society, allowed the government to exercise a considerable degree of social and political control over Indonesian society at large, even down to the smallest hamlets and neighbourhoods.[8]

The Political Economy

To a large extent the political system depended on the government's control and distribution of economic favours. A boom in oil prices from the mid-1970s provided the government with access to financial resources on a previously unprecedented scale, which enabled it to build up a political economy where economic rewards were exchanged for political loyalty. The system encompassed both national elites and those community leaders and local and regional politicians who were willing to comply with the government's wishes. Economic rewards and political patronage flowed downward in the system, while political loyalty flowed upward in what resembled a giant pyramid of patrimonial relations.[9]

In the early 1980s the international oil prices slumped, but the fall in government revenue was soon offset by increased revenues from tourism and non-oil exports. The income from these sectors combined with foreign aid revenues allowed the government to maintain and consolidate the political economy throughout the 1980s and the first half of the 1990s.

---

8. On the corporatist character of the New Order, see MacIntyre (1994). See also Antlöv (1995) for a study of the system in practice on the local level.
9. On the political economy of the New Order, see Robison (1986) and (1990) and Winters (1996).

However, from the end of the 1980s, popular resentment against the government's economic policies also increased, largely due to the increasingly obvious and rampant corruption and nepotism which thrived in the system. A great deal of the resentment focused on President Suharto's blatant favouritism of his own relatives. In the 1980s, several of the president's children had founded conglomerates, big groups of companies related by ownership rather than by their economic activity. The children's companies were active in a wide range of economic fields. For example, Suharto's eldest daughter, Siti Hardiyanti [Hardijanti] Rukmana, also known as Tutut, held interests in telecommunications, agribusiness, toll road construction and ship manufacturing. The president's second son, Bambang Trihatmojo [Trihatmodjo] controlled the large Bimantara group which was active in telecommunications, real estate, agribusiness, food retailing, construction and electronics. Suharto's youngest son, Hutomo Mandala Putra, known as Tommy Suharto, had interests in shipping, agribusiness, petrochemicals and air travel, only to mention some of the most important fields.[10]

In the 1990s, several cases of blatant favouritism of Suharto's children and other relatives inspired public animosity, and had a significant influence on the president's personal legitimacy. In 1996 a presidential decree gave Tommy's company, P. T. Timor Putra Nasional, the task of developing a national car. P. T. Timor, however, did not have any experience with car production, and the company did not seem to be able to put together an assembly line or other facilities needed to start the domestic car production. Instead the government gave P. T. Timor a licence to import Kia cars from South Korea, exempt from luxury tax and import duties, which allowed the company to sell the cars

---

10. So far, the most comprehensive studies of the business interests of the Suharto family are Aditjondro (1998) and Soesilo (1998), both of which are critical to the Suharto family. For a valuable survey, see Schwarz (1994: 133–161), or *Asiaweek* (12 April 1996) and *Warta Ekonomi* (1 June 1998) for more recent surveys.

for around half of the price of its competitors. The whole affair looked like a tax break to enable Tommy Suharto to import a foreign car and sell it under the name of a national car. The project drew much criticism both domestically and internationally, and the car did not sell well, probably because it quickly became a prime symbol for the nepotism of the Suharto family.[11]

Tutut, Bambang and Tommy were the three Suharto offspring who had the most extensive business interests, but Suharto's other children, Sigit Harjoyudanto [Hardjojudanto], Siti Hediati Hariyadi [Harijadi] and Siti Hutami Endang Adiningsih, each had their own business conglomerates as well, as did some other relatives, such as Suharto's half-brother Probosutejo [Probosutedjo] and one of the president's grandsons, Ari Harjo Wibowo, also known as Ari Sigit.

Most of the family businesses benefited from state contracts or regulations, such as trading monopolies or import licences. In addition, they often benefited from cheap loans from state banks which demanded little or no security. These benefits were also obvious to foreign and domestic investors, who often preferred to hook up in joint ventures with members of the Suharto family. Typically, the presidential relatives contributed little in terms of skill or capital, but instead provided access to the corridors of power and a display name for the venture which smoothed things out in dealings with official authorities. Suharto said that his children were free to do business like anybody else, but it was obvious that they were greatly favoured by their political connections. Although first family nepotism was a definite taboo to write about for the Indonesian press, awareness of the president's favouritism towards his children was widespread in Indonesia. Throughout Suharto's last years this persistent nepotism seriously tainted the president's public image, as well as the image of the regime at large.

---

11. For the Timor case, see Abimanyu and Goodfellow (1997: 129–133). and Manning and Jayasuriya (1996: 18–21).

Although the first family's businesses were huge, they faded in comparison with the business empires which were owned by a handful of Chinese Indonesian business tycoons close to Suharto. They controlled the vast majority of Indonesia's large conglomerates, and ethnic Chinese owned an estimated 50–70 per cent of Indonesia's domestically-owned private corporate sector. The biggest of the Chinese tycoons was Suharto's long-standing friend and business partner, Liem Sioe Liong, who led the huge Salim group with over 300 companies active in areas as diverse as cement production, banking, food manufacturing and distribution, electronics and car production. In 1994, the Salim group had sales of nine billion dollars, accounting for five per cent of Indonesia's GDP.[12]

Since the colonial period, Indonesia's ethnic Chinese population, which makes up around three per cent of the total population, had dominated large sectors of the modern economy. The New Order took up the policy of the colonial regime of economically favouring the ethnic Chinese over indigenous ethnic groups. Under the New Order, Chinese Indonesian businessmen were thus able to benefit for example from the awarding of state licences and contracts as well as easy access to credit. Meanwhile, the Chinese Indonesians in general contributed in major ways to Indonesia's economic development, for example by providing capital, access to international business

---

12. Naisbitt (1996: 24). For Liem Sioe Liong and the Salim group, see Schwarz (1994: 109–115). For a discussion of the economic dominance of the Chinese, see Schwarz (1994: 109). The Indonesian economist Sjahrir (1993: 24 n. 3) estimated that in 1993, at least 80 per cent of the companies listed at the Jakarta stock exchange were owned by ethnic Chinese. Of Indonesia's top 25 conglomerates in 1994, 21 were owned by Chinese Indonesian, and the two largest of the non-Chinese conglomerates were owned by Bambang Trihatmojo and Tommy Suharto respectively; see Hill (1997: 111). See also Schwarz (1994: 98–132), Wibisono (1995) and Suryadinata (1997b: 32–75) for the economic role of the ethnic Chinese in New Order Indonesia.

networks and managerial and technical skills. However, the government's conscious policy to favour Chinese Indonesians over indigenous ethnic groups gave rise to much resentment on behalf of indigenous businessmen, as well as among non-Chinese Indonesians at large. Although there were very few Chinese Indonesians who directly benefited from the president's patronage, the resentment against them reflected on Indonesia's ethnic Chinese population in general. Since most Chinese Indonesians were Catholics or Buddhists, just as under the colonial era, Islam provided a focus for anti-Chinese sentiments, which contributed to fanning fundamentalist Islamic undercurrents.[13]

For Suharto, betting on the Chinese fulfilled a political purpose. Given the latent racist sentiments against the Chinese in Indonesia, the latter were unlikely to be able to translate their economic power into political power. Rather, as their favours depended on the state, or in many cases more specifically on their relationship with the president, the arrangement served to secure the political loyalty of the leaders of the business community. If threatened by racist violence and social unrest, the Chinese would be inclined, in the interest of their own safety, to throw their support behind the authoritarian regime. For Suharto, favouring the ethnic Chinese business community served to obstruct the rise of a powerful indigenous capitalist class which might translate their economic wealth and power to political opposition and challenge the regime.

It is not known exactly how far Suharto's own business interests extended. He was in charge of several non-profit foundations, *yayasan*, which in principle were not required to disclose any information about their holdings or economic activities. Before her death in April 1996 Suharto's wife, Tien Suharto, also controlled a number of *yayasan*, as did the

---

13. For the historical background of the ethnic Chinese in Indonesia and especially the New Order's policy towards the Chinese Indonesians, see Coppel (1983).

president's children and other relatives. Officially the *yayasan* mostly had social or religious purposes, but for Suharto their main purpose was political. Allocating economic resources and handing out favours served to secure the loyalty of those dependent on the president, be they ministers, bureaucrats, military officers or private entrepreneurs. This patrimonial system was reproduced throughout the chain of power, so that it created, in the words of Andrew MacIntyre, a 'pyramid-like network of patron-client relationships.'[14]

The exchange of favours and loyalties flowed throughout the state apparatus and its extensions of corporatist organisations, and it served to maintain the New Order just as much as did repression or attempts at symbolic legitimation. As long as the economy was growing at a high pace the system seemed to work well in securing support among the national and local elites for the political status quo. However, the system was also at the heart of much of Indonesia's economic and political ills, and public resentment against the corruption, collusion and nepotism embedded in the system was on the rise well before Asia's economic crisis hit Indonesia.

President Suharto

Suharto was born in 1921 in a small village near Yogyakarta in central Java.[15] He had six years of primary school education, and then worked briefly as a bank clerk until he joined the Royal Netherlands' Indies Army, KNIL (*Koninklijk Nederlandsch Indisch Leger*) at the age of nineteen. Thereafter his career was almost completely within the army, and during the war for independence from the Dutch (1945–49) he rose swiftly in

---

14. MacIntyre (1991: 7). For the patrimonial model, see further Crouch (1979) and (1980). About the *yayasan*, see Robison (1993: 48) and Aditjondro (1998: 3–78).
15. See Vatikiotis (1993: 1–31) and McIntyre (1996) for Suharto's biography.

rank. After Indonesia became independent he held different commanding positions, until he became Major-General and commander of the Army's Strategic Reserve, Kostrad (*Komando Strategis Angkatan Darat*) in 1964. In the wake of the abortive coup in October 1965 and during the army's subsequent campaign against the Communist Party, PKI, Suharto emerged as the dominant figure in ABRI. In March 1966, after five months of widespread communal violence largely orchestrated by the army, President Sukarno, under military pressure, handed over power to Suharto and instructed the latter to take all necessary steps to re-establish public order and to safeguard the president. Two years later Suharto replaced Sukarno as full president. In the course of the next decade Suharto's position gradually developed from that of a *primus inter pares* to one of complete and unchallengeable political dominance. Several factors influenced this development. At the heart of Suharto's power and legitimacy was the country's positive economic development and the president's access to revenues which he could distribute in exchange for political loyalty. Other important factors were Suharto's tactical political skill and his demonstrated ability to crush or sideline all potential challengers to his position. A proven staunch anti-Communist, Suharto could furthermore enjoy the support of the United States and other western countries as long as the cold war dominated the international political arena.

Little is known about Suharto's inner personality. He is reserved and shut-off in his manners, and while in office he would rarely show his feelings or lose his temper. He usually appeared dignified, calm and soft-spoken, without revealing his inner thoughts. One senior politician who had watched him closely for several years commented: 'No one knows what that man thinks [...] That is the secret of his power.'[16]

Culturally, Suharto came from a background of Javanese mysticism known as *kejawen*, and held strong personal mystical

---

16. Mackie and MacIntyre (1994: 45).

beliefs and world-view. During his first years in power, Suharto was helped by a group of spiritual advisers who helped the president achieve the concentration of spiritual power known in Javanese as *wahyu*. Suharto therefore collected various heirlooms, such as what was said to be the death mask of Gajah Mada [Gadjah Mada], the great prime minister of the fourteenth-century Javanese kingdom of Majapahit. The death mask was believed to contain the power and wisdom of Gajah Mada himself. Another heirloom collected by Suharto was a swagger stick which had belonged to Sukarno, and which was said to give its owner great power. Throughout his tenure of power, Suharto also frequently visited various holy places in Java to meditate and absorb spiritual power.[17]

Several observers have likened Suharto's style of leadership to that of a Javanese king. Ideally, as described in the old Javanese court chronicles, a king should possess spiritual powers, *wahyu*, which supposedly allowed him to rule without visible effort. As long as the king possessed these powers people would automatically follow his wishes, invisibly guided by the divine energy.[18]

In line with these ideals, Suharto, it seems, strove to exercise his power as discreetly as possible. As a rule, he was removed from the everyday squabbling of politics, which instead was left to ministers, generals and other officials. He would rarely talk to journalists, and he almost never let himself be questioned. Suharto rather made statements, either directly in speeches, or indirectly when government ministers and officials quoted him after audiences in the presidential palace. Thus, in many respects until the final stages of the 1996–98 crisis, the president seemed

---

17. Lyon (1993: 225–230); cf. also Ramadhan (1996: 308–309) and Soeharto (1989: 441–442). For *kejawen*, see Mulder (1978).
18. For discussions of Suharto's leadership in terms of that of a Javanese king, see e.g. Schwarz (1994: 45–46), Maurer and Raillon (1994: 118), Mulder (1996: 64) and Kingsbury (1998: 75). For the Javanese idea of power, see Anderson (1972) and the discussion below in Chapter 2.

detached from causes of the crisis and from the political, social and economic ills which plagued the country.

The image of Suharto being detached from real politics was, however, misleading, as the president was much more than a mythical Javanese king. Policy making under Suharto was in general not very transparent, but it seems that the president exercised crucial personal influence on policies in most important fields. Although not always in a direct or formal way, the president managed to keep close watch on policy implementation regarding a wide range of issues, while he was able to avoid becoming tied up in details.[19]

Suharto was also an extremely skilful statesman and political tactician who understood how to play different interests and individuals against each other, so that by the mid-1990s he seemed virtually irreplaceable. Numerous potential challengers to Suharto were demoted after having become too critical or too influential in their own right. It has even been suggested that the core of Suharto's tactics while in office was to try to make himself indispensable by carefully eliminating all the alternatives.[20] Whether or not this was Suharto's intention, it seemed indeed to be the situation towards the end of his presidency. Together with the fear of a repetition of the communal violence around the only previous presidential succession, the expected power vacuum after Suharto created great uncertainty and anxiety about the country's political future. This situation caused analysts throughout the 1990s to describe Indonesia as a nation 'in waiting'.[21] Political actors engaged themselves in a double game through which they tried to achieve political goals and benefits in the short term, while

---

19. Cribb (1998a: 229). See also MacIntyre (1991: 30–31) and Winters (1996) for the process of policy making within the government, and Liddle (1987) for a bottom-up perspective.
20. Halldorsson (1998: 18).
21. For example, Cribb (1990: 24), Crouch (1992: 61–62); Schwarz (1994) and Eklöf (1997: 1195).

simultaneously trying to position themselves for the inevitable presidential succession.

Indonesia in the 1990s

The first half of the 1990s saw a period of relative political openness, or *keterbukaan*, in Indonesia. It was an Indonesian type of *perestrojka* with greater freedom of expression and a more open climate of debate than during the previous decade. The new openness was related to a struggle between the military and Suharto, both of whom tried to improve their political standing by courting institutions and organisations outside the state structure.[22] Up to the first years of the 1990s, ABRI was very much under the influence of Leonardus Benyamin 'Benny' Murdani [Leonardus Benjamin Moerdani], a Catholic general who was commander-in-chief of ABRI from 1983 to 1988. Benny Murdani was a protégé and close confidant of President Suharto up to the second half of the 1980s, when the relations between the two men became markedly cooler. From 1988 to 1993 Murdani served in the less influential position of defence minister, before he was dropped by Suharto from the cabinet in 1993. However, Benny Murdani was widely believed to continue to exercise considerable influence over ABRI also after his retirement, mainly through his personal ties with the leaders of the officer corps.[23]

---

22. See Lane (1991), Robison (1995a: 49–53) and Bertrand (1996) on *keterbukaan* and its relation to the conflict between Suharto and ABRI.
23. It is difficult to assess to what degree Benny Murdani continued to exercise influence in ABRI. Immediately after his departure as defence minister in 1993, Suharto initiated a campaign of 'de-Bennyisation', purging the military of officers loyal to the former general; see the Editors (1994: 83–85) and (1995: 104–105). In May 1997, Benny Murdani claimed that the campaign forced him to go far away from the capital to play golf, in order that no one should be seen with him and thus become a victim of the purge; Said (1998: 544 n. 20). In late 1998, Benny Murdani claimed that he had no influence whatsoever in ABRI, as he no longer knew any of the senior active officers; interview, Jakarta (4 Dec 1998).

There were two main conflict issues between ABRI and the president. One concerned the political influence and autonomy of ABRI. At the beginning of the 1990s it was clear that the political influence of the military had begun to wane in favour of the president and a number of families from the politico-bureaucrats who dominated the state apparatus. ABRI thus started increasingly to look like a political instrument in the hands of the presidency and the state bureaucracy, and not, as ABRI envisioned and as the *dwifungsi* doctrine prescribed, an independent political institution and actor in its own right. The other issue which gave rise to increasing resentment among military officers concerned Suharto's blatant economic favouritism of his own family members and a small circle of selected crony businessmen.

In order to strengthen his position vis-à-vis the military and to broaden his political support, Suharto decided in 1990 to sponsor a newly formed Association of Indonesian Muslim Intellectuals, ICMI *(Ikatan Cendekiawan Muslimin se-Indonesia)*. His long-standing protégé and friend, Minister for Research and Technology B. J. Habibie, was elected chairman of the organisation, whose official aim was to promote cultural and educational activities among Indonesian Muslims.[24]

Suharto's sponsoring of ICMI meant a new and much improved role for Islam in the national political life. Suharto, with his background in Javanese mysticism, had previously not stood out as a devout Muslim, and his policies had for most of his tenure in power seemed designed to contain or emasculate Islam as a political force. The culmination of the struggle between the regime and Islam had been in the lead-up to the enactment in 1985 of a law which required all social and political organisations to recognise *Pancasila* as their sole fundamental

---

24. For ICMI, see Anwar (1992), Hefner (1993), Wessel (1996), and Ramage (1995: 75–121). The following paragraphs draw mainly on the latter.

ideological foundation. The main purpose of the law was to prevent Islam from becoming the basis for independent organisation, and the fiercest resistance to it had come from modernist Islamic scholars and activists. Now, for many of these, ICMI represented a turn-about and an unprecedented forum for channelling Islamic political and cultural aspirations. In general, the founding of ICMI was greeted with great enthusiasm by Indonesian Muslim leaders and intellectuals.

However, one of Indonesia's most influential Islamic leaders, Abdurrahman Wahid, chairman of the country's largest organisation, the traditionalist Islamic NU *(Nahdlatul Ulama*, Rise of the Islamic Scholars) emerged as one of ICMI's severest critics. He branded the organisation as fundamentalist, suspecting that some of its members tried to promote the idea of an Islamic state. Wahid, a staunch proponent of democracy and of inter-religious tolerance, saw ICMI as a dangerous and undemocratic organisation aspiring to transform itself into a political party. ICMI was also met with considerable scepticism from the military, largely for the same fear that Wahid harboured of Islamic political aspirations.

Both Abdurrahman Wahid and the military realised that Suharto's sponsorship of ICMI was an attempt on behalf of the president to build a new constituency in the face of waning support from the military, as well as other groups. Most ICMI activists also seemed to realise this, and they tended to regard the alliance with the president as temporary. For them, ICMI was primarily a means for promoting their own political agenda rather than for supporting the president. In addition, Habibie's Muslim credentials were questioned both within ICMI and by its critics outside the organisation. Cynics even alleged that when Habibie lived in Germany in the 1960s and 1970s he used to eat pork and drink beer.[25]

---

25. Informants in Jakarta, March 1997; cf. also Ramage (1995: 75) and Liddle (1996a: 56).

Aside from his engagement in ICMI, Habibie was disliked among many military leaders for other reasons. He was resented for being a civilian who exercised great political influence through his close relationship with the president. As Minister of Research and Technology, moreover, he also came into conflict with ABRI over military equipment acquisitions. In 1993, Suharto seems to have been intent on having Habibie elected as vice-president, but as this plan met with much resistance from the military, the president was forced to back down and instead accept ABRI's choice, the military commander-in-chief, General Try Sutrisno [Soetrisno], as vice-president. A year later, in 1994, the conflict between Habibie and the military again came to head with a deal brokered by Habibie, in which the navy was forced to acquire 39 used warships from former East Germany. The conflict indirectly led to the incident which generally is regarded as the end of the period of openness in Indonesia. In June 1994 the government banned three weekly publications, among them Indonesia's leading news magazine *Tempo*, for its reporting on the warships affair.[26]

In the context of the power struggle between ABRI and himself, Suharto undertook a series of reshuffles in the military from the early 1990s. In doing so, the president aimed at eliminating the influence of the Benny Murdani faction and instead he placed officers more sympathetic to ICMI, Habibie and himself in key positions. Feisal Tanjung [Tandjung], who was appointed commander-in-chief of ABRI in May 1993 was widely considered to be sympathetic to ICMI, as was General R. Hartono who became army Chief of Staff in February 1995. Both were personal friends of Habibie, and the latter was also close to Suharto's eldest daughter, Tutut. In December 1995,

---

26. On the conflict between Habibie and the military, see e.g. Robison (1997: 53) and Shiraishi (1996: 179). On the conflict surrounding the 1993 MPR session, see Liddle (1993: 31–34), and on the press bannings, see Romano (1996) and Hanazaki (1998).

Suharto's son-in-law, Prabowo Subianto [Soebianto] took over the command of the elite unit Kopassus *(Komando Pasukan Khusus*, Special Forces Command). At the age of 44, Prabowo also became the youngest general in the armed forces. These three, Feisal Tanjung, Hartono and Prabowo, were considered to be the key figures in a group of 'green' (Islamic) officers, in contrast to the 'red and white' (nationalist) officers more suspicious of ICMI and of Islamic political aspirations. For Suharto, the green officers forged a link between his old constituency in the military and his new supporters in ICMI. However, the distinction between the two groups of officers was not clear-cut, and there were tensions within each group as well. Several of the leaders of both the green and the red and white groups were furthermore former bodyguards or personal adjutants to the president, such as the Kostrad commander, Lieutenant-General Wiranto, who gradually emerged as the leader of the red and white group of officers. Overall, thus, the ABRI leadership was, more than before, personally loyal to Suharto. In addition, the president understood how to use the rivalry among the officers, balancing individuals and factions against one another. In this way, he obstructed the rise of a new unitary faction of ABRI officers which might threaten his hold on power.[27]

By the mid-1990s Suharto had emerged as winner in the struggle between himself and the military. With the unquestioned loyalty from the leadership of the armed forces, with the support of influential Muslim leaders, and with no feasible alternative to his national leadership, his position in early 1996 seemed secure and virtually unchallengeable. However, groups from outside the state apparatus were becoming increasingly

---

27. For the reshuffles in the military, see the Editors (1993, 1994, 1995 and 1998), and for the recent factionalism in ABRI, see Mietzner (1998a) and Bourchier (1998a); see also Liddle (1995: 18) and Mallarangeng and Liddle (1996: 113–114). Officially the military denied that there was any split or factionalism within the armed forces.

vocal in their criticism of the regime and of the president's national leadership. The dissidents included students, intellectuals, journalists, labour activists and members of the numerous non-government organisations (NGOs) which had sprung up and flourished since the end of the 1980s.[28] The regime seemed both unable and unwilling to accommodate these new social and political aspirations. Although probably not powerful enough seriously to threaten Suharto or the regime, the oppositional forces might have the potential to disturb the smooth running of the upcoming general election scheduled for May 1997 and the subsequent MPR session and presidential election scheduled for March 1998. Consequently, from Suharto's point of view, it was necessary to deal with them well in time before election. These challenges and the regime's responses to them triggered the 1996–98 political crisis which eventually, when fuelled by the regional economic downturn from mid-1997, led to the fall of Suharto.

---

28. For the NGOs in Indonesia in the 1990s, see Eldridge (1995) and for the related phenomenon of the pro-democracy movement, see Uhlin (1997).

CHAPTER 2

Dealing with the Opposition

On 20 June 1996 some 700 delegates of the Indonesian Democratic Party, PDI, gathered in the Pangkalan Mansyur hall in Medan in North Sumatra to hold a national congress. The congress had been preceded by an extensive public debate in the media about the need for the PDI to hold a congress, and about the legality of arranging one. The party's central board was split in two, with the majority supporting the congress. However, the event was boycotted by the party's chairperson, Megawati Sukarnoputri [Soekarnoputri], along with her supporters. Minister of Home Affairs Yogie S. M. opened the congress, encouraging the delegates to deliberate in order to reach a consensus which would solve the party's internal problems. The commander-in-chief of ABRI, General Feisal Tanjung, spoke next, denying allegations that the military had meddled in the party's affairs. He also said that the military cared for the PDI. On the front rows in the congress hall, together with the organisers of the congress, sat the North Sumatra Governor Raja Inal Siregar as well as several high-ranking military officials.[1]

The congress went off completely without incident. There were no visible lines of division between the delegates, and all the issues on the agenda were quickly settled. Most important, a new central board was elected, and Suryadi [Soerjadi], the party's former chairman from 1986–93, was unanimously elected to replace his successor, Megawati Sukarnoputri, as chairperson. The congress closed on 22 June, two days earlier than scheduled,

---

1. *Merdeka* (21 June 1996) and *Jakarta Post* (21 June 1996).

with Suryadi thanking the government and the military for helping to arrange the congress. Minister Yogie declared the government's full support for Suryadi's leadership, and the military chief of social and political affairs, Major-General Syarwan Hamid, said that ABRI was prepared to ensure the full implementation of the congress' decisions.[2]

The smooth running of the congress was unique in the party's history. All the party's previous four congresses had been chaotic and marred by disagreements and deadlocks. At the last ordinary congress, which was held in the same venue in 1993, opponents of Suryadi had gate-crashed the congress hall in a jeep, and several delegates were injured in the fighting that followed.[3] In 1996, by contrast, military security around the congress was tight, and Megawati's supporters refrained from trying to disturb the occasion.

It seemed strange that the party should hold a congress at this time. The preparations for the general election in May 1997 had already started, and most analysts seemed to think that the PDI under Megawati had a good chance of doing well in the polls. Megawati also seemed to enjoy a broad support among the rank-and-file of the party. Therefore, to political observers it was obvious that the initiative to hold a congress, and to depose Megawati, came from outside the party, that is from the government.[4]

---

2. *Jakarta Post* (23 June 1996) and *Suara Karya* (24 June 1996).
3. See Halawa (1993:107–114), van Klinken (1994) and Zulkifli (1996: 87–91).
4. See for example the editorial in *Jakarta Post* (6 June 1996). Even Suryadi himself admitted that the congress demonstrated that there had been outside interference; *Forum Keadilan* (1 July 96). Later Suryadi said in an interview that under the New Order there was not one congress of the PDI, PPP or Golkar which was free from government interference; *Tempo Interaktif* (1 August 1998). Van Dijk (1997: 411), however, stops short of drawing this conclusion, saying only that the congress was 'described in some newspapers as a government-sponsored one'.

It was somewhat less obvious exactly why the government felt the need to have Megawati deposed. She led the smallest of Indonesia's two legal non-government parties. In the 1992 election the PDI had won 14.9 per cent of the votes. Golkar, meanwhile, had gained 68.1 per cent.[5] Even if the PDI under Megawati could be expected to make substantial gains in the 1997 election, it would not be able to threaten Golkar's majority. Nor was Megawati remarkably confrontational towards the government, and her political statements were always within the boundaries of what was permissible in the political life of the New Order.

Megawati, Sukarno and the PDI

Megawati was the eldest daughter of Indonesia's former president Sukarno. She first entered politics in 1986 when she was invited by Suryadi to campaign for the PDI in the 1987 election. She drew large audiences in Central Java, where she put forward her father's ideas in short but cogent speeches, punctuated with slogans such as 'Long Live Sukarno' (*Hidup Sukarno*). Thousands of young people gathered at the rallies carrying pictures of the late president.[6]

At this time, Megawati was chiefly a vote-getter for the PDI, and she did not belong to the inner circle in the party. She was not particularly active in parliament, to which she was elected in 1987 and again in 1992. One of her biographers even described her as a woman who was 'weak, meek and plain'.[7] Her popularity was largely derived from her name and from the notion among her supporters that she represented the ideas and the charisma of her late father.

---

5. See Baroto (1992: 250) for the 1992 election results.
6. Van de Kok and Cribb (1987: 161) and *Far Eastern Economic Review* (30 April 1987).
7. Bahar (1996: 32); cf. also Brooke (1995: 87).

Megawati rose to the PDI chair in 1993 after the government rejected Suryadi's re-election to the post at the party's congress in July the same year. Although Suryadi was later to be widely despised as a government stooge for his role in the events of 1996–97, he enjoyed in 1993 considerable support within the PDI. He had led the party in two successful elections, in 1987 and 1992, and he had acquired a reputation as an independent-minded leader who dared to challenge the government to some extent. However, this earned him the disapproval of the government, which declared his re-election in July 1993 void. An extraordinary party congress was assembled in December the same year, at which the majority of the delegates expressed their overwhelming support for Megawati, in spite of the government's attempts to manipulate the event. A few weeks later, after intense lobbying and deliberations with government and military representatives, Megawati was formally elected chairperson of the PDI by a meeting of provincial party leaders.[8]

Although Megawati's election to a considerable degree was due to support from the rank-and-file of the party, she also depended on support from within the military for her ascendancy to the party chair. This support seems to have been related to the struggle between Suharto and the military, which came to a head at the Golkar congress in October the same year. At the congress, Suharto had one of his most personally loyal aides, Information Minister Harmoko, elected as the Golkar chair. Harmoko was the first civilian ever to lead the organisation, and his election was obviously unpopular with large parts of the officer corps. After the congress, one of ABRI's deputy faction leaders in parliament, Major-General Sembiring Meliala, even hinted that ABRI might shift its support for Golkar to the PDI, in which case, he said, the PDI would certainly win the 1997 election.[9]

---

8. See van Klinken (1994) and Haribuan (ed.) (1996: 2–16).
9. Van Dijk (1994: 412).

Megawati's popularity and her election to the party chair should also be seen in the context of what has been described as the 'second life' of Sukarno in the New Order. The regime had always had difficulties with the position to be awarded to the nation's first president in history. On the one hand, he was a national hero who led the struggle for independence and proclaimed the Indonesian state in 1945. On the other hand, he was also the leader of the regime that preceded the New Order, the left-leaning, chaotic Old Order, which the new regime claimed to be a correction against. On many instances throughout the New Order Sukarno had come to symbolise opposition to the regime and President Suharto. It was widely believed that Sukarno had devoted himself completely to the common people and that he never used his position to enrich himself or his family. In this way, the first president's rule and personal life was consciously regarded by many Indonesians as a contrast to the contemporary conditions and the rule of President Suharto.[10]

The PDI was particularly well placed to exploit the popularity of the first president. The largest of the parties which merged to form PDI in 1973 was the Indonesian Nationalist Party, PNI (*Partai Nasional Indonesia*), which had been closely associated with Sukarno. The PDI could thus be considered as the successor of the PNI, and the PDI successfully used Sukarno's image in the election campaign in 1987, which led to serious concerns on behalf of the government. In the 1992 election campaign, the government prohibited all use of pictures of Sukarno, as well as text references to his person.[11]

With Megawati leading the PDI, many of her supporters identified in her the virtues associated with her late father. Megawati was seen as living in a simple, humble life style, and

---

10. Aspinall (1996: 7–8). About Sukarno's standing in the New Order, see Labrousse (1994) and Brooks (1996).
11. Liddle (1988: 186–187) and van Dijk (1992a: 249).

her image was that of a person close to the people, *Mbak* (Sister) Mega, just as her father had been *Bung* (Brother) Karno to all the Indonesian population.[12]

In addition, Megawati had, or acquired, qualities of her own which accounted for some of her popularity. She had a reputation for decency, patience, calm and righteousness, qualities in a leader which seemed to find cultural resonance and appreciation among many Indonesians. Her being a woman may also have been a positive factor for her popularity, standing in contrast to most of the New Order's political life with its dominance of men with military backgrounds.[13]

For all her strengths, Megawati was never a dominant leader within the PDI. Many followers of Suryadi resented his exclusion from the leadership in 1993 and he maintained regional power bases within the party. There were also several conflicts on the local and regional levels in the party, and rival boards even sprang up in several provinces and districts. In 1995, a rival central board was set up on the initiative of Yusuf Merukh, a West Timorese PDI leader and mine owner who was well connected with the government. It seems that both Yusuf Merukh's rival board and several of the rival boards in the provinces were sponsored by the government as parts of a campaign to destabilise Megawati's leadership of the PDI.[14]

---

12. Indonesians like using abbreviated nicknames for people such as Mega for Megawati, or Karno for Sukarno. *Mbak* is the common Javanese form of address to a woman of the same status and age as oneself. *Bung*, which means brother and carries the connotation of comrade, is used affectionately as a title for popular leaders, especially leaders of the independence struggle 1945–1949. By contrast, Suharto is commonly referred to as *Pak* Harto; *Pak* literally means father and is the common form of address to an older man or a man of higher status than oneself.
13. See McIntyre (1997: 1–3).
14. See Bastaman (1995: 17–26), Haribuan (ed.) (1996:18–51) and *EIU Country Report Indonesia*, 3rd quarter (1995: 11)

Challenging Suharto

A few months before the PDI congress, at the end of January 1996, suggestions began to circulate that Megawati would be nominated as a candidate for the presidential election in 1998. The idea gained wide attention, and was vigorously debated by politicians and analysts in Jakarta for a few weeks. At the time, it was not known from whom the suggestion had originated and this seemed, if anything, to make the issue even more interesting.[15] However, most analysts did not seem to think that Megawati had any serious chance of actually becoming elected. After all, the incumbent President Suharto would control the appointment of over half of the delegates of the MPR which would elect the new president.

Megawati herself appeared to take the matter lightly, and in an interview she said:

> I do not yet think about the nomination. [...] My priority is to prepare the PDI for the general election that is going to take place. Even if I want to nominate myself, that will be after the 1997 general election, after seeing whether the situation is favourable or not.[16]

Even this seemingly diplomatic stance, however, was an indirect challenge to Suharto. In suggesting that she might stand, Megawati implied a possibility of dissatisfaction with Suharto, who had been the sole candidate for the presidency on every previous occasion. The Indonesian political system under the New Order was in theory non-confrontational, and the PDI, like most other socio-political organisations, had repeatedly stated its support for the New Order under the leadership of

---

15. Aberson Marle Sihaloho, a PDI parliamentarian known as one of the 'radicals' in the party, later admitted that he had taken the initiative to make a questionnaire in which the suggestion was made of nominating Megawati. The forms had been spread among several of the PDI branches in Central Java after October 1995; Haribuan (ed.) (1996: 138) and *Forum Keadilan* (12 February 1996).
16. *Forum Keadilan* (12 February 1996).

President Suharto. At the time of the debate, more than two years before the presidential election, a number of organisations had already publicly expressed their support for Suharto.[17] In this context, for Megawati not to reject explicitly the idea of her nomination amounted to a challenge to Suharto.

The debate in the media eventually ebbed away after mid-February. Not surprisingly, President Suharto himself did not enter the debate. The reaction from other government representatives and the military was cautious, but not directly condemning. The official attitude seemed to be that the nomination of Megawati, or anyone else, for president was no big matter, and that it was within the boundaries of what was permitted in the country's democracy. However, all the officials stressed the importance of the nomination and presidential election following the proper formal procedures.[18] That meant channelling the nomination through the MPR controlled by Suharto, which in effect would exclude the slightest chance of Megawati being elected.

The nomination of Megawati was by no means the first attempt to challenge Suharto's sole candidacy. On various occasions under the New Order, people had put themselves forward as potential presidential candidates, and in 1978 Suharto's single candidacy led to violent student protests in Jakarta. After the 1992 general election Megawati's younger brother, Guruh Sukarnoputra [Soekarnoputra], tried unsuccessfully to nominate himself as the PDI's candidate for the 1993 MPR session. None of the previous attempts, however, had ever led to a formal nomination in the MPR, and the government could safely ignore

---

17. *Jakarta Post* (24 January 1996). The PDI's support for the New Order under President Suharto was part of the party's political platform and was adopted and confirmed on its congresses; e.g. DPP/PDI (1993: 89).
18. For example, *Jakarta Post* (27 January 1996), *Kompas* (1 February 1996), and *Gatra* (3 February 1996).

them, as the persons who nominated themselves generally lacked the support of large or influential groups in society.[19]

However, as the PDI would comprise a faction in the MPR, the party would have the formal opportunity to nominate its leader as a presidential candidate. This could force the MPR for the first time ever to hold a vote to decide between two presidential candidates. If the PDI performed strongly in the elections, the party might also try to put force behind Megawati's candidacy by mobilising large masses of people to demonstrate in their support of her. From the point of view of the regime, this could mean opening a Pandora's box of populist mass politics, triggering a development which might easily go beyond the control of the government.

A further problem for Suharto was the prospect of the MPR taking a vote to elect the president and vice-president. The suggestion touched on something of an Achilles' heal for the president, because voting was exactly the procedure for taking decisions in the MPR that was prescribed by the constitution. Indonesia's 1945 constitution occupied a central place in the political rhetoric of the New Order and President Suharto himself frequently referred to it, tirelessly stressing the importance of constitutional forms and procedures. From this perspective his own repeated election by acclamation stood out as an anomaly.[20]

---

19. For Guruh's candidacy, see *Tempo* (20 June 1992). However, when a minor civil servant, Sawito Kartowibowo, in 1976 received the support of several influential politicians, among them the former vice-president Mohammad Hatta for his nomination, the matter gained much attention, and the government took stern measures to meet the threat. Sawito was eventually sentenced to eight years' imprisonment for subversion. For the so-called Sawito affair, see Bourchier (1984) and Cala (1988).
20. The relevant article in the constitution reads: 'All decisions of the People's Consultative Assembly are taken through majority vote.' *UUD. 1945* (undated: bab II, pasal 3). On Suharto's and the New Order's attempts to acquire constitutional legitimacy, see Liddle (1985: 84 and 1992: 448–449).

From Suharto's perspective as a traditionally oriented Javanese believing in the mystical qualities of power, the idea of the MPR voting for two or more candidates would also be hard to accept. According to traditional Javanese notions of power, as described by Benedict Anderson, power is only one and indivisible.[21] The source of power, in the traditional Javanese thinking, is the mystical divine energy, *wahyu*, which can be absorbed by a person through mental exercises and asceticism. The concentration of *wahyu* in the power holder needs to be absolute, as the dispersal of power implies the ruler's loss of divine sanction and consequently of his legitimacy. Therefore, the mere existence of opposition against the ruler is seen as a sign of the dispersal of his power. A presidential election in which Suharto did not obtain 100 per cent of the votes would from this perspective be seen as a sign that his power and authority were unravelling.

Although Anderson sets out to describe a cultural phenomenon, or a culturally constituted idea of power, it is probably better to treat it as an ideology of power. The complex of ideas described by Anderson, and the ones that have made most mark in the literature, are more than anything else the ideas of power held by those in power.[22] Just as much of this complex of ideas used to belong to the court elites of the ancient Javanese kingdoms, in modern day Indonesia they belong to the mostly Javanese political elite, and perhaps most conspicuously in this context to Suharto himself. However, the regime's attempts to monopolise the definition of traditional Javanese culture and ideas of power did not go unchallenged, as illustrated by the views of two Indonesian political scientists, both writing in 1996:

> ... many of our political elite [...] are *paranoid*. [...] I think this *paranoia* sickness comes as a result of the impact of the concept of power. On one hand there is the elite which is

---

21. Anderson (1972).
22. See Quarles van Ufford (1987: 150) for a similar argument.

isolated with the idea that the origin of power is God. Power is one and cannot be divided. Because of this, they believe that political legitimacy goes together with the proximity to the centre of power.[23]

Democracy demands a certain attitude. The nomination of a candidate to challenge another candidate, even if he or she is the incumbent, may well be a challenge to a certain cultural values [*sic*] here, where it is considered inelegant, disconcerting and perhaps even "unethical" to do so. Not all cultural values and traditions deserve to be preserved. [...] I loathe the tendency on the part of those in power to abuse or manipulate what they call "national identity" or traditional "cultural values", which they themselves define, though vaguely, and thus they alone pretend to understand, primarily to justify and maintain their power.[24]

Knowing that Suharto was a believer in and practitioner of Javanese mysticism, it is reasonable to believe that he would interpret political events within this cultural framework. Not only was he threatened by the prospect of not getting a unanimous support for his re-election in 1998; what may very well have been worse from his point of view was that the threat came from Megawati Sukarnoputri, the daughter of the man he himself had toppled 30 years before. There thus opened up a possibility that Suharto's reign would be bracketed between two Sukarnos, which in historical perspective would make Suharto look like an illegitimate usurper.[25]

It may be, as several analysts argued both in Indonesia and abroad, that the challenge from Megawati was not very significant, and that the chance of her seriously threatening Suharto was minimal. After all, the president would control the line-up of the MPR, the military was firmly in his hands, and he had secured the support of influential leaders of the Muslim

---

23. Imawan (1996: 6–7); italics in original.
24. J. Sujati Jiwondo in *Jakarta Post* (1 February 1996).
25. I owe this observation to Patrick Walters, Jakarta correspondent for *The Australian*; personal communication, Jakarta (14 March 1997).

community. However, it does not necessarily follow that Suharto himself felt secure. In traditional Javanese thinking, one of the characteristics of *wahyu* is that it may easily pass on from a power holder to someone else, especially someone coming from a formerly powerful family.[26] Furthermore, as Suharto had built up a reputation for complete political dominance during more than two decades, even a relatively small challenge to his power might be considered as a sign that his power was unravelling. The president's age and the general feeling that his presidency was nearing its end also combined to strengthen such perceptions.

The issue of Megawati's nomination highlighted some of the contradictions in Indonesia's political life in the late Suharto era. While the regime ostensibly adhered to modern democratic ideas and paid lip service to the constitution, it simultaneously drew on a different, essentially non-modern, political culture, to achieve legitimacy and maintain the political status quo. On the surface, the government reacted calmly to the suggestion of nominating Megawati for president, mainly pointing out that the proper, quasi-democratic political forms and procedures would have to be adhered to. On a deeper level, however, the affair was interpreted as a sign of opposition to the regime, and especially to the position and personal rule of President Suharto. It highlighted the incompatibilities of, on the one hand, the efforts of the government to portray itself as a modern democratic regime, claiming legitimacy on legalistic and constitutional principles and, on the other hand, its paternalistic character and claims to legitimacy based on traditional Javanese mystical ideas.

Removing Megawati

According to Megawati, the plans to have her removed from the PDI chair were drawn up at an ABRI leadership meeting which

---

26. Anderson (1996).

was held at the end of March 1996.[27] The meeting was held to discuss ABRI's strategy for guaranteeing the security and success of the 1997 general election and the 1998 MPR session.

Soon after the meeting, the local branches of the PDI began to experience pressure from local authorities, and from the end of April the party's central board received letters of complaint from several branches about the external intervention. The letters told a remarkably similar story from different parts of the country: local branch leaders were invited to the local authorities and advised to accept the holding of a party congress. The purpose of this congress was not specified, but most people suspected that it would be used to depose Megawati. They were given little information but that everything was already organised and that they should wait and see. Leaders of the provincial chapters, as well as members of the central board, were also approached by military authorities. In a speech on 26 May Megawati attacked the covert campaign, accusing internal as well as external elements for trying to disrupt the party's consolidation in order to turn it once more into a small insignificant party.[28]

On 3 June the call for a congress became public. A delegation of around 40 PDI cadres visited the Ministry of Home Affairs in Jakarta and delivered statements which they claimed represented 215 of the party's 305 local branches, all demanding that a congress be held. A spokesman for the ministry immediately agreed to the request of the delegation. It also became clear who

---

27. Interview in Haribuan (ed.) (1996: 168). Megawati actually sets the meeting in April; however, since there was no national ABRI leadership meeting in April, it is most likely that she meant to refer to the one held at the end of March.

28. Soekarnoputri (1996a: 14). See *Merdeka* (8 June 1996) for reports on pressure on the local PDI branches in North Sumatra, West Java and West Nusa Tenggara. The head of PDI's research department, Kwik Kian Gie, claimed in the beginning of May that he had evidence of the action, and he said that Sabam Sirait and Sukowaluyo, two members of the central board, had been pressured by the authorities to agree to hold a congress; see *Jakarta Post* (2 May 1996).

among the party's leaders supported the action. Suryadi, who served as the party's deputy speaker in parliament, immediately declared himself to be a vanguard figure in arranging the congress, and on the next day Fatimah Achmad, leader of the PDI's faction in the parliament, formed a congress committee. The supporters of the congress claimed, without much credibility, that it was necessary according to the party's statutes to hold a congress, and that it was not the intention to depose Megawati.[29]

It was obvious that the move to arrange a congress was the result of a conspiracy. The delegation went directly to the Ministry of Home Affairs, bypassing Megawati and the party's central board.[30] The statements from the local branches had been collected throughout the previous month, again bypassing Megawati and the central board. Furthermore, the government and the military clearly sided with the proponents of the congress, and consistently ignored the protests of Megawati's camp. Military and government officials held briefings with media representatives, advising them to report favourably about the congress. The press was also advised not to use Megawati's last name, Sukarnoputri, because of its association with the former president, but rather to refer to her as Megawati Taufik Kiemas after her husband. The biased stance of the government drew criticism from several observers and analysts, as well as independent NGOs and the National Commission for Human Rights, Komnas HAM.[31]

---

29. *Jawa Pos* (4 June 1996), *Bisnis Indonesia* (4 June 1996) and *Suara Pembaruan* (5 June 1996).
30. *Kompas* (4 June 1996). Van Dijk (1997: 407) claims that the delegation first visited the PDI headquarters to put forward their demands. Van Dijk does not give a source for this information. The report in *Kompas* for example does not mention that the delegation went anywhere except to the ministry, and I have not been able to confirm the information elsewhere.
31. Haribuan (ed.) (1996: 57), Indonesian Legal Aid Foundation (1997: 2–3), *Jakarta Post* (12 June 1996), *Weekend Australian* (15/16 June 1996), *Suara Pembaruan* (19 June 1996) and Indonesian National Commission on Human Rights (1997: 22–23). Sukarnoputri literally means 'daughter of Sukarno'.

On 12 June Megawati made an unprecedented outburst against the government. Talking to a group of foreign journalists, Megawati said that she would sue the government for endorsing the plans to organise the congress. She also said that it was beyond doubt that individuals in the military had played an active role in encouraging party members to request a congress. Furthermore, Megawati said that the PDI 'could bring tens of millions of people into the streets of every major city and town in the country', closing thousands of factories, offices and schools nation-wide and bringing normal activities to a halt. However, Megawati said, the PDI would refrain from taking to the streets, because the party loved the constitution, both the constitution of the party and of the nation. At the press meeting, Megawati was accompanied by Abdurrahman Wahid, leader of the more than thirty million strong NU. Ostensibly he was there only as Megawati's friend, but his presence served to put extra force behind Megawati's threat to bring people out on the streets. Together the two could command the loyalty of millions of people, mainly in the politically sensitive and crucial Java.[32]

The threat was meant as a warning to the government and to Suharto that a 'people power' revolution, such as in the Philippines in 1986, might occur in Indonesia as well. Nothing more came of it, however. Both Abdurrahman Wahid and Megawati had lived through the upheavals in the mid-1960s, and both were anxious to avoid another wave of uncontrolled bloodshed, which many feared might easily be the result of attempting to initiate a 'people power' revolution against the military.

A week later, the PDI congress went ahead as smoothly as planned. President Suharto was careful not to involve himself in the matter, and he did not, as was customary, open the party's congress, nor did he send a written address to be read at the occasion. In spite of Suharto's seemingly detached stance,

---

32. *Jakarta Post* (13 June 1996), *The Australian* (15/16 June 1996) and *Merdeka* (13 June 1996).

most politically educated Indonesians had no doubts about why the manipulative operation was put into action. Megawati and the PDI were not to be in a position to disturb Golkar's election victory and Suharto's uncontested re-election as president in 1998.

The Opposition Gathers Momentum

Whereas the congress in Medan went very smoothly, the event triggered large protests among Megawati's supporters in Jakarta. On the day of the opening of the congress, thousands of Megawati's supporters demonstrated in the capital against the congress, and against the government's support for it. Outside Gambir railway station in Central Jakarta, riot police and soldiers blocked the way of the demonstrators. A number of unidentified people in black started hurling stones at the troops, who answered by attacking the demonstrators with batons and rattan sticks. Over 70 demonstrators were injured, five of them severely. The military claimed that 55 of its troops were injured. After the clash, which became known as the Gambir incident, an agreement was reached between the Jakarta military commander, Major-General Sutiyoso, and Megawati's central board to avoid further incidents. According to one of Megawati's aides, their side promised not to hold any more street demonstrations, but was permitted to hold activities in the compound of the party's headquarters in the suburb of Menteng in Central Jakarta.[33]

Megawati refused to acknowledge the result of the Medan congress, or the 'Medan Meeting' (*Rapat Medan*), as her supporters preferred to call it.[34] She still claimed to be the legal chairperson of the PDI, in spite of the government's recognition of Suryadi as party leader. Megawati's lawyers launched a suit

---

33. *Jakarta Post* (22 June 1996), Indonesian Legal Aid Foundation (1997: 4).
34. For example, Silaban *et al.* (1997: 297).

in the Jakarta central district court to have the congress declared illegal, and they charged both the Suryadi camp and representatives of the government, among them Minister of Home Affairs Yogie S. M. and the military commander-in-chief, General Feisal Tanjung, who had supported the congress. However, the first session was cancelled, allegedly because the judge had a toothache.[35] The case was adjourned for three weeks, and then in several stages until it eventually was declared by the court to be outside its jurisdiction.

On 26 June support for Megawati gathered strength, as the representatives of 30 NGOs announced the formation of an umbrella organisation called MARI (*Majelis Rakyat Indonesia*, Indonesian People's Assembly) in support of Megawati. According to one of the founders, MARI was formed in response to the government's interference in the PDI. It set forward a number of political demands, including an end to corruption and collusion, as well as a reform of political legislation. MARI represented a wide spectre of NGOs, mostly on the political left, and all drawn from groups critical of the government. Among the leading figures were Muchtar Pakpahan, the leader of an independent worker's union, and Budiman Sujatmiko [Soedjatmiko], the leader of a small unrecognised leftist-intellectual party, the PRD (*Partai Rakyat Demokrat*, Democratic People's Party). There were also several student activists among MARI's founders, and Megawati's younger sister, Sukmawati [Soekmawati], who was the most radical and militant member of the Sukarno family, was also among the founders. She admired Che Guevara and a few years earlier she had declined to join the PDI because she considered the party to be too accommodating to the government.[36]

---

35. *Republika* (2 August 1996); see further Luwarso (ed.) (1997: 202–211) for the trials.
36. On the formation of MARI, see Luwarso (ed.) (1997: 153), and for Sukmawati's radicalism, see McIntyre (1997: 9).

Megawati's supporters continued to occupy the PDI's central headquarters in Jalan Diponegoro in central Jakarta, guarding it day and night against an expected attack from Suryadi's supporters or the military. A free-speech forum was erected in front of the office which, after a cautious start, gradually became more bold and critical of the government. It was a unique occurrence, because it was the first free-speech forum outside a university campus in several years. Speakers from the PDI as well as from the NGOs in MARI spoke at the forum, criticising the government, corruption and lack of democracy. Hundreds of pro-democracy activists and supporters of Megawati gathered each day to listen to the speeches and to sing political songs.[37] The government's treatment of Megawati had brought about a broad coalition of pro-democracy forces which seemed to be growing in strength day by day.

The government also realised the danger. On 22 July General Feisal Tanjung branded the free-speech forum as unconstitutional, saying that the speakers planned to overthrow the government. He also said that the speeches did not reflect Indonesian values and that the jargon of the speakers was similar to that used by the outlawed Indonesian Communist Party (PKI). Meanwhile, Feisal's statements in themselves illustrated a jargon typical of the New Order: branding political opponents as subversive and un-Indonesian and accusing them of having links with the PKI, the government's political ghost *par excellence*.[38]

Two days later, on 24 July Jakarta's chief of police formally banned the free-speech forum. The next day President Suharto

---

37. See Antlöv (1996: 9), YLBHI (1997: 11–19) and the editorial in *Jakarta Post* (24 July 1996) about the free-speech forum. The platform was denoted either as the 'free platform' *(mimbar bebas)* or the 'democracy platform' *(mimbar demokrasi)*. Government and military representatives normally used the former term, trying to project an image of the forum being free in the sense of wild *(liar)* and irresponsible *(tidak bertanggungjawab)*; see Wardhana (1997: 28).
38. *Jakarta Post* (23 July 1996). For the anti-Communist ideology of the New Order, see Goodfellow (1995).

received Suryadi in the presidential palace, thus giving him the definite seal of official approval as party leader. After the meeting Suryadi quoted the president as warning against the 'bald devils' (*setan gundul*) who were creating problems in the PDI. Suharto, as cited by Suryadi, accused the NGOs in MARI of being outside the New Order and of using the PDI for their own purposes. The president also commented on the historical parallel with the revolt of the PKI in 1965.[39] With the culprits thus singled out, the military hinted at immediate action against the free-speech forum and against Megawati's supporters at the party headquarters.

The Grey Saturday of 27 July

Shortly after dawn on 27 July 1996, a number of yellow trucks pulled up in front of the PDI headquarters in Jalan Diponegoro.[40] The trucks unloaded hundreds of young men with head bands and red t-shirts reading 'Supporter of the Fourth Medan Congress' (*Pendukung Kongres IV Medan*).[41] Many of the men were well-

---

39. *Suara Karya* (26 July 1996). The president's analysis may have been less off the mark than it first appears. The PRD, which was the leading organisation in MARI, was outside the New Order in that the party aimed at overhauling the regime in favour of a more democratic system. The parallel with the PKI is relevant with respect to the class-based political strategy which the PRD employed. At the time it was also the tactic of the PRD to try to mobilise the large masses of Megawati supporters for their own political struggle; confidential interviews with two PRD activists, Jakarta (November 1998).
40. This rendering of the events of 27 July is, where not otherwise stated, based two first-hand accounts: *Tempo Interaktif* (3 August 1996) and *Kabar dari PIJAR* (27 July 1996), and two summaries of the events based primarily on first-hand sources (among them *Tempo Interaktif*); Luwarso (ed.) (1997: 22–35) and YLBHI (1997:18–26). The overall sequence of events is similarly described in all of these.
41. The Medan congress was in fact the fifth in the party's history. However, its supporters, somewhat confusingly, claimed that it was a continuation of the last ordinary congress (the fourth) which was held in the same venue in Medan in 1993.

built and with short crew-cut hair, leading some observers to suspect that they were in fact soldiers out of uniform.[42] Several of the men were armed with long wooden sticks. They started to throw stones and other objects unloaded from their trucks at Megawati's supporters inside the building, who returned the assault in the same way as best they could. The stone throwing was accompanied by verbal insults between the two groups. Shortly afterwards some 500–1,000 anti-riot police, backed up by armoured vehicles, arrived on the scene. They did not attempt to stop the attack and the stone throwing, but instead split into two groups sealing off Jalan Diponegoro on both sides of the party headquarters. Passers-by and supporters of Megawati who had heard of the attack began to assemble outside one of the cordons, near Cikini railway station.

After about an hour of stone throwing the chief of the Central Jakarta police command, Lieutenant-Colonel Abu Bakar, intervened and called a cease-fire between the two groups. He urged Megawati's supporters to evacuate the building and surrender it to the police, promising that it would be considered as in a condition of status quo. He telephoned Megawati, who seems to have agreed to let her supporters evacuate the building under the observation of foreign and domestic journalists.[43] Before the agreement went ahead, however, the attack started again with intensified stone throwing. Dozens of anti-riot police then broke down the fence around the PDI headquarters and charged in, interspersed with the red-shirted young men. Large parts of the building were destroyed in the attack and by a fire

---

42. For example, Aspinall (1996: 5) and *Suara Independen*, no. 1/III (August 1996). This was also the opinion of Megawati herself; Soekarnoputri (1996b). The men in red seem to have been commanded by the commander of central Jakarta district military command, Lieutenant-Colonel Zul Effendi; Luwarso (ed.) (1997: 22–23) and YLBHI (1997: 18). See also the discussion below about the identity of the attackers.
43. Soekarnoputri (1996b).

which broke out during the mêlée. Several people were killed or injured, both by fire and blows from batons and rattan sticks. Although the military afterwards claimed that no firearms were used in the attack, at least one of Megawati's supporters died from gunshot wounds. The National Human Rights Commission, Komnas HAM, found that five people, all Megawati supporters, were killed in the attack. In addition, another sixteen people were still missing more than a year after the event.[44]

Around 9 a.m. the police had captured the building and closed the area around it to the public and to reporters. Some of the more seriously injured of the defenders were carried off in ambulances, while dozens of others were detained and taken to the Jakarta police headquarters.

Meanwhile, the crowd of people outside the cordons continued to swell. A free-speech podium was erected, and the speakers expressed their support for Megawati and the need to fight for democracy and justice. People sang protest songs, and some minor clashes with security forces took place. Rumours also began to spread that up to 50 people had been killed in the attack on the PDI headquarters, and that the corpses had been heaped up in a mass grave.

As the situation grew increasingly tense, Lieutenant-Colonel Abu Bakar agreed to let five people go and see the PDI building accompanied by security forces. After fifteen minutes the five envoys came out again. One of them told a journalist that 'there is nothing inside, but blood is spilled everywhere.'[45] As the group tried to address the crowd, one of them was hit by a rock. At this, the crowd began to throw stones, wood and parts of a demolished iron fence at the troops. Some of the crowd began to advance towards the line of policemen who fought back with their batons and shields.

---

44. Indonesian National Commission on Human Rights (1997: 22) and *Suara Merdeka* (5 September 1997).
45. *Tempo Interaktif* (3 August 1996).

The crowd eventually calmed down somewhat. Prominent leaders of Megawati's PDI faction came to the scene and tried to negotiate with the authorities. Meanwhile the number of people near Cikini railway station continued to grow, swollen largely by high-school students on their way home from school. From a few thousand people in the morning, it was estimated that the crowd grew to over 10,000 people in the afternoon.

At around 2.30 p.m. the stone throwing started again, more intensely than before. The police troops were forced to retire from their blockade line in order to protect themselves. However, the counter attack came shortly afterwards, with the police using tear gas, water cannons and batons. Chased by the security forces, the crowd ran eastward along Jalan Diponegoro, setting fire to a couple of buses which were parked on the street. Several people were caught by the security forces and beaten with sticks and batons.

On reaching the intersection of Jalan Diponegoro and Jalan Salemba the crowd split into two, one heading south and the other north. More buses and other vehicles were set on fire, and several traffic lights were smashed with stones. Several buildings had their windows destroyed or were set on fire. Among the buildings burnt down by the crowd were several banks, a building belonging to the Ministry of Agriculture, a Toyota auto showroom and an office belonging to the official organisation for army wives. The riots continued well into the evening with many smaller shops being looted or set on fire. The reinforced security forces, meanwhile, concentrated on sealing off the riot-hit areas to prevent the unrest from spreading. Gradually during the evening the troops moved in and the rioters dispersed. Around 1 a.m. the police and the military had regained full control over the city, and the fires and looting came to an end.

'People Power' or Government Manipulation?

The unrest on 27 July began with a planned operation to seize the PDI headquarters from Megawati's supporters and to put an end to the increasingly bold free-speech forum. The role of the government and the security forces in the operation was conspicuous. Using hindsight, it is obvious how the momentum was built up for the attack with government and military officials condemning the use of the PDI headquarters. The attack came as no surprise to the defenders of the building, and Megawati herself later claimed that she knew of plans for the attack two days before it happened.[46]

The take-over was apparently intended to look like an internal showdown between the rival supporters of Megawati and Suryadi. It was also apparent that the security forces were prepared for the attack and thus could arrive on the scene with large numbers of anti-riot personnel only a few minutes after the attack started. However, instead of trying to stop the attack, the troops participated in it.[47]

A question mark concerns the identity of the Suryadi supporters who attacked the building. As mentioned, their physique and hair cuts led some observers to conclude that they were soldiers in mufti. Although this is possible, later events suggested that a

---

46. Megawati gave this information when testifying in the Jakarta state court in November 1996; *Kompas* (12 November 1996).

47. The Komnas HAM concluded that '[t]he July 27, 1996 take-over of the [PDI headquarters] was an act accompanied by violence carried out by the [central board of the] PDI of the Medan Congress and their supporters, and was carried out jointly with the security apparatus.' Indonesian National Commission on Human Rights (1997: 23).

The Editors (1997: 105) [of the journal *Indonesia*] suggest that military officers from the 1974 class of graduates from the Military Academy, *Akmil (Akademi Militer)* in Magelang, Central Java were behind the attack. This group of ambitious officers, led by Suharto's son-in-law and commander of the elite unit Kopassus, Major-General Prabowo Subianto, dominated the staff and command postings in and around Jakarta at the time of the attack. However, Prabowo's profile in the affair was very low key, and available evidence does not suggest that he was directly involved in the attack. Suspicions of high-level military involvement rather focused on General Feisal Tanjung and Major-General Syarwan Hamid, the two senior officers who seemed to take most interest in the affair.

number of the attackers were criminal thugs (*preman*) hired for the purpose. The use of hired thugs is a long-standing tactic in Indonesian politics dating back at least to the 1940s. Under the New Order, thugs have been used on several occasions by the government and the military. They typically form alliances with influential political patrons, and they get financial compensation and political protection for their murky services. These services may include staging violent demonstrations and riots or intimidating political opponents by, for example, attacking their residences or offices.[48]

In May 1997, 49 men who claimed to have taken part in the attack on the PDI headquarters filed a law suit against Suryadi and four other PDI functionaries for not paying the allegedly agreed financial compensation. According to their leader, Seno Bella Emyus, he met with several leaders of Suryadi's central board a week before the attack. At the meeting it was allegedly agreed that a number of Seno Bella's followers dressed in red T-shirts would take part in the attack, which they did. Seno Bella claimed that he received a total of 11.5 million rupiah (4,800 U.S. dollars) as a down payment for this service, and that he was promised another 200 million (83,000 US dollars) to be paid after the attack, an amount which was never paid. Suryadi, although he admitted that he knew Seno Bella, claimed that there had never been an agreement between them, and that he would not hire thugs who were not PDI members for the attack. Instead he suspected that the accusation was part of an attempt to slander him in connection with the election.[49]

---

48. For some observations about the *preman* phenomenon and its political implications, see Bresnan (1993: 146), Cribb (1996: 8), Randall (1998), *Digest* 13 (30 May 1996) and *Tapol Bulletin*, no. 123 (June 1994). For the historical roots of *preman*ism in Jakarta, see Cribb (1991).
49. *Kompas* (27 May 1997, 15 July 1997, 12 August 1997, 15 August 1997 and 9 September 1997) and *Tempo Interaktif* (31 May 1997). The law suit was filed three days before the election day, and Seno Bella's thugs were represented in court by Megawati's chief lawyer and close aide, R.O. Tambunan.

In the end, the court rejected Seno Bella's suit, ruling that there had not existed any legally binding agreement between Seno Bella and Suryadi. However, the court believed it to be true that Suryadi had hired the thugs for the attack, and that Seno Bella had received the down payment of 11.5 million.[50]

If the crowd which attacked the PDI headquarters in the morning of 27 July were hired thugs and soldiers, the people who went on the rampage later in the afternoon were a different crowd. They consisted of supporters of Megawati who assembled outside the police cordons around the PDI headquarters, residents of the slum areas around the Cikini railway station and passers-by who stopped on their way home from work or from school. Whereas the attack on the PDI office was a planned and co-ordinated action involving elements of the military and the government, the rioting that followed in the afternoon was unplanned.

In handling the riot, the security forces acted according to what seems to be a formal ABRI tactic in riot control: to seal off the riot area thus preventing the unrest from spreading to other areas and then to wait for the rioting to abate, while reinforcements arrive. The troops then move in, disperse the crowd and arrest some rioters who are caught red-handed. The use of firearms is deliberately avoided and is only a last resort. This 'softer' tactic seems to have been adapted and implemented by the military after massive international and domestic criticism after the Dili massacre in East Timor in 1991.[51]

In part as a result of ABRI's riot control tactic, for a few hours in the afternoon of 27 July an area of Central Jakarta was a lawless area where young men could vent their frustrations in

---

50. *Kompas* (21 October 1997 and 13 November 1997).
51. See *Forum Keadilan* (24 February 1997) and Amnesty International (1998b). According to Haseman (1997: 130) senior ABRI officers were proud that the 27 July riots could be contained with a minimum of casualties and considered this outcome as a tribute to the professionalism of the military in controlling riots.

an orgy of destruction directed at the symbols of wealth and power. It was not a coordinated or ideologically coherent action, and hopes among some Western commentators that 27 July would be the start of a 'people power' revolution in Indonesia were unfounded. The unrest was not primarily directed toward the police or the military, and the hatred and confrontational behaviour of demonstrators in, for example, South Korea in the 1980s was largely absent in Jakarta.[52] This observation does not diminish the seriousness of the rioting or the frustrations that underlay it. It was primarily a class-related protest against the symbols of wealth and inequality, as demonstrated by its targets, such as banks and car outlets. However, the violence and the protesting lacked political direction and organisation, and therefore the 27 July lacked the clout to become a starting point for a popular political movement which might challenge the regime.

The PDI Affair and the Legitimacy of the New Order

Megawati's ousting was the result of a conspiracy supported by elements within the regime. In order to preserve the political status quo, Megawati could not be allowed to lead the PDI, possibly making substantial gains for the party in the election and openly challenging Suharto for the presidency. Therefore, an operation was staged which aimed at ousting Megawati in what was meant to look like a constitutionally handled internal party affair. However, as the involvement of senior government and military officials was exposed, the event damaged the image of the regime and its already shaky democratic credentials in the eyes of many Indonesians. The affair also demonstrated the regime's unaccommodating attitude towards the increasingly vocal calls for political reform and more democracy from students, intellectuals and various activists.

---

52. I owe this observation to Jim Della-Giacoma, correspondent for *Reuters* in Jakarta, personal communication, Jakarta (September 1997).

The 27 July riots were worrying to many analysts as the unrest gave an indication of the social and economic discontent which was brewing in society, mostly among young urban poor people. In the New Order's corporatist society these groups lacked adequate channels for their social and political aspirations. In contrast to the regime, Megawati had come to represent the plight of the poor, both through her link with Sukarno and through her own repeated attacks on corruption and social and economic injustice. Against this background, many of Megawati's supporters conceived of her unjust removal as symbolic of a general pattern of injustice in society.

The blatant demonstrations of manipulation and repression by the regime were mostly damaging to its image domestically. The international community largely treated the affair as an internal problem and refrained from taking sides. Investors quickly recovered from a minor shiver caused by the sudden outburst of violence in Jakarta on 27 July. Overall, Indonesia was still seen as a socially and politically stable nation with very promising economic prospects.

Remarkably, President Suharto seemed to stand above all the commotion, in spite of a widespread realisation that his invisible hand had guided the events, as it did all major political events in Indonesia. Suharto deliberately did not involve himself in the PDI conflict, and the bad publicity from the affair did not reflect directly on his personal legitimacy. He was still, in the eyes of Indonesia and the world, the most powerful man in Asia.

CHAPTER 3

Riots and Conspiracies

In 1996 and early 1997 several riots occurred in various parts of Indonesia. The 27 July riot in Jakarta was the incident which made the biggest headlines in the national, as well as international media. The Jakarta riot, however, was not the most serious disturbance that year neither in terms of the number of casualties nor in terms of the economic damage it caused. In Situbondo (East Java), Tasikmalaya (West Java), and Sanggau Ledo (West Kalimantan), thousands of people went on the rampage, killing, burning and looting in sudden outbursts of communal violence. Riots flared up in several other locations as well, such as on 9 June, when crowds attacked and destroyed several churches in the East Java capital Surabaya.[1] However, this incident was not reported in the media, and therefore it had little political impact on the national level. By contrast, the riots in Situbondo and Tasikmalaya, and to a lesser extent the riots in West Kalimantan, were extensively reported and discussed in the media. The riots caused great uneasiness among analysts and social commentators about the country's social and political future. Ethnic, racial and religious tensions were obviously central motives in all of the riots, but more sophisticated theories of explanation were put forward as well. Economic and social divisions were popular explanations among intellectuals in Indonesia, as were various politically motivated conspiracy theories. With the general election approaching, it seemed that some mysterious 'third party' or

---

1. See YLBHI (1997: 76–81) and Rani *et al.* (eds) (1997: 23).

parties were instigating the riots in order to promote some hidden political agenda or murky political aspirations.

Churches Ablaze in East Java

It started with an affair reminiscent of a heresy case in medieval Europe. On 12 September 1996, in the small East Java town of Situbondo, a young gardener by the name of Saleh was brought to trial on charges of having insulted religion, or more specifically Islam. According to his accuser, a local Islamic teacher, Kiai Haji (K. H.) Achmad Zaini, Saleh claimed to be the messenger of Allah and denied that Muhammad had been Allah's prophet. Kiai Zaini also accused Saleh of having said that the Koran was a work of mankind, and that it was not necessary for man to do the daily prayers (*solat*). According to the accusations, Saleh claimed to have received his spiritual teachings from a highly respected local Islamic leader (*kiai*), the late K. H. R. As'ad Syamsul Arifin. Saleh also said that the latter's passing away had not been perfect (*ta'kacer*) as he had died in a hospital and not at home.[2]

---

2. YLBHI (1997: 55). It is not clear where Saleh got the latter idea from. According to one source, he had got it from a Madurese whom he had met but did not know; *Kerusuhan Situbondo* (1996: 19).

The reconstruction of the events in Situbondo are, where not otherwise stated, taken from YLBHI (1997: 54–75), Rani *et al.* (eds) (1997: 19–23) and *Detektif & Romantika* (19 October 1996). Hariyanto (ed.) (1998: 5–25) provides a more detailed account based on second-hand sources and literature. See also the white book, *Kerusuhan Situbondo* (1996), produced by the East Java branch of NU's youth organisation *Gerakan Pemuda Ansor*.

The weekly *Detektif & Romantika* was originally a popular magazine featuring, as the name implies, criminal and romantic stories. However, in 1996, the magazine's publishing licence was bought by the Grafiti Pers group and turned into a serious news magazine intended to fill the place of *Tempo*, the group's flagship which was banned by the government in 1994. In this way, Grafiti Pers could get around the difficulties in obtaining a publishing licence from the government for a new magazine.

At the trial, Saleh denied all accusations that he had disgraced Islam, but he maintained his opinion that K. H. R. As'ad Syamsul Arifin's death had not been perfect. It seemed that many people were angered by Saleh's defamation of the *kiai*'s memory, and at the fourth court session on 3 October a large crowd assembled outside the court house, calling for Saleh's death. After the session a handful of people even managed to break into Saleh's cell from the roof and beat him up.

For the next session on 10 October an even larger crowd, estimated at 3,000 people, gathered outside the court house.[3] Many of them apparently came from outside the town of Situbondo. It seemed that Kiai Zaini had distributed photo copies of the announcement of the trial in order to assemble more people. Also present were around a hundred soldiers from the Military District Command, Kodim (*Komando Distrik Militer*), to maintain order for the trial.

At the trial the prosecutor demanded five years' imprisonment for Saleh, the maximum penalty for insulting religion according to the law. The crowd, however, was not satisfied, and demanded the death penalty for Saleh. Some people started to throw stones at the court house. The security forces withdrew inside the building, and eventually fled out the back over a river, together with the judges and Saleh himself. At this point someone set fire to the court house and to a car belonging to the prosecutor.[4] The rumour then spread that Saleh was hiding in the nearby Bukit Sion Church. The angry crowd moved to the church and set it on fire, using gasoline from a nearby petrol station.

From the Bukit Sion Church, the masses moved on to attack the other churches in town. In one day 23 churches, out of 26 in the Situbondo district, were destroyed mostly by fire, but some also by stone throwing and by people tearing down the

---

3. *Far Eastern Economic Review* (25 October 1996).
4. *Tempo Interaktif* (25 January 1997).

walls. In one of the churches a minister and his family were burned alive, resulting in a death toll of five people. Several cars, schools, shops, and a Christian orphanage were attacked and set on fire as well.

The security forces were slow to respond, and did not attempt to stop the rioting until reinforcements arrived in the afternoon, around five hours after the unrest had started. When the police and military had restored order in Situbondo, however, the crowd moved to nearby villages and towns where they continued the destruction. Apparently big trucks arrived to transport the rioters. All the churches that were attacked were situated in the Situbondo district. In some places the rioting continued well into the night.

There were many unclear circumstances around the Situbondo riot. For one thing it seemed to come right out of the blue. There had not been any serious instances of rioting or inter-religious tensions earlier in the district. Situbondo was a strong *santri*, or orthodox Muslim area, with around 98 per cent of the population officially adhering to Islam. Most of the population were descendants of Muslim migrants from the nearby island of Madura, and Christians made up only a little more than one per cent of the population.[5] Although many ethnic Chinese, who were on average better off than the majority of the population, were Christians, there is nothing to indicate that economic jealousy or racism were driving motives behind the incident. A few shops, some of them probably owned by Chinese, were attacked, but these were marginal features of the riot. Neither did Chinese people or their private property seem to have become targets for the rioting. People who participated in the riots afterwards said that they did not do it out of hatred. For example, two youngsters who were detained by the police in the riot, said in an interview afterwards that they and their friends just went along. Another, anonymous, resident of Situbondo

---

5. YLBHI (1997: 57) citing the official statistics.

who took part in the riot said: 'There was no feeling of hatred toward a certain group. We just felt that it was a rare occasion and that being a part of it carried the emotions away.'[6]

Still, the systematic way in which the destruction targeted the churches was striking. The rioters did not confine themselves to the town of Situbondo where the rioting sparked off, but they also took care to destroy the churches in other towns and villages in the district. It also seems that someone organised transport for the rioters.

According to some sources the church attacks in some villages several kilometres from Situbondo even happened at precisely the same time as the court house was set on fire in Situbondo. This was the opinion of Situbondo's territorial military commander, Lieutenant-Colonel Imam Prawoto. Another curious circumstance was that, according to the *Suara Pembaruan* daily, several molotov cocktails were later found behind some of the destroyed churches; these had apparently been placed there beforehand for use in the attacks.[7]

Political Implications of the Situbondo Riot

On the following day there was no word in the press of the riots. Neither East Java's leading papers, the *Jawa Pos* and the *Surabaya Post*, nor the big national newspapers, carried anything on the story. Ethnic and religious violence was something which newspaper editors dealt with cautiously for fear of losing their publishing licences. Only three weeks earlier, on the opening of a ten-day *Pancasila* ideology course for mass media executives, Suharto had called on the media to handle stories about unrest and riots with care.[8]

---

6. *Detektif & Romantika* (2 November 1996) and Rani *et al.* (eds) (1997: 21).
7. Rani *et al.* (eds) (1997: 21–22). See also *Tempo Interaktif* (25 January 1997) describing the riots as a systematic operation.
8. *Jakarta Post* (21 September 1996).

However, the government decided to bring the news of the Situbondo riot to public knowledge. On 11 October, State Secretary Murdiono [Moerdiono] held a press conference, expressing the government's regret over the incident and asking that all religious leaders intensify the guidance of their congregations to avoid a repetition of similar incidents. Several other ministers and government representatives also expressed their concern over the Situbondo violence, stressing the role of religious leaders in forestalling inter-religious violence. Minister of Religious Affairs Tarmizi Taher said that the incident showed that the religious leaders were unable to lead their congregations properly. The East Java Governor Basofi Sudirman [Soedirman] asked Islamic leaders, *ulama*, to be active in nipping such outbreaks in the bud.[9]

The obvious message from these official statements was that the *ulama* had failed in leading their communities. The ill-concealed target of government criticism was the Nahdlatul Ulama (NU) and its outspoken leader, Abdurrahman Wahid. The NU, with its more than 30 million members, had its stronghold in the rural areas of East Java. It was centred on the revered orthodox Islamic leaders, *ulama*, and their religious schools, *pesantren*. Thanks to the network of *ulama* and *pesantren*, the NU had a unique grass-roots organisation with a far-reaching potential to function as a channel for political mobilisation. The NU had previously been a political party, and had formed the largest component of the PPP when it was founded in the party merger in 1973. However, after serious divisions in the new party, the NU withdrew from the PPP in 1984, declaring itself a non-political organisation. It also declared that its members were free to vote for either Golkar, the PPP or the PDI.[10]

---

9. *Kompas* (12 October 1996 and 13 October 1996).
10. For NU and its role in politics, see Ramage (1995: 45–74), Barton and Fealy (eds) (1996) and van Bruinessen (1998).

With the general election in May 1997 approaching, all three election contestants were eager to win the voter support of the NU members. Thus, in the years preceding the Situbondo riot, the *pesantren* had increasingly become a focus of political activity, especially from government representatives. President Suharto as well as Minister of Research and Technology B.J. Habibie, who was also chairman of the Association of Indonesian Muslim Intellectuals, ICMI, and other high-ranking politicians had made widely publicised visits to the religious schools. For several years in a row, during the fasting month of Ramadan, Golkar's chairman Harmoko toured the *pesantren*, as did several high-ranking army officers.[11] East Java was a key province for Golkar in the upcoming election, as the organisation was keen on winning back the large number of votes which it had lost there in the 1992 election.[12]

In spite of NU's formal withdrawal from politics, its long-standing chairman, Abdurrahman Wahid, was one of the most vocal and prominent political commentators and debaters in Indonesia. As a leader of an orthodox rural-based Muslim organisation, Wahid was something of a contradictory figure. On one hand, he had strong traditionalist credentials as a charismatic leader and the grandson of NU's legendary founder, K. H. Hasyim [Hasjim] Ashari. At the same time, he was one of Indonesia's leading intellectuals and highly respected for his social and political thinking internationally as well as domestically. In this respect, Wahid represented one of the most significant developments in Indonesian Islam in the last few decades, the emergence of neo-modernist thought. Neo-modernism seeks to make Islam compatible with modernisation of society in the

---

11. Van Dijk (1996: 111).
12. In the 1992 election, Golkar's share of the votes in East Java dropped from its 1987 percentage of 71.2 to 58.8 per cent; see Baroto (1992: 250) for the results. This was by far the largest loss for Golkar in any province. Cf. also Afan Gaffar's (1992) study of the realignment of Javanese voters in the 1992 election.

economic, social, cultural and political fields, emphasising pluralism and inter-religious tolerance, as well as a commitment to the core values of democracy.[13]

Abdurrahman Wahid was also one of the strongest proponents of *Pancasila* as the ideological foundation for the Indonesian state. He was furthermore one of the severest critics of ICMI, which he saw as a vehicle for Islamic fundamentalists trying to Islamise the state, as well as all of society, a programme which he believed risked alienating Christians and other religious minorities.[14] Throughout the 1990s Wahid had also stood out as a one of Suharto's most outspoken opponents, and the president had not tried to hide his displeasure with the NU leader. Since Wahid was re-elected as NU chairman in 1994, Suharto had not received him, thus denying him the customary official seal of approval as leader of the country's largest organisation. The relationship between the two men seems to have become particularly infected by Wahid's critical remarks of Suharto as cited in Adam Schwartz' book *A Nation in Waiting* (1994), where Wahid did not stop short of calling the president stupid.[15] However, just before the Situbondo riot occurred Wahid had started to show himself more conciliatory towards the government. Most importantly, in early October, he distanced himself publicly from Megawati by calling for her to withdraw the law suits which she and her lawyers had launched against the government.[16]

Ironically, when the Situbondo riot occurred, Wahid was in Rome to pray for world peace together with other religious leaders from around the world. The riot, with thousands of NU members burning churches, was an embarrassment to Abdurrahman

---

13. See Barton (1994), (1996) and (1997).
14. Ramage (1995: 45–74) and van Dijk (1996: 142–143).
15. Schwarz (1994: 188). See also van Dijk (1996: 142–143), Fealy (1996: 275) and *Forum Keadilan* (2 December 1996) about Wahid's comment.
16. *Kompas* (4 October 1996).

Wahid, who also showed great public concern over the incident. On his return from Rome on 13 October, the NU leader publicly apologised for the incident, accepting moral responsibility for what had happened. Reconciliation meetings were arranged between the *ulama* and the military as well as between the *ulama* and Christian leaders in East Java. Abdurrahman Wahid was keen to arrange and take part in these meetings and to use them to improve relations between the government and the NU.[17]

In early November, the new improved relationship between the government and the NU became manifest, as Suharto turned up at an NU meeting in a *pesantren* in Genggong, East Java. There the president gave Wahid the long-awaited sign of approval by symbolically taking the NU leader's hand and holding it for a long time in front of the press and TV cameras.[18]

Shortly after the meeting with President Suharto, Wahid met the army chief of staff, General R. Hartono in Situbondo. The meeting was significant in two ways. First, it confirmed the government's acceptance of Abdurrahman Wahid as the leader of the NU, and that the confrontation had come to an end. Hartono had been a particularly outspoken adversary of Wahid, and it appears that he actively campaigned against the latter's re-election as NU chairman in 1994. Second, whereas Hartono was a friend of Habibie's and sympathetic to ICMI, he was also a staunch supporter of Golkar and close to Suharto's eldest daughter, Tutut, who was Golkar's election coordinator for the provinces of East and Central Java and Yogyakarta. In all of these important provinces the NU would have significant influence over the outcome of the election, and it was hardly

---

17. See *Kompas* (14 October 1996), and *Surabaya Post* (31 October 1996) for some of the meetings.
18. *Kompas* (3 November 1996) and *Media Indonesia* (4 November 1996); see also *Digest* 25 (13 November 1996).

conceivable that Golkar would be able to meet its election targets with the help of the NU.[19]

Several parties conducted investigations into who instigated the Situbondo riot. The National Commission [on] Human Rights, Komnas HAM, at first found that [there] had been no third-party involvement, and that the riot was [a s]pontaneous reaction caused by several background factors. This analysis was contradicted by the military which claimed that their investigation showed that the riots had been planned beforehand and engineered. Abdurrahman Wahid also said that there was a third party behind the riot, and he gave the initials of four alleged instigators: L. H., D. S., A. R. and A. S. This fuelled much speculation as people tried to match the initials with people of flesh and blood. The *Gatra* weekly suggested that the initials might mean Lukman Harun, Din Syamsuddin, Amien Rais and Adi Sasono, all leading ICMI activists. Not surprisingly, all four denied involvement, and Wahid himself refused to elaborate further when contacted by the magazine, saying he was tired.[20]

Finally, for the record of conspiracy theories, the East Java branch of NU's youth organisation, the Ansor Youth Movement (*Gerakan Pemuda Ansor*), produced a white book (*Kerusuhan Situbondo*), which concluded that there was a conspiracy of several groups behind the riot, among them criminal thugs

---

19. For the meeting between Hartono and Wahid, see *Kompas* (14 November 1996); for the 1994 NU congress and Hartono's opposition to Wahid, see Bastaman (1995: 29–32) and Fealy (1996). On Hartono's background and relationship with ICMI and Habibie, see Mallarangeng and Liddle (1996: 113–114) and Liddle (1995: 18).
20. *Kompas* (17 October 1996) and *Gatra* (16 November 1996). The Komnas HAM, however, in its annual report for 1996, did not exclude the possibility that the riot had been planned, and concluded that the 'rioting was a surge of anger of the crowds coinciding with simultaneous movements in several places (using trucks and motorcycles)'; Indonesian National Commission on Human Rights (1997: 53).

(*preman*), *Kiai* Zaini's group, and the bureaucracy as well as sections of the military were also implicated in the conspiracy. The book was not produced and sold openly. ICMI, as East Java's territorial military commander, Major-General Imam Utomo, reacted by denying the issue altogether. '[T]he white book never was, and its contents was certainly not true', he was quoted by the *Surabaya Post* as saying.[21]

While speculation and conspiracy theories went around, the police in Situbondo arrested six people accused of being involved in the rioting. All six were local residents and previously known to the police. Before the trials against them started one of them died in custody, officially from a mysterious, unidentified disease. More credible reports say that he was tortured to death.[22] The other five were brought to trial and each sentenced to five months' imprisonment for their participation in the riot. More trials followed, but there was nothing to indicate that any of the accused were part of the hidden conspiracy that instigated the rioting.[23]

The Tasikmalaya Riot

Only a couple of months after the Situbondo riot, on 26 December, religiously motivated violence flared up again, this time in Tasikmalaya, a district capital with 250,000 inhabitants in West Java. Compared with the Situbondo riot, in which the

---

21. *Surabaya Post* (1 February 1997). A few days later, however, Imam Utomo conceded that evidence had been found showing that the book did exist after all; *Surabaya Post* (6 February 1997). For a summary of the book's contents, see *Tempo Interaktif* (25 January 1997). Cf. also Wahid's clarification about the white book; *SiaR* (3 February 1997). The book does exist; *Kerusuhan Situbondo* (1996).
22. Indonesian Legal Aid Foundation (1997: 24–25).
23. *Surabaya Post* (12 December 1996 and 23 December 1996) and *Kompas* (18 December 1996). The trials continued in the first months of 1997, but the accused were only tried for their participation in the riot, not for having instigated or masterminded it.

attacks were primarily and systematically aimed at Christian property and symbols, the targets of the Tasikmalaya riot were more diverse and the destruction seemed less systematic, even though it was much more extensive. A number of churches were destroyed in Tasikmalaya, as were some Christian schools. Much of the anger, however, was directed at the police, and fifteen police stations around town were attacked with stones or set on fire. Another target which seems to have been more pronounced in Tasikmalaya was the city's ethnic Chinese population. One woman of Chinese descent was burned to death as rioters set fire to her shop, and another shop owner, also of Chinese descent, died of heart failure as her baker's shop was attacked by rioters. Another two people died in traffic accidents in connection with the riot, leaving a total death toll of four people. Numerous shops, banks, factories and auto showrooms were attacked and burned, as were hundreds of vehicles. In terms of material destruction, the Tasikmalaya riot was by far the worst in 1996, with losses estimated at 85 billion rupiah (c. 35 million US dollars). This was almost twice as much as for the 27 July riot in Jakarta, and seventeen times more than in Situbondo.[24]

The background of the outburst was a trivial incident in a *pesantren* in Tasikmalaya. One of the students, a boy of fifteen, was caught stealing from his fellow students, and was disciplined according to the rules of the school by being beaten and soaked in water. The boy's father, who was a police officer, did not approve of his son's punishment. On 23 December, the teacher and two senior students responsible for disciplining the son were called to Tasikmalaya's central police station, where they were severely beaten by the boy's father and three fellow policemen. The teacher, Mahmud Farid, was so badly wounded that he had to be treated in hospital.

---

24. YLBHI (1997: 84) and Hadad (1998: 29). The reconstruction of events as related here is, where not otherwise stated, based on YLBHI (1997: 75–90), Hadad (ed.) (1998: 9–28), Rani *et al.* (eds) (1997: 32–36) and *Tempo Interaktif* (7 January 1997).

The next couple of days the atmosphere in the town became increasingly tense. The Tasikmalaya chief of police, Lieutenant-Colonel Suherman, visited the *pesantren* to apologise for the four policemen's behaviour, and the four policemen were detained on the afternoon of the day of the incident, but this failed to relieve the tension. Instead, a false rumour spread that Mahmud Farid had died from his wounds in hospital. People from surrounding areas came to Tasikmalaya to check on the rumour, or perhaps just to see what was going on, and tension increased further.

On 26 December a prayer meeting was arranged in the Jami Mosque in central Tasikmalaya. Thousands of people attended the meeting which was arranged by two local Muslim organisations, the Santri Communication Forum (*Forum Komunikasi Santri*) and the Tasikmalaya Islamic Young Generation (*Generasi Muda Islam Tasikmalaya*). As the meeting proceeded, another unknown group of people apparently gathered in front of the Tasikmalaya central police station which was situated only a few hundred metres from the mosque. As the prayer meeting ended, the crowd from the mosque dispersed or joined the crowd outside the police station. Growing restive, the crowd started to throw sandals and small stones across the fence of the police station. From there on the demonstration turned into a riot, with some people apparently taking initiative and urging the crowd to attack churches, police stations, shops and vehicles.

In contrast to the Situbondo incident, the military was quick to respond. The West Java territorial commander, Major-General Tayo Tarmadi, immediately came to Tasikmalaya from his headquarters in Bandung, bringing 800 military troops to restore order. Nonetheless the rioting continued throughout the afternoon, until 5 p.m. when the security forces managed to regain control of the town. Rioting continued in the evening outside Tasikmalaya in small towns up to 50 kilometres from the district capital. In the evening, Major-General Tayo Tarmadi visited the *pesantren* to check on the condition of Mahmud

Farid. He also met with Mahmud's father, the 74-year-old *kiai* who headed the *pesantren*, and arranged for the latter to hold a radio speech in which he denied the rumour that his son had died. The rest of the night and the following days were calm, with security tight in the whole Tasikmalaya area.

Abdurrahman Wahid and the Green Dragon Theory

Again it seemed that NU members had taken to rioting, attacking not only the police but also Christians and Chinese. This time, however, there was a marked difference in the official reactions to the riot. Unlike after the Situbondo riot, government and military spokesmen did not try to implicate the NU in the riot. Instead, several officials were keen to stress that NU members were not involved in the riot. The governor of West Java, H. R. Nuraiana, immediately said that Islamic groups were not at all responsible for the riot. Major-General Tayo Tarmadi said that no *santri* were involved, but that a certain party wanted to cause disunion, using Islam as a tool. Perhaps most significantly, General Hartono said that there were no indications of involvement of NU members in the Tasikmalaya riot. He also said there were no signs of the riots being engineered with the purpose of destabilising NU or Abdurrahman Wahid.[25]

The NU leader for his part stepped up his campaign against ICMI. He perceived a connection between the riots in Surabaya, Situbondo and Tasikmalaya, all of which he said had been engineered to show that NU members could not live in peace with other parts of society. He then launched his sensational dragon theory, which gained much attention. According to Wahid, there existed two operations, one 'red dragon operation' (*Operasi Naga Merah*) and one 'green dragon operation' (*Operasi Naga Hijau*). The red dragon operation had been conducted,

---

25. *Pikiran Rakyat* (28 December 1996), *Tempo Interaktif* (7 January 1997), *Media Indonesia* (15 January 1996).

successfully, to oust Megawati from the PDI, and now, Wahid feared, the green dragon operation was staged to destabilise the NU. The idea was to instigate riots in NU constituencies in order to create a crisis which would force Wahid to step down as NU leader. According to Wahid, the unrest would first occur in NU core areas and then spread to other places around Java and the rest of the country.[26]

At first, Wahid declined to elaborate on whom he believed to be behind the dragon operation against the NU. However, after a few weeks, Wahid publicly accused the Humanika Foundation (*Yayasan Humanika*), a foundation and discussion forum associated with ICMI, together with ICMI's secretary-general, Adi Sasono, of having instigated the Tasikmalaya riot. He did not rule out that other parties might be involved as well, but he claimed that, so far, he had evidence of the involvement of the Humanika and of Adi Sasono. Adi Sasono and leaders of the Humanika denied Wahid's accusations, and the Humanika Foundation reported Wahid to the police for slander.[27]

Only two days later, on 30 January, a riot occurred in another town, Rengasdengklok, in West Java. Although no one was killed in the riot, several churches, shops, schools and factories were destroyed or looted. The involvement of Muslims in the riot was made explicitly clear, as even the normally cautious *Kompas* daily reported that the targets of the riot had the words 'property of infidels' *(milik kafir)* sprayed on their shop windows.[28]

---

26. *Kompas* (5 January 1997) and *Suara Merdeka* (13 January 1997).
27. *Tempo Interaktif* (1 February 1997) and *Kompas* (30 January 1997 and 1 February 1997); see also *Gatra* (15 February 1997). More than a year later, the police had still not questioned Abdurrahman Wahid over the slander charges, fuelling suspicions that the police feared the possible political consequences of such a questioning; see Hadad (ed.) (1998: 50–51).
28. *Kompas* (31 January 1997). For the Rengasdengklok riot see Harsono (ed.) (1998).

Things then took a somewhat unexpected turn when Abdurrahman Wahid met with the president's daughter Tutut at the Ministry of Religious Affairs in Jakarta on 7 February. The meeting was believed to have been arranged by General Hartono. According to the daily *Jawa Pos*, Wahid's appearance was extraordinary. The newspaper noted that he wore shoes instead of sandals, that he arrived on time, and that he did not fall asleep during the meeting, as was the old man's habit. At the meeting, Wahid invited Tutut to visit six *pesantren* with him.[29] Although Wahid denied that their meeting and the arrangement would have anything to do with the election, it was obvious that for Tutut the purpose of the visits was to boost Golkar's election effort in East and Central Java. Perhaps by coincidence the religious riots in NU areas stopped after the meeting.

Killing Fields in Kalimantan

By far the worst case of social unrest in Indonesia for decades occurred in the province of West Kalimantan from late December 1996 to early March 1997. Probably around 500 people were killed in ethnic violence between indigenous Dayak groups and transmigrated Madurese. Those killed were mostly Madurese, and it appears that the Dayaks waged a ritual war against the Madurese communities, reportedly involving grim practices such as severing the heads of their victims and eating their livers.[30]

Friction between Dayaks and Madurese was not a new phenomenon. West Kalimantan was one of Indonesia's poorest

---

29. *Far Eastern Economic Review* (27 March 1997) and *Jawa Pos* (8 January 1997).
30. This account of the West Kalimantan unrest is, where not otherwise stated, taken from Human Rights Watch/Asia (1997), which so far is the most comprehensive and balanced account of the events. In contrast with the relatively extensive reporting on the Situbondo and Tasikmalaya riots, press reporting on the West Kalimantan unrest was severely restricted by the government, apparently out of fear that media coverage might exacerbate the tensions.

provinces, and a major part of the background to the conflict was the on-going economic and political marginalisation of the Dayaks, caused primarily by discriminatory government policies. This marginalisation triggered a heightened sense of ethnic solidarity among the Dayaks and an increased polarisation vis-à-vis other groups including the Madurese. The violence which was sparked off in December 1996 had also been prodded by a number of incidents in the preceding decades. For example, in 1979 a dispute over a debt escalated into widespread violence between Dayaks and Madurese, claiming the lives of twenty people according to official figures, although unofficial estimates ran into the hundreds.

The violence in 1996–97 started with what seemed a trivial incident on 29 December 1996. In a village in the Sanggau Ledo district close to the Malaysian border, two Dayak youths were attacked and slightly injured by a gang of Madurese youths in an argument over a girl. The two were treated in hospital and then sent home the same evening. Rumours spread, however, that the two boys had died, and large crowds of Dayaks in war dress assembled outside the district police station, demanding retribution. The Dayaks then attacked the homes of Madurese settlers and some houses were set on fire, in the course of which several people were killed. Smaller groups of Madurese men in their turn responded by attacking Dayak homes. The unrest continued until 4 January 1997 when the police and military finally managed to gain control over the situation. The unrest caused extensive material damage, and up to twenty people were killed in the clashes.

After the unrest, the government tried to negotiate a number of peace agreements between the warring sides. However, these did not succeed in reducing tensions in the area, and at the end of January violence once again erupted, this time more fiercely and over larger parts of the province. The incident which triggered the second wave of violence seems to have been an attack by a group of Madurese on a Christian social work foundation in Siantan, a suburb of the West Kalimantan capital Pontianak. After the attack, some Madurese set up roadblocks south of Pontianak, stopping Dayak road-users and attacking them with knives. After a Dayak was killed at one such roadblock, retributions started, and on 31 January one of the bloodiest attacks took place in the town of Pahuaman, where at least 148 Madurese were killed. The conflict spread, and massacres, mostly by Dayaks of Madurese, took place in several locations. The conflict was most intense in late January and early February, and eventually, at the beginning of March, heavily reinforced security forces were able to impose a tense order in the province. By that time, however, hundreds of people had been killed, thousands had seen their homes destroyed, and tens of thousand had fled, seeking shelter at military bases. The violence was the worst instance of communal violence in Indonesia since the 1960s, and it raised serious concerns about the future of inter-ethnic relations in Indonesia. The issue was all the more critical in the light of the country's uncertain political future and the recent eruptions of violence in places like Situbondo and Tasikmalaya.

Several explanations were put forward for the violence. Once again, reference to social and economic divisions was common, as were cultural explanations. The cultural argument emphasised the Madurese disposition towards violence and the Dayak tradition of collective blood-feuds. In addition, there were the familiar conspiracy theories focusing on hidden political agendas. Since the population of Situbondo was overwhelmingly Madurese, and Madurese transmigrants were involved in the unrest in West Kalimantan, there was some scope for speculation about possible connections between the two events. However, most analysts considered the Kalimantan unrest as a separate incident from the riots in Java in the preceding months. This was for example the view of the Komnas HAM, as well as of Abdurrahman Wahid.[31]

---

31. *Kompas* (19 February 1997) and *Tempo Interaktif* (25 January 1997)

It appears, however, that some elements within the military tried to scapegoat the PPP for the riots, presumably with the intention of damaging the party for the election. In West Kalimantan, a journalist and legislative candidate for the PPP, Zainuddin Isman, was arrested for his writing on the conflict. General Hartono said that there were elements from East Java agitating in West Kalimantan, and one of his staff members showed photographs to the press of two of the alleged instigators, bearing the initials A. I. and A. D. It seems that the army leaders were trying to pull the same trick as Abdurrahman Wahid by naming initials of suspected instigators, thus implicating political adversaries without directly accusing them. The move prompted an immediate reaction from the PPP's leader, Ismail Hasan Metareum, who guessed that the two implicated instigators were the PPP parliamentarians K. H. Amin Imron and K .H. Abdullah Schal, although it was not clear how the initial A. D. could translate to the latter's name. A couple of days later, however, General Hartono denied that he had ever tried to implicate the PPP in the riots, and the military commander-in-chief, General Feisal Tanjung denied that the initials were at all relevant.[32]

Conspiracies

The riots and the politicking and allegations in their wake point to a complex picture. Ethnic or religious tensions played a role in all of the riots, but there were other factors as well. As mentioned, economic and social divisions were popular explanations among Indonesian analysts, as well as among foreign observers. However, some analysts have questioned the value of

---

32. *Kompas* (18 February 1997, 19 February 1997, 21 February 1997 and 22 February 1997). Initials are commonly used in Indonesian media to represent the accused in trials. Naming the initials of political foes in public statements could thus serve to represent them as suspected criminals.

this explanation and the extent of social and economic disparity in Indonesia in general.[33] A problem for resolving the issue is that the last official figures measuring economic inequality are from 1990, and therefore they do not say anything about the change in income distribution during the 1990s. However, an unofficial study from 1997 found that inequalities had increased noticeably from 1990 to 1996.[34] There is also an abundance of so-called anecdotal evidence of growing inequalities. The blatant displays of wealth by Indonesia's upper classes were by the mid-1990s very evident to the public, especially in the bigger cities. It was also a widespread and deeply held view in Indonesia that the benefits of the economic development were very unevenly distributed. At the same time, it seems that social tolerance towards economic disparities has declined in recent years, and that resentment against inequalities has become more manifest.[35] Therefore, it seems likely that economic divisions and the popular resentment they inspired were important parts of the background to the social unrest in 1996 and early 1997.

---

33. For example, Mallarangeng and Liddle (1997: 171–172).
34. Tjiptoherijanto (1997). According to the study, Indonesia's average Gini ratio, which is the standard measurement for measuring economic inequality, increased from 0.32 in 1990 to 0.3568 in 1996. Cf. also ILO, Jakarta Office (1998: 4). A study by Indonesia's Central Bureau for Statistics, BPS (*Biro Pusat Statistik*), found that for Jakarta the Gini coefficient increased from 0.305 in 1990 to 0.423 in 1993; cited by Booth (1998: 37 n. 57). Although probably part of the increase is attributable to an increase in the basic data sample, the 1993 figure, which presumably was the more accurate of the two, indicated that income distribution indeed was very skewed in Jakarta.
35. Thee Kian Wie (1998: 134) and Booth (1998: 38). An illustrative example is the widespread resentment against a spate of golf course construction in Indonesia since the late 1980s, often involving compulsory land clearances. It is widely perceived that the victims of the golf course projects mainly are poor subsistence farmers who are forced from their land without adequate financial compensation in order to give way for vast leisure fields for the upper classes. For the popular resentment around the golf courses and other land disputes in the 1990s, see Lucas (1997).

It has also been argued that if social and economic divisions were decisive, the unrest would more likely occur in the big cities where inequalities were larger and more conspicuous, rather than in small or mid-sized towns such as Situbondo or Tasikmalaya.[36] This is probably a correct observation, and several instances of unrest did occur in big cities in 1996 and early 1997, indicating a growing resentment among urban groups who felt that they were being comparatively disadvantaged by the economic development.[37] As for Situbondo and Tasikmalaya, however, there is nothing to indicate that social divisions were particularly serious in the two towns, and no warning signs of increasing social tensions seem to have occurred before the riots erupted. The same was true of inter-religious and inter-ethnic tensions. These circumstances, together with the reports and eyewitness accounts from the riots, rather indicate that the Situbondo and Tasikmalaya riots were caused by deliberate instigation, presumably with political motives.

To an outside observer, the flourishing of conspiracy theories is one of the most conspicuous and intriguing elements of Indonesia's political life. There is an inclination to interpret all political events and acts in terms of manipulation by a hidden mastermind *(auctor intellectualis)*, or *dalang* (puppet master). In some instances such suspicions seem well founded; Indonesia's

---

36. Mallarangeng and Liddle (1997: 171–172).
37. In May 1996, student protests in Ujung Pandang, South Sulawesi, against a hike in bus fares turned into rioting and a military crackdown which resulted in the fatal shooting of at least six people; see *Asiaweek* (17 May 1996). The Surabaya riot on 9 June when nine churches were burned down has already been mentioned. Apart from the 27 July riot in Jakarta, street hawkers in the Tanah Abang district in Central Jakarta rioted in January after they were ordered by the police to move their stalls; see *Kompas* (28 February 1997). In the same month, thousands of workers in Bandung, West Java, went on the rampage after a conflict with the factory management; see *Pikiran Rakyat* (1 February 1997). For a comprehensive list of major riots in Indonesia from 1995 to May 1998, see Hadad (ed.) (1998: 31–36).

modern political history contains numerous examples of more or less overt political manipulation. However, it is often difficult to assess the degree of truth in the conspiracy allegations in each case. Hard evidence is often scarce or contradictory, and the various more or less plausible theories often rest on very precarious empirical ground. As already demonstrated, the conspiracy allegations, true or not, tend themselves to serve various political purposes. This is a warning to be cautious in evaluating the conspiracy theories, however alluring they may be with their inner logic and pretensions of revealing a deeper hidden truth behind seemingly inexplicable events.[38]

This said, Abdurrahman Wahid's green dragon theory warrants further comment. As a conspiracy theory it seemed to hold particular fascination, especially because of its red dragon analogy, the conspiracy to oust Megawati. In the minds of most politically aware Indonesians, there was no doubt that Megawati's ousting indeed was the result of a conspiracy supported or initiated by elements within the government and the military. As Megawati and Abdurrahman Wahid had long been two of the most potent opponents of the government and of Suharto, the two theories together did indeed make sense.

The green dragon theory was elaborated by the illegal news magazine *Suara Independen*.[39] According to the magazine its hidden actors were primarily from parts of the military and

---

38. For some notes on these and related facets of Indonesian political culture, see Siegel (1993), Mulder (1996: 115–117) and Kingsbury (1998: 16). On the political history of manipulation under the New Order, see e.g. MacDonald (1981), Jenkins (1984) and Crouch (1993).

39. *Suara Independen* no. 3/III (January 1997). *Suara Independen* was the mouthpiece of the unrecognised Indonesian Journalists Alliance, AJI (*Aliansi Jurnalis Independen*). Some of the magazine's articles are of high quality, albeit generally biased against the government. As the magazine was illegal it operated outside the ordinary restrictions and self-censorship of the Indonesian press; see Stanley (1996) for some notes on the alternative press.

government elite, who, together with groups in ICMI, saw Abdurrahman Wahid as a thorn in the side. The military group identified as hostile to Wahid was centred around General Hartono and the group of 'green' officers within ABRI who were widely considered to be sympathetic to ICMI. The magazine also cited an anonymous source within the military who claimed that only the military had the technical ability to instigate the riots.

In the end, nothing in Wahid's accusations proved ICMI's involvement in the riots. It is doubtful that ICMI would have the technical and organisational skills to instigate riots on the scale that occurred in Situbondo and Tasikmalaya. Concerning the possibility of ABRI involvement, the military had an interest in keeping up a public notion that there existed latent and perennial threats to the national security and stability. Such a notion served to legitimise ABRI's central political role and the authoritarian regime at large. Furthermore, the Indonesian military had previously, on several occasions, employed manipulative and repressive tactics in its dealing with social and political challenges to the regime. In 1990, Richard Tanter identified 'intermittent but persistent state terror' as a major political tactic employed by the New Order to exercise control of the population.[40] Against this background it is reasonable to take allegations of military involvement in the riots seriously.

If there was a green dragon operation, and if its purpose was to oust or marginalise Abdurrahman Wahid, it did not succeed. Instead the riots contributed to pushing Wahid closer to Suharto and making him support Golkar in the election. According to Wahid himself, he did his touring with Tutut in order to counter the influence of Islamic fundamentalists.[41] From the point of view of Wahid's political adversaries in ICMI, Wahid's improved relations with the government and Suharto were a

---

40. Tanter (1990: 214); see also *ibid.* (*passim*) for numerous examples of state terror by ABRI intelligence bodies. Cf. also Lowry (1996: 6, 147).
41. Interview, Jakarta (7 October 1997).

less than desirable outcome. Wahid emerged as the undisputed chairman of the NU, even more than before, after having held Suharto's hand before the press cameras.

In the wake of all the politicking and speculation, Suharto suddenly reiterated his warning from eight years earlier that he would clobber *(tak'gebug)* anyone who tried to unseat him unconstitutionally.[42] It was uncertain whom, if anyone in particular, Suharto had in mind in making this harsh statement. However, at the same time, there were signs that Habibie's and ICMI's standing with the president was declining. The most important sign was the resignation of Amien Rais, leader of Indonesia's second largest Muslim organisation Muhammadiyah and one of the most outspoken members of ICMI, from the organisation. His resignation was a result of Suharto's intervention, and it was widely interpreted as a warning to Habibie to curb his own political ambitions.[43] The opaque nature of palace politics makes

---

42. *Kompas* (1 March 1997). In 1989 the president made a similar statement against the background of an intensive debate about the presidential succession, and the main target then seems to have been Benny Murdani and his allies in the military; see Cribb (1990: 25) and Liddle (1996b: 211).
43. *EIU Country Report Indonesia*, 2nd quarter (1997: 16). In this context, it is worth noting a document allegedly produced by the Centre for Policy and Development Studies (CPDS), a think-tank associated with ICMI and Hartono's group in the military. The supposedly top secret document which was widely circulated in Jakarta before posted on the internet by the alternative news agency *SiaR* (*ISTIQLAL*) on 28 March. It contained an analysis of the political constellation among the elites, where people and groups were classified as pro-Suharto or anti-Suharto. The anti-Suharto groups, termed the 'Rainbow Coalition' consisted of high-ranking civilian and military officials, Christians, Sukarnoists and student activists, among others. The alleged coalition seemed to coincide with the political adversaries of ICMI. Among those named in the Rainbow Coalition were Lieutenant-General Wiranto, retired General Benny Murdani, Megawati Sukarnoputri and Abdurrahman Wahid. According to *SiaR* (11 April 1997), Suharto was angry with the CPDS and Hartono after reading the document. For a summary and analysis of the CPDS document, see *Digest* 29 (29 March 1997).

it impossible to tell whether these developments were linked to a suspicion on behalf of Suharto that ICMI, Amien Rais or perhaps Habibie, had been conspiring with parts of the military to fan communal violence. If so, they certainly seem like possible targets of the president's clobber threat.

Whatever the truth of the allegations and conspiracy theories, they demonstrated some of the deep-seated mistrust and mutual suspicions between different groups of the political elites in Indonesia. The animosity between ICMI and Abdurrahman Wahid was exacerbated as a consequence of the riots and of the politicking in their wake. If anything, Wahid rather than ICMI came out strengthened from the affair, although the price he paid was to support Golkar in its election effort.

CHAPTER 4

A Festival of Democracy?

On 29 May 1997, Indonesia was scheduled to hold its sixth parliamentary election under Suharto.[1] The formula was to be the same as in earlier New Order elections. In the word of the government it should be a 'festival of democracy' (*Pesta Demokrasi*). This meant a national ritual designed to reproduce the legitimacy of the regime without contesting its hold to power. The campaign period preceding the poll would offer a catharsis during which political frustrations could be vented in a tense and sometimes chaotic and violent atmosphere. This would be followed by a 'quiet week' during which no political activities were allowed. The quiet week would set the atmosphere for the election day, which, in contrast to the campaign period, should take on a solemn, peaceful character; showing the orderly participation of the whole nation in a ritual act which again made manifest national unity and social harmony. Election day thus marked the restoration of order after the upheavals and chaos of the election campaign.[2]

Preparations

As we have seen, the twelve months preceding the election were characterised by heavy interference and manipulation of one of the three contestants, the PDI, as well as apparent attempts to destabilise the politically important NU. A year earlier, Suharto's

---
1. The text in this chapter borrows heavily from an article which appeared in the December 1997 issue of *Asian Survey*: Eklöf (1997).
2. For descriptions of earlier New Order elections as rituals, see Schulte Nordholt (1980), Pemberton (1986) and Labrousse (1993).

two most potent opponents had been the leaders of these two organisations, Megawati Sukarnoputri and Abdurrahman Wahid. The two were personal friends, and if Wahid had lent his support to a PDI led by Megawati in the election, this alliance might have rearranged Indonesia's entire political landscape. As it was, however, the regime had forestalled this threat by the exclusion of Megawati and her supporters from the election. Abdurrahman Wahid, meanwhile, had been manoeuvred into granting Golkar access to NU's *pesantren* network as a platform for its election campaign. These measures seemed set to guarantee another landslide victory for Golkar.

Aside from these manipulative measures, more overtly repressive means had been employed to silence the opposition in anticipation of the election. A wave of political trials in the year preceding the election had either locked up in jail most vocal critics of the regime or frightened them to silence. The 27 July riot provided the government with a pretext for cracking down on a number of opponents that long had been a thorn in the side of the government. Several of the NGO activists in MARI who had declared their support for Megawati after the Medan congress were brought to trial on charges of subversion or other political offences. The organisation worst hit by the crack-down was the Democratic People's Party, PRD, which was accused of having masterminded the 27 July riots. In all, more than a dozen activists, among them the PRD leader Budiman Sujatmiko and the labour leader, Muchtar Pakpahan, were tried and several were sentenced to long prison terms for political offences.[3] The

---

3. For the trials, see Luwarso (ed.) (1997: 294–318), *Far Eastern Economic Review* (26 December 1996 and 27 February 1997), IRIP News Service (1997) and Jones and Jendrzejczyk (1997). The trials were often farcical, with the prosecution being ill-prepared and the judges at times falling asleep during sessions.

Indonesia's anti-subversion law was introduced by President Sukarno in 1963, and has been much criticised by lawyers and human rights activists both in Indonesia and internationally. The law has been used by the government on several occasions to get rid of political opponents; see Thoolen (ed.) (1987: 85–94) and Amnesty International (1997).

government thus turned the 27 July riot into a clean-up action directed at pro-democracy activists, student leaders and NGOs critical of the government in order to ensure the smooth running of the general election and the subsequent presidential election in 1998. The result was that the opposition was forced underground or inside the university campuses, where the regime allowed a somewhat broader scope for political activities than outside the campuses.

In the 1997 election, 425 out of the 500 seats in the national parliament were contested, the remainder being reserved for ABRI representatives. Up to 1997, ABRI held 100 seats, but this number was set to be reduced following the recommendations from the Indonesian Academy of Sciences, LIPI (*Lembaga Ilmu Pengetahuan Indonesia*), which had been commissioned by President Suharto in 1995 to investigate the future of the sociopolitical role of ABRI. The reduction of the number of ABRI representatives in parliament was also related to the longer development dating back to the 1980s, through which the military had become less independent and influential as a political force.[4]

Other than this change, there was little new in the formal electoral system. As earlier, only the three officially recognised contestants, Golkar, the PDI and the PPP, were allowed to take part in the election, and all their candidates had to be screened and approved beforehand by the government. All three contestants furthermore had to adhere to the state ideology *Pancasila* as their sole ideological basis, thus obstructing the PPP from formally using its association with Islam to boost its popularity.

Megawati was barred from participating in the election, and she consistently refused to acknowledge the result of the

---

4. For LIPI's investigation, see Samego (1996). LIPI also conducted an investigation commissioned by the president about the election system. The result was presented to the president in early 1996, but was not made available to the public until it was published by LIPI after Suharto's resignation more than two years later; Tim Peneliti Sistem Pemilu (1998).

government-engineered congress the year before. The lawsuits which she had filed against the government and against the Suryadi camp gained widespread media attention, but most of the cases were rejected by the courts as being outside their jurisdiction. Although Megawati and her supporters probably did not hold any high hopes of succeeding in their legal endeavour, it was a way for Megawati to try to stay in the public limelight, while simultaneously boosting her public reputation for fairness and justice.[5]

As the election approached, the PDI was paralysed by its internal split between Megawati and Suryadi. The government acknowledged Suryadi's chairmanship, but his attempts to consolidate the party failed. On several occasions he had to flee from egg-throwing crowds of angry Megawati supporters, who regarded him as a government puppet. However, a month before the election Suryadi remained publicly optimistic about the party's election prospects, predicting that the PDI would increase its share of the votes and overtake the PPP to come second in the election.[6]

The situation in the PPP was quiet by comparison. After a few surprisingly confrontational statements by the party's leader Ismael Hasan Metareum in the year before the election, and a subsequent failed push in parliament to reform the election laws, the party was much less in the spotlight than the PDI. In places around Java, however, local PPP supporters competed, sometimes fiercely, with Golkar supporters in marking out party territories with flags. Like the other election contestants, the PPP held numerous small campaign rallies, thinly disguised as 'cadre meetings'. As the start of the official campaign period in late April drew nearer, clashes between PPP and Golkar

---

5. Interview with Kwik Kian Gie, member of Megawati's central board, Jakarta (17 March 1997).
6. Luwarso (ed.) (1997: 254–257) and *Forum Keadilan* (5 May 1997).

supporters became more frequent, and even led to rioting in some places in Central Java. The PPP was nevertheless optimistic about its prospects for the election, hoping to benefit from the wave of Islamic resurgence in Indonesia, and from the transfer of votes from supporters of Megawati. The party hoped to obtain at least 28.8 per cent of the votes, which would match its best result ever in the 1982 election.[7]

Golkar's campaign had meanwhile been under way informally for a long time. Over the preceding years, Golkar's chairman Harmoko had visited all of Indonesia's 27 provinces in a nationwide 'safari' conducted in the fasting month of Ramadan each year. Moreover, in Central Java, the regional authorities had several years earlier launched a 'yellowisation' (*kuningisasi*) programme to support Golkar's election effort. Each of the three election contestants had a campaign colour: yellow for Golkar, red for the PDI and green for the PPP. In the previous election in 1992, the colours were used mainly for election rallies, but in 1997 a much wider 'colour war' took place as a result of the yellowisation scheme. All over Central Java details on government buildings and offices in the province, as well as kerbs and even trees in public parks and along roads were painted yellow, the colour of Golkar. In Solo, Central Java, PPP supporters protested against the apparent Golkar campaign by repainting the yellow public buildings, trees and other public facilities around the city's central square, so that they once again became a neutral white. The war of colours escalated when PDI supporters then painted parts of the kerbs around the square red so that they became red and white, the colours of the Indonesian flag.[8]

In the months leading up to the election, Golkar's unofficial election campaign intensified. Tutut, who was one of Golkar's seven deputy chairs and the organisation's coordinator for the

---

7. *Forum Keadilan* (5 May 1997).
8. *Kompas* (14 January 1997, 18 January 1997 and 22 February 1997).

provinces of Yogyakarta, Central Java and East Java, was often seen on the state-controlled TV news, engaged in cadre meetings for Golkar, or touring the *pesantren* with Abdurrahman Wahid. Frequently wearing a yellow head scarf, she led an effort to enhance Golkar's Islamic appeal. The organisation aimed at obtaining at least 70.02 per cent of the votes, which would amount to a moderate increase of less than two percentage points over its 1992 result.[9]

The Campaign

The official campaign period, which started on 27 April, was limited to 27 days. However, to limit the possibility of violent clashes between supporters of different parties, each of the three contestants was only allowed to hold campaign activities on every third day in each province throughout the country. The regulation also served to prevent any of the parties from developing a momentum in their public meetings. Street rallies were outlawed in favour of campaign activities in enclosed premises, which were expected to draw smaller crowds and to be easier to handle for the security forces.

There was also an idea that the campaign should be conducted in what was supposed to be politically more mature forms of 'dialogue' campaigning, with debates and campaigning by the contestants in the media. Television broadcast time was set aside for each of the three contestants for this purpose, and in comparison with earlier elections, the debate element was more pronounced in the 1997 campaign. For the government, strengthening the debate element was an attempt to respond in a limited way to the increasing demands in society for more democracy and a more open political climate. However, the scope of the political debates was severely circumscribed because, as in previous elections, the contestants were not supposed to

---

9. *Kompas* (29 November 1996).

criticise the government or government policies. The political dialogue consequently contained little in terms of debate over concrete policies or political programmes. The themes advanced by the three election contestants were remarkably similar, expressing their commitment to such universal goods as economic development, social justice, clean government and democracy. However, the messages of the three election contestants contained little in terms of concrete suggestion of how to achieve these objectives.[10]

Golkar's main theme in the campaign was the success of economic development, for which the organisation, as representing the government in the election, claimed much of the credit. Although Golkar also brought up its commitment to fighting corruption, its image as a government party made it vulnerable to criticism of the negative aspects of the country's modernisation. These included the apparently increasing social and economic gaps between rich and poor and the widespread corruption and collusion, not least in the government and civil service.[11]

The PDI's rallies were quiet and sparsely visited. Suryadi was shown on television in all but empty stadiums, addressing only a few hundred supporters. At a rally in Bali, only 110 people showed up to listen to Suryadi, a crowd far outnumbered by the 600 security personnel present. Another rally in Surabaya was cancelled after supporters of Megawati had entered the premises and ascended the podium, causing a commotion.[12] A joke circulated that Suryadi campaigned like a panther – it moves at night and no one ever sees it. The PDI's unsuccessful campaign was in great contrast to its previous election campaign in 1992, when the party had attracted huge crowds at its rallies, especially

---

10. See the *Far Eastern Economic Review* (15 May 1997) for the TV campaigns. See also the interview with political scientist Syamsuddin [Sjamsuddin] Haris in *Sinar* (31 May 1997) for a critique of the dialogue element in the campaign.
11. *Forum Keadilan* (19 May 1997).
12. *Forum Keadilan* (19 May 1997).

in the larger cities in its traditional areas of stronghold in Java, Bali and parts of Sumatra.

With the PDI hampered by its internal problems, the PPP could effectively take over the PDI's former role as a party for the small people. The PPP also focused on the lack of democracy in the implementation of the election, and threatened not to accept the result if the election were rigged. The party's rallies drew large crowds, especially in Jakarta and other cities in Java. Many of Megawati's supporters seemed willing to channel their political aspirations through the PPP. In early May the new informal coalition between the PPP and Megawati's supporters became manifest with the apparently spontaneous emergence of the so-called *Mega-Bintang* (Mega-star).[13] The symbol, which was carried at PPP rallies around Java, combined the PPP's party symbol of a star with the red colour of the PDI. Pictures of Megawati were also displayed at the PPP's rallies, and the word *Mega-Bintang* was used as a political slogan. The government, evidently cautious of the emergence of the new coalition, banned the *Mega-Bintang*. The use of pictures of people in the election campaign had already been banned since the 1992 campaign.[14]

Like the PPP, Golkar focused its campaigning on Java. The organisation was keen to win back the large number of seats in the national and regional parliaments it had lost there, mostly to the PDI, in 1992. Tutut, who was Golkar's coordinator for the provinces of East Java, Central Java and Yogyakarta, seemed largely to overshadow Golkar's chairman Harmoko. Comfortable with large crowds and relaxed in her addressing campaign rallies, she made good use of her agreement with Abdurrahman Wahid, and their appearance together on several occasions probably had a significant influence on Golkar's electoral success especially

---

13. *Mega-Bintang* literally translates as 'Mega-star', but the word also means 'superstar'.
14. This was a reaction against the PDI's successful use of Sukarno's picture in its 1987 campaign; see Brooks (1995: 75–76, 84–89).

in Central Java. Before the campaign, Abdurrahman Wahid had called Tutut 'one of the leaders of the future' and he also arranged for her to meet Islamic community leaders. These meetings also served to rally voter support for Golkar from the NU constituencies, although Tutut herself claimed that they were merely courtesy visits.[15]

Also campaigning for Golkar were government ministers, as well as popular entertainers and TV personalities, such as Rhoma Irama, a popular *dangdut* singer who previously had campaigned for the PPP. The East Java governor Basofi Sudirman also recorded *dangdut* songs to boost Golkar's performance.[16]

In spite of the attempts at regulating the campaign to prevent clashes between supporters of the three contestants, the campaign turned out to be the most violent ever under the New Order. Frequent clashes occurred between supporters of Golkar and the PPP, and between supporters of Megawati and Suryadi. According to official figures, at least 273 people were killed, many of them in traffic accidents as campaign rallies often continued as unruly street processions with excited youngsters on trucks and motor bikes. The pattern of gratuitous and exuberant violence predominantly by young men and teenagers had been prominent in earlier election campaigns as well, but as indicated by the high death toll, the level of violence was remarkably high in 1997. In addition to the 273 people killed in incidents directly related to the election, at least 123 people died when a shopping complex was set on fire in riots in Banjarmasin in South Kalimantan on 23 May. A military spokesman explained the riots as having been provoked by third-party instigators, and just as after the 27 July riot the year before, the Democratic

---

15. *Forum Keadilan* (2 June 1997).
16. *Kompas* (29 April 1997). See also *Mutiara* (5 February 1997) about Golkar's use of *dangdut* music in the election campaign. *Dangdut* is a modern Indonesian and Malay music style which blends influences from Indian popular film music, Middle Eastern and indigenous melodies; see Frederick (1982).

People's Party, PRD, was accused of having masterminded the unrest. However, against the background of the several instances of unrest preceding the election campaign, it seems that the high level of violence can largely be explained by social and economic grievances which were vented during the tense political atmosphere of the election campaign.[17]

The campaign period was followed by a week-long cooling-off period before the ballot day on 29 May. The campaign had been marked by riots and violence, but had contained little political debate of any substance. The main themes brought to the fore by the three contestants were remarkably similar, albeit with some difference in emphasis. The main themes were the commitment to continued economic development, the need to address problems of growing social and economic divisions and corruption, and the need for greater democracy and respect for human rights. The three contestants all declared their commitment to addressing these issues, but none of them seemed to be able to present any concrete solutions or policy formulations.

The Election and Its Results

Whereas earlier elections in general had been quiet on the polling day, the 1997 election day was marked by violence in several places around the country. In the East Java island of Madura, riots involving supporters of the PPP occurred in several towns, leading to the destruction of buildings and vehicles. A number of ballot boxes also disappeared or were destroyed in the riots, forcing the government, for the first time ever, to hold a re-vote in the areas concerned. In East Timor, the polling day marked the start of a series of attacks on Indonesian security forces by East Timorese independence fighters. In the Sumatran

---

17. The official death toll figures are cited in *Jakarta Post* (3 June 1997). For the campaign violence, see *Forum Keadilan* (16 June 1997), and for the Banjarmasin riot, see Salim *et al.* (1997).

province of Aceh, at least one person was killed in a shoot-out at a polling station.[18] The election went smoothly at most polling stations around the country and the situation was calm in Jakarta, but the impression from media reports was rather that the election day was marred by disturbances.

Predictably, the official result of the election showed a landslide victory for Golkar, which gained 74.5 per cent of the votes. This was Golkar's best result ever and a substantial increase over its 68.1 per cent in 1992. The PPP fared relatively well according to the official count, securing 22.4 per cent of the votes, an improvement by 5.4 percentage points. The PDI, on the other hand, declined disastrously, collecting only 3.1 per cent of the votes, down from 14.9 per cent in 1992. The official turn-out remained high at around 90.6 per cent, an insignificant decline of 0.3 percentage points from the 1992 turn-out.[19]

Several tendencies in the official result were largely unexpected, and together with several other circumstances these raised serious doubts about the validity of the official result. Most analysts, for example, had before the election estimated that the so-called *Golput* (*Golongan Putih*, literally the 'white group'), consisting of people choosing not to exercise their voting rights, or casting invalid votes, would increase substantially.[20] The possibility of an increase in non-voters was enhanced as Megawati, after much speculation about her stance, declared a week before the election that she would not vote.[21] Although she did not explicitly urge her supporters to abstain, which would have been illegal, her announcement was expected to influence many people. It seems that many of her supporters, especially in Java, followed her example and chose not to vote. According to the official

---

18. *Reuters* (29 May 1997) and *Jakarta Post* (30 May 1997).
19. For the 1997 election results, see *Kompas* (24 June 1997) and for the 1992 results, see Baroto (1992: 250).
20. Estimates typically seemed to range from twelve to twenty per cent of the vote; see *Forum Keadilan* (19 May 1997).
21. *The Australian* (23 May 1997).

figures, the turn-out in Jakarta, for example, decreased from 93.5 per cent in 1992 to 88.1 per cent, and in East Java it dropped from 88.9 per cent to 85.0 per cent. These figures also concealed considerable local variation; in the East Java capital of Surabaya, for example, the turn-out was only 78.5 per cent. According to the official figures, however, the fall in turn-out in Java was offset by increases in other provinces, so that nationally, the turn-out remained high at over 90 per cent.[22]

Another surprise was the scale of the PDI's decline. Estimates of the party's performance had ranged from a low of 5 to 6 per cent to around 10 to 12 per cent, but hardly anyone had predicted that the party would get as little as 3.1 per cent nationwide. In fact, a rumour in political circles in Jakarta before the election had it that the result would be rigged in favour of the PDI, allowing the party to gain approximately the same share of the votes as in 1992. As 25 more parliamentary seats were contested in 1997 than in 1992, this would still allow the PDI to increase its representation in the body, something which would save the face of the evidently unpopular Suryadi, while at the same time slamming Megawati and her supporters.[23] A member of the unofficial Independent Election Monitoring Committee, KIPP (*Komite Independen Pemantau Pemilu*), in Yogyakarta also believed that votes from the *Golput* group in Yogyakarta would be added on top of the PDI's result.[24]

---

22. For the 1997 turn-out figures in the provinces in Java, see *Forum Keadilan* (16 June 1997) and *Jakarta Post* (3 June 1997).
23. Personal communication with PDI politicians in both camps and political analysts, Jakarta, March 1997.
24. *South China Morning Post* (12 May 1997). KIPP was formed on the initiative of a group of intellectuals early in 1996 and was intended to be an independent broad popular movement for monitoring the elections. However, the organisation was rejected by the government, and it did not manage to monitor more than a few hundred polling stations. For KIPP, see Yanuarti (1996) and Human Rights Watch/Asia (1996).

Apparently this did not happen. Instead, the PDI performed disastrously all over the country, possibly with the exceptions of East Timor and West Kalimantan, where the party dropped only moderately from 16.0 to 13.5 per cent and from 21.5 to 15.1 per cent respectively. The party's number of seats in parliament dropped from 56 to eleven and it achieved representation from only eight of the country's 27 provinces, compared with 20 in 1992. The party even failed to gain representation from its former stronghold Jakarta, where it obtained less than two per cent of the vote. This meant that Suryadi, who had topped the party's Jakarta list, failed to win a seat in parliament. Furthermore, according to the provisional election results of 5 June, it seemed that the PDI would gain only ten seats in the parliament, which would mean that the party would not have enough parliamentarians to be represented in all the eleven commissions in parliament. A government-backed suggestion to correct this by simply transferring some thousands of Golkar votes to the PDI was rejected by the PPP, and was also legally dubious. However, in the final vote count, the PDI's number of votes in the province of North Sumatra increased substantially, enabling the party to get two parliamentary seats instead of one from the province, and thus a total of eleven seats in the national parliament. The PPP seriously questioned the vote count, but the authorities would give no plausible explanation for the large discrepancy between the provisional and final results. Perhaps by coincidence, the eleventh seat went to Fatimah Achmad, who a year earlier had led the committee which organised the Medan congress to depose Megawati.[25]

According to the official result, Golkar increased its share of the votes in all of the country's 27 provinces. In general, the organisation made its largest gains in the former strongholds of the PDI, such as Jakarta, Central Java, Bali, North Sumatra and

---

25. The PDI's final result for the province of North Sumatra exceeded the provisional result by 64,000 votes, or 19.4 per cent; see *Kompas* (19, 20 and 22 June 1997).

South Sumatra. However, in East Java and West Java the organisation's gains were less pronounced. The PPP, meanwhile, made large gains all over Java, where the party officially gained 30 per cent of the total votes. These gains were crucial, because slightly over half of the contested seats in parliament came from the five provinces in Java, and the PPP could consequently increase its representation in parliament substantially, from 62 to 89 seats.[26]

Election Rigging and the Golkar Victory

To some extent, Golkar's large majority no doubt reflected popular support for the government and its success in leading the country on its path toward modernisation and economic development. In May 1997 the Indonesian economy was still doing very well, and analysts were convinced that economic growth would continue unabated well into the twenty-first century.[27] Many voters no doubt also saw a vote for Golkar as a vote for continued political stability, regarding the authoritarian regime as an essential vanguard against perceived threats of extremist political aspirations, primarily interpreted as Communism and fundamentalist Islam, as well as the threats of increasing ethnic and religious tension and upheaval.

The government regarded the election result as a powerful manifestation of popular support. Immediately after the first preliminary election figures were made public, Harmoko claimed Golkar's large victory as a sign of popular approval for the government's policies. He also dismissed allegations that systematic violations of the election laws and vote rigging had occurred.[28]

---

26. Previously, the number of parliamentary seats from Java was limited to half of the contested seats, i.e. 200 out of 400. In 1997, however, as the number of parliamentary seats contested in the election was increased from 400 to 425, Java's number of parliamentary seats increased to 216, i.e. 50.8 per cent.
27. For example, Guinness Flight (1997: 10).
28. *Reuters* (1 June 1997).

However, in spite of Harmoko's denial, several circumstances indicate that systematic manipulation and election rigging in fact accounted for a large part of the outcome of the election. The heart of the problem was that the organisers of the election were the bureaucracy whose members were obliged to support Golkar. According to the so-called doctrine of mono-loyalty, all civil servants were required to be loyal only to the government, and not to hold membership in any political organisation without permission from their superiors. All civil servants also had to join the Indonesian Civil Servants' Corps, Korpri (*Korps Pegawai Republik Indonesia*) which was one of the three main support organisations of Golkar (the other two being the military and Golkar's own cadres). In practice, it was difficult for civil servants to get permission to join any of the two non-government parties, and it would certainly not have been beneficial for their career. Essentially, the doctrine of mono-loyalty meant that the country's six million civil servants, and often their families as well, were required to support Golkar, including actively taking part in Golkar's election efforts.[29]

Golkar's support from the civil service was especially important in remote rural areas, where the organisation, through the bureaucracy, thus had an informal permanent political representation. The PPP and the PDI, by contrast, faced great difficulties in establishing political representation in rural areas. According to the so-called 'floating mass' doctrine of the New Order, party politics were banned from rural areas between elections. However, as the ever-present bureaucracy represented Golkar, the doctrine strongly favoured Golkar over the other two election contestants. The allocation of state resources at the local levels were furthermore often linked to voter support for Golkar. Numerous reports

---

29. For the mono-loyalty doctrine, see van Dijk (1992: 59–61).

tell of villages being promised, for example, electricity or a surfaced road in exchange for supporting Golkar.[30]

Golkar's support from the bureaucracy also gave the organisation access to state resources, such as official buildings and vehicles for its campaign. In addition, Golkar could more easily obtain permits to hold meetings and other campaign activities. Through its close association with the government and certain business conglomerates, Golkar also had access to financial resources on a completely different scale from the PPP and the PDI, both of which had to rely mainly on the scarce funding provided by the government. Furthermore, according to two independent studies ahead of the 1997 election, Golkar got substantially more coverage in the news broadcasts of the state owned TVRI (*Televisi Republik Indonesia*) compared with the PPP and the PDI.[31]

The military, which was officially supposed to be neutral in the election, also gave more or less open support to Golkar. Whereas in 1992 the military was widely praised for its neutrality in the election, its stance in 1997 was more ambiguous. Already in March 1996, the army Chief of Staff, General Hartono, had said that all members of ABRI were Golkar cadres. The statement sparked a lively debate which questioned the political neutrality of the military in the upcoming election.[32]

In addition to the more or less overt support from the bureaucracy and the military, outright violations of the election codes also contributed to Golkar's victory. A common type of

---

30. For example, Cederroth (1994: 148), van Dijk (1992: 58) and informants in Yogyakarta and Bali 1996–97. For the floating mass doctrine, see Moertopo (1982: 97–99).
31. *Tempo Interaktif* (18 April 1997), and *Jakarta Post* (27 May 1997). TVRI had a virtual monopoly on television news broadcasts, as all Indonesian TV channels were required to re-broadcast TVRI's news programmes; see Kitley (1997). For the issue of campaign funding, see for instance the editorial in *Jakarta Post* (10 March 1997).
32. On the military's role in the 1992 election, see *Tempo* (13 June 1992) and for the reactions to Hartono's remark, see Simanjuntak (ed.) (1996).

violation in 1997 seems to have been double or multiple voting. Many civil servants were issued two voting cards, and cast their votes at two separate polling stations, one in their residential area and the other at their work place.[33] This practice may to some extent explain the unexpectedly high turn-out figure in the election.

Many reports also tell of harsher methods being employed by members of the bureaucracy and the military in order to ensure Golkar's victory. These included threats, coercion, unlawful detention, destruction of property, and outright physical abuse. This intimidation affected voters as well as party candidates and the scrutineers from the political parties who were supposed to monitor the vote count at each stage.[34]

In earlier elections the vote count had often been manipulated, especially at the local polling stations at the village levels. Scrutineers from each of the three contestants were supposed to be present at the vote count at every polling station, as well as at subsequent stages in the vote count up to the level of province. However, the PPP and the PDI could not manage to provide scrutineers for all of the more than 300,000 polling stations around the country. Moreover, the scrutineers often became the victims of intimidation by members of the bureaucracy or the military, or they were denied access to the vote count. They also often faced bureaucratic obstacles in obtaining official permits

---

33. The Komnas HAM noted after the 1997 election that multiple voting was widespread; *Kompas* (14 June 1997), and it was also a common violation in earlier elections. An Indonesian study of the 1992 election compiled over 400 cases of various violations, the majority of which were committed by members of the official bodies organising the election. The members of these bodies were almost exclusively drawn from the bureaucracy; Irwan and Edriana (1995). Other recent studies documenting violations against the election procedures are Wenban (1993), Antlöv (1995: 170–182), Zaidun and Aribowo (1996).

34. Irwan and Edriana (1995: 14–28); see also the other studies cited in footnote 33 above.

as scrutineers. Another problem was that the scrutineers were not always issued a copy of the result of the vote count, so they could not contest the count if the figures were manipulated afterwards.[35]

The last stage of the vote count was the least transparent. In 1997, only five senior government officials were granted access to the national election results database set up by the General Election Committee, LPU (*Lembaga Pemilihan Umum*), in Jakarta. Among the five officials were President Suharto and Harmoko, the latter officially in his capacity as minister of information. While Harmoko simultaneously was Golkar's general chairman, Suharto was Golkar's supervisor and chairman of its advisory board, and in reality the organisation's most powerful figure. The leaders of the PPP and the PDI were meanwhile denied access to the database, ostensibly because of the costs it would incur to connect them on-line.[36] It was the result published by the LPU three and a half weeks after the election which was the final and legally valid result of the election, not the vote counts reported directly from the polling stations.

According to Alexander Irwan, co-author of an Indonesian study of violations against the election procedures in 1992, the violations did not occur haphazardly, but rather systematically with the purpose of ensuring Golkar's victory.[37] Civil servants on different levels in the administration were even issued targets for Golkar's election performance in their respective areas of administration. For example, according to the *Jakarta Post* before the May 1997 election, the regent of Banyumas in Central Java promised one ox for each polling station in the regency where

---

35. For the difficulties faced by scrutineers from the PPP and the PDI in 1992, see Irwan and Edriana (1995: 24) and *Tempo* (13 June 1992 and 4 July 1992).
36. *Jakarta Post*, (28 May 1997). For Suharto's role in Golkar, see Robison (1995a: 55–58) and Suryadinata (1997a).
37. Interview with Alexander Irwan in *Tempo Interaktif* (2 June 1997); see also Irwan and Edriana (1995: 26) and footnote 33 above.

Golkar gained at least 95 per cent of the votes, and two oxen where Golkar gained 100 per cent. After the election the regent reportedly gave away more than 400 oxen.[38]

Suspicions over plans to manipulate the election results also arose in the beginning of the campaign period in May, when the PPP discovered a document, dated 2 March 1997, which showed detailed election data from all 125 polling stations in a subregency in the city of Bengkulu in Sumatra. According to the document, which was signed by the subregent, who was also chairman of the election committee in the area, Golkar would gain 82.29 per cent of the total votes. The subregent and the government claimed that the document was only an estimation, but this explanation did not satisfy the PPP, and the affair fuelled suspicions that the election results would be manipulated.[39]

Complaints over election irregularities were handed by the official Committee for the Supervision of Election Implementation, Panwaslak (*Panitia Pengawas Pelaksanaan Pemilu*), a body headed ex officio by the attorney general. Few of the complaints filed by the political parties with the Panwaslak had in the past led to any sanctions or legal proceedings. Even if they did, they would not affect the validity of the election results.[40]

Just as after previous elections, both the PPP and the PDI made numerous allegations of vote rigging and of violations against the election laws by the organisers of the election. The PPP was especially outspoken in its criticisms. However, on 23 June 1997, representatives of all three contestants signed their approval of the final result of the 1997 election. Not signing would have meant that the parties' legislators would not be able to take up their seats in parliament, scheduled to open in October. Suryadi, who had failed to win a seat, was conspicuously absent

---

38. *Jakarta Post* (5 June 1997).
39. *Kompas* (11 May 1997).
40. Irwan and Edriana (1995: 71) for example observed that, to their knowledge, none of the 462 instances of violations compiled in their study had led to legal action three years after the election.

at the ceremony, and the PDI was instead represented by the party's secretary-general, Buttu Hutapea. The PPP leader Ismael Hasan Metareum expressed his disappointment with the implementation of the election, especially concerning the vote count. He apologised to the party's voters for signing the approval in spite of the party's many allegations of irregularities in the election process.[41]

The Significance of the 1997 General Election

The 1997 election followed the same overall pattern as earlier elections under the New Order, being a carefully rigged affair designed to ensure a large victory for Golkar, thereby serving as a demonstration of the government's continued legitimacy. However, the election rigging and manipulation was too extensive and too conspicuous for the election to fulfil its purpose. It failed to convince a growing number of politically educated Indonesians of the government's continued political legitimacy. Suryadi was widely seen as a government stooge and the party's disastrous result was, more than anything, a consequence of voter distaste with the government's manipulation of the party's internal affairs ahead of the election. The government's treatment of Megawati appalled many Indonesians who earlier might have believed that the country, however slowly, was moving in the direction of greater democracy. It was also obvious to most politically educated Indonesians that Golkar's result as well as the high turnout figure to a large extent was explainable by the extensive manipulation of the election procedures and the vote count.

Several combined factors made the election a failure from the government's point of view, despite Golkar's unprecedently high vote. Higher levels of education and political awareness among

---

41. *Kompas* (24 June 1997). As of 24 June, the PPP claimed it had reported 1,033 cases of violations in the election to the Panwaslak; *PPP Online* (24 June 1997).

the population at large helped to highlight the shortcomings of the election to a wider political public. Furthermore, the heavy manipulation and repression preceding the election led to what Suryadi after the election called 'overkill'.[42] The result was undesired even from the regime's point of view, as both Golkar's increase and the PDI's decline were too drastic and implausible to be convincing indicators of popular political sentiments. In comparison with the previous election in 1992, the impression of the 1997 election was that it was more characterised by government manipulation and election rigging. The election therefore represented a reversal of the hopes among some observers that the election system was moving towards greater freedom and honesty.

There was in 1997, already before the economic crisis set in, a widespread feeling that the Suharto era was approaching its end. Calls from outside the regime for improving democracy and for addressing problems of growing social and economic injustice were gaining strength. The regime responded to these calls by increasing its levels of repression and manipulation, all in order to try to maintain the status quo of power and social relations. There were no attempts to try to accommodate new political aspirations or to bring in even moderate proponents of reform into the government. If anything, the May 1997 election served to undermine the already shaky legitimacy and democratic credentials of the regime. The election demonstrated the increasing alienation of the regime from society at large and its disability to adjust to the new social and political demands which had emerged in the wake of three decades of economic transformation.

---

42. Interview, Jakarta (7 October 1997).

CHAPTER 5

Economic Crisis

In the second half of 1997 a series of events in Indonesia and the surrounding world thoroughly transformed the Indonesian political landscape. During these months the cracks in the façade of the regime became increasingly obvious, and the long-suppressed resentment and opposition against President Suharto began to be aired publicly with a previously unheard vigour and outspokenness. The two crucial factors in this transformation were the Asian economic crisis, which began to affect Indonesia from August 1997, and worries about the president's health which seemed to be deteriorating in the last month of the year.

Immediately after the election, however, this development seemed far away. The economy was still booming and the opposition had been silenced by a combination of repression and manipulation. It seemed to be 'business as usual' in Indonesia. In the middle of August one prominent Indonesia watcher concluded: 'The [New Order's] old formula of combining economic benefits with tough authoritarian controls is proving remarkably durable, despite wider changes in society.'[1] By the end of 1997, this durability seemed less certain, and the anti-Suharto opposition seemed to feel that the winds of change were gathering momentum.

---

1. Andrew MacIntyre in *The Australian* (15 August 1997). The expression 'business as usual' is Bertrand's (1997), who used it to describe Indonesia before the election.

'Business as Usual'

Immediately after the election, Harmoko had claimed Golkar's victory as a sign of popular support for the government. Meanwhile, Suharto was conspicuously quiet on the subject. Instead he removed Harmoko from his position as minister of information only a few days after the election, replacing him with General Hartono, who thus retired from the military. It was a remarkable move by the president; only once before, in 1995, had Suharto removed a cabinet minister in mid-term.[2] Meanwhile, no official explanation was given for Harmoko's removal, which led to much speculation of the background and meaning of the move. He retained his ministerial status, and a few weeks later he was assigned the task of preparing the new parliamentarians for their inauguration in October. He thus seemed set to become the chairman of the parliament and the MPR for the coming five-year term.

Soon after Harmoko's removal another event shed new light on the cabinet reshuffle. In a constitutionally dubious move, Suharto refused to sign the country's first broadcasting law which had been passed by parliament in December the year before. Harmoko had led the process of drafting the bill, and had reportedly been very satisfied with the outcome. However, the law had inexplicably been stalled for six months, awaiting

---

2. Wiratman and Hasibuan (1997: 227). Minister of Trade Satrio Budiarjo Yodono [Budiardjo Joedono] was removed from his post in December 1995, ostensibly to allow the merger between the trade and industry departments. However, he was widely acknowledged to have performed poorly in his portfolio, and it was rumoured that his refusal to grant favours to well-connected businessmen, including members of the Suharto family, hastened his removal; Fealy (1997: 26). As Yodono was close to Habibie, and as his dismissal came the day before the opening of ICMI's congress, it was also widely interpreted as a signal from Suharto to Habibie for the latter to curb his political ambitions; see *EIU Country Report Indonesia*, 1st quarter (1996: 10). In contrast to Harmoko's removal, Yudono's was final with no hint at a future career.

the president's signature. After the election, one of the first tasks of Harmoko's successor, Hartono, was to take the legislation bill back to the parliament together with a letter from the president in which he described the law as 'technically difficult to implement'. Among other things, the law stipulated that private TV stations would not be allowed to cover more than 50 per cent of the population, and that operating licences would only be granted for a period of five years at a time.[3]

Although Suharto offered a technical reason for rejecting the bill, most observers believed that the reason, as cautiously put by the *Jakarta Post*, was that all of Indonesia's five private TV stations were 'owned by politically connected people'.[4] In fact, four of them were partly owned by relatives of Suharto. Tutut held the majority share holding in one company, TPI (*Televisi Pendidikan Indonesia*), while the president's second son, Bambang Trihatmojo, had majority share holdings in the largest station, the RCTI (*Rajawali Citra Televisi Indonesia*), as well as interests in a third station, *Indosiar Visual Mandiri*. Bambang's wife held 22.5 per cent of the shares in yet another station, the SCTV (*Surya Citra Televisi*).[5]

A special committee was quickly set up in parliament, and the legislation was duly amended to allow operating licences to run over ten instead of five years, while the limitation on the stations' coverage was scrapped. In addition, an original provision which would have permitted the state-run television, TVRI, to run commercials was scrapped. On 18 September, the new law was passed unanimously in parliament, after Deputy House Speaker Sutejo had rejected a request by some MPs to make additional comments. Hartono, meanwhile, thanked the house for its kindness in reconsidering the bill, and described the process as active, dynamic and coloured with lively debate.[6]

---

3. *Far Eastern Economic Review* (4 September 1997).
4. *Jakarta Post* (19 September 1997).
5. *Far Eastern Economic Review* (4 September 1997).
6. *Jakarta Post* (19 September 1997).

Suharto's move to reject the broadcasting bill was embarrassing, because it demonstrated the influence which Suharto's children seemed to have over the president and over national policy making. It also demonstrated the fact that their private economic interests often took precedence over national economic or political interests. The affair with the broadcasting bill came on top of several other high profile examples of first-family nepotism in the preceding years, including, most notoriously, the privileges awarded to Tommy Suharto's national car project. To the public the affair with the broadcasting bill served as a reminder of the lengths to which Suharto was prepared to go in order to favour his family.

The Onset of the Economic Crisis

In the second half of 1997 much of East and Southeast Asia entered the severest economic downturn in the region since the 1930s. The currencies of several of the previously vigorous 'tiger' economies collapsed and the countries worst hit, Thailand, Indonesia and South Korea, all had to turn to the International Monetary Fund (IMF) for help, resulting in large bail-out packages for each of them. In Southeast Asia, most leading economies entered severe recessions, and the rest of the East and Southeast Asia experienced a sharp slowdown. Of all countries affected by the crisis, Indonesia was worst hit, with GDP expected to contract by fifteen per cent in 1998.[7]

---

7. For surveys and analyses of the Asian economic crisis in general, see Henderson (1998), Jomo K. S. (ed.) (1998), McLeod and Garnaut (eds) (1998) and World Bank (1998). Biers (ed.) (1998) provides a collection of articles from 1997 and early 1998 from the *Far Eastern Economic Review* on the crisis. Richard Mann's (1998a) account is so far the most detailed survey of the development of the economic crisis in Indonesia, although it is curiously uncritical of the Indonesian government's handling of the crisis and therefore seems somewhat biased. Booth (1998) and McLeod (1998) provide shorter but more balanced accounts.

The Asian economic crisis did not originate in Indonesia, but in Thailand with the collapse of the baht in early July 1997. After speculators had identified several weaknesses in the Thai economy, including an overvalued currency fixed to the dollar, a troubled banking system, large unhedged short-term foreign debts, declining returns on investment and a general lack of transparency in business and finance transactions, the baht came increasingly under attack from currency speculators. On 2 July, the central bank unexpectedly announced that it would no longer defend the currency, resulting in an instant devaluation of nearly fifteen per cent to the dollar.[8]

The immediate effects of the Thai currency crisis were small in the rest of the region. The small depreciation which affected the rupiah in July and early August seemed to be effects of contagion rather than a sign of any fundamental problems within the Indonesian economy. On 8 July, six days after the floating of the baht, the Jakarta Stock Exchange hit an all-time high.[9] Most analysts seemed to agree that the Indonesian economy overall was in good shape. The main macro-economic indicators, such as economic growth, inflation, export growth and budget and current account balances, were strong, and Indonesia was seen as the most promising country in the region. Shortly before the crisis set in, Indonesia was described as 'one of the most remarkable development success stories in the last third of the 20th century.'[10]

However, in early August the Indonesian rupiah came under increasing pressure, and on 14 August the central bank allowed

---

8. For the Thai crisis, see e.g. Lauridsen (1998) and Warr (1998).
9. *Far Eastern Economic Review* (21 August 1997).
10. Hill (1997: 1); cf. also Hill's (1998) analysis of the causes of the crisis. For other examples of generally positive assessments of the Indonesian economy shortly before the crisis, see the World Bank (1997), Guinness Flight (1997: 10) and *Far Eastern Economic Review* (21 August 1997). For the phenomenon of contagion and its sources in the context of the Asian crisis, see Garnaut (1998: 14–16)

the currency to float, resulting in a devaluation from around 2,600 to nearly 3,000 rupiah against the US dollar. Still, the Indonesian government was widely praised for its handling of the situation. In contrast with Thailand, the Bank of Indonesia did not waste large sums on defending the currency. The devaluation was swiftly followed up with cuts in government spending, higher interest rates and a deregulation package in early September, all of which were applauded by international investors and analysts as well as by the IMF. A team of experienced free-market economists, Indonesia's so-called technocrats, was appointed to manage the crisis and to boost the confidence of international investors.[11]

There were, however, niggling doubts about the government's and President Suharto's commitment to the deregulation package and to cutting government spending. A few days after the rupiah's float Suharto had declared his support for a plan to build the world's longest bridge between Sumatra and Malaysia. Suharto's second daughter and the wife of the Kopassus commander Major-General Prabowo, Siti Hediati Hariyadi, officially presented the plan to the president, and she seemed set to play a major role in the project. The controversial national car project headed by the president's son, Tommy Suharto, was not affected by the reforms. In addition, several cartels and monopolies controlled by the Suharto family or politically well-connected businessmen were allowed to continue. These circumstances signalled that the president saw no need to let the reforms affect the business interests of his family and crony businessmen.[12]

---

11. *Far Eastern Economic Review* (4 September 1997), *The Economist* (11 October 1997) and *Kompas* (18 September 1997). For the development of the Indonesian crisis up to March 1998, see Soesastro and Basri (1998).
12. *Kompas* (21 August 1997 and 6 September 1997) and *Far Eastern Economic Review* (16 October 1997). The plan for the bridge was later, on 23 September, postponed, together with a number of other infrastructure projects; McLeod (1997: 45).

Throughout September the rupiah continued to depreciate, driven by high demand for US dollars among domestic companies, many of which held high short-term debts in dollars. The rupiah's fall was also triggered by domestic capital flight, as wealthy Indonesians and companies moved their capital offshore, fearing a further decline in the rupiah's value.[13] Even if the government was lauded by the international community for its handling of the crisis, it seems that it failed to win back the confidence of the domestic business community. In early October, *The Economist* observed:

> The government seems to have lost the confidence not so much of the international markets, as of its own businessmen. Many of them believe that the web of patronage, cronyism and corruption that binds the economy together prohibits effective government action.[14]

Such sentiments probably contributed significantly to exacerbate the currency crisis and to turn it into a general economic crisis. In the preceding years the prevalence of corruption and nepotism had become increasingly evident to the Indonesian public, including the Indonesian business community. As the rupiah slid downwards throughout September, the broadcasting bill was being reconsidered in parliament, serving as a reminder of the precedence of private economic interests over national interests. Consequently, cynicism and scepticism of the government's ability and willingness to deal effectively with the crisis was widespread, and hindered the restoration of confidence in

---

13. Johnson (1998: 12); see also Cole and Slade (1998: 63–64). The capital flight seems to an extent to have been driven by a debate over a proposition, announced on 15 July, to move the large Indofood, a food processing company belonging to Liem Sioe Liong's conglomerate, the Salim group, to Singapore; Johnson (1998: 12) and Lindblad (1997: 12).
14. *The Economist* (11 October 1997).

the rupiah and in the economy in general among the Indonesian business community.[15]

As the rupiah continued to fall, there was no serious hint that the currency troubles might affect the static political order. In mid-September the list of delegates for the MPR was announced. Amongst the 500 appointed delegates endorsed by the president were four of his children, as well as the wives of several senior government and military officials. As expected, Harmoko was appointed chairman of both the MPR and the parliament. Conspicuously absent from the MPR line-up were the NU leader Abdurrahman Wahid and the Muhammadiyah leader Amien Rais. The MPR was sworn in by President Suharto on 1 October and the assembly immediately started work in committees on drafting, among other things, a decree which would delegate sweeping emergency powers to the president in the interest of national security. The suggestion was presented as a response to the many instances of social unrest which recently had occurred throughout the country.[16]

---

15. Cf. Thee Kian Wie (1998: 126). See Robison (1997: 48–51) for some of the high-profile cases of corruption and mismanagement linked to the regime in the preceding years. It was also the opinion of Indonesia's Finance Minister Mar'ie Muhammad that the loss of confidence in the rupiah initially was driven by domestic capital flight; interview (16 November 1998).

It may be argued that the prevalence of corruption, collusion and nepotism, KKN (*korupsi, kolusi dan nepotisme*) did not cause the economic crisis in Indonesia. The problems were much older than the crisis, and Indonesia had experienced strong economic growth for several years up to mid-1997 with market participants all along being aware of the KKN factor. However, once the crisis started in August, the prevalence of KKN quickly became the focus of market interest, and therefore the government's commitment to taking on the problems became a crucial factor for restoring market confidence and thus for solving the crisis. See Hill (1998: 99–100) and Johnson (1998: 14) for similar lines of argument.

16. *Jakarta Post* (16 and 20 September 1997). For the discussions on the decree, see Swantoro (1997: 360–361). The leaders of the NU and the Muhammadiyah had on previous occasions been included in the line-up for the MPR.

On the same day, 1 October, Suharto was bestowed with the rank of a five-star general together with two of the other central figures in the history of the armed forces, General (retired) Abdul Haris Nasution and, posthumously, General Sudirman [Soedirman]. While Sudirman was regarded as the founding father of the Indonesian military and was intimately associated with the independence struggle 1945–49, Nasution had been a leading figure in the armed forces during the 1950s and 1960s. The move to promote the three generals apparently served to link Suharto to the two senior historic figures of ABRI in a symbolic trinity where each of them represented three successive periods in Indonesian history: Sudirman for the independence struggle, Nasution for the Old Order, and Suharto for the New Order. The ceremony to confer the fifth star on Suharto was conducted by the commander-in-chief, General Feisal Tanjung, who afterwards cited the president's pride over the conferral. Feisal did not seem to attach any importance to the fact that Suharto himself had taken the decision to have himself promoted.[17]

The efforts to prepare the way for Suharto's re-election also proceeded. On 16 October, Harmoko, in his capacity as Golkar's chairman, announced that Suharto was the organisation's only candidate for the presidency, and that it was the wish of the people that the president be re-elected for another five-year term. Suharto responded by asking that the five months up to the MPR session be used to further investigate if the people really still trusted him. This stance precipitated an expected chorus of support for his candidacy from Golkar, as well as from numerous other state-sponsored social and political organisations.[18]

The First IMF Package and Its Aftermath

Meanwhile, on 8 October and after the rupiah had hit a low of almost 4,000 to the dollar, Indonesia announced its intention

---

17. *Kompas* (2 October 1997).
18. *Suara Pembaruan* (16 and 20 October 1997); see also *EIU Country Report Indonesia,* 4th quarter (1997: 12).

to seek assistance from the IMF. The decision was followed by two weeks of negotiations and work on drafting an agreement before it was announced on 31 October. It was said to be the IMF's biggest rescue package ever, reportedly providing up to 43 billion US dollars in assistance over three years. However, the figure was overblown, as it included five billion from Indonesia's own assets. Furthermore, much of the rest of the money, around 20 billion dollars, consisted of stand-by loans from several governments which were preferably not to be used.[19] The announced size of the package was meant to restore market confidence in the Indonesian economy quickly and decisively. Like previous IMF packages, including that for Thailand in August, the Indonesian agreement aimed at tight fiscal and monetary policies. It targeted a budget surplus of one per cent of GDP during the fiscal year 1998–99 and a current account deficit of less than three per cent of GDP within two years. The package also included a restructuring programme for Indonesia's troubled financial sector. In addition, the agreement included structural reforms for the economy as a whole, including the elimination of import and marketing monopolies and the privatisation of government enterprises. Such reforms were traditionally not the business of the IMF and had not been part of the Thai agreement. It is unclear if the initiative to include the reforms in the agreement came from the IMF or if they were proposed by the Indonesian negotiators in a bid to strengthen the credibility of the package.[20]

---

19. McLeod (1998: 40). The full text of the agreement was not made available to the public; for a summary of the main (public) contents, see *IMF Survey* (17 November 1997).
20. According to Soesastro and Basri (1998: 16), the reform measures were voluntarily proposed by Indonesia, but according to Finance Minister Mar'ie Muhammad, who took active part in the negotiations, the initiative came both from the IMF and the Indonesian negotiators; interview, Jakarta (16 November 1998).

The package initially succeeded in restoring some confidence in the rupiah, which strengthened against the US dollar as the news of the package broke. However, several aspects of the agreement weakened its capacity to restore enduring confidence in the rupiah or in the announced structural reforms. The fiscal and monetary austerity prescribed by the agreement seemed likely to worsen the crisis by exacerbating the fall in demand which was already apparent. It was also unclear how the funds provided should be used, and there was no pronounced strategy for achieving a strengthening of the rupiah to a realistic level at which Indonesian borrowers would be able to repay their loans in foreign currencies.[21] The problem of large private sector debt in foreign denominations was not covered by the agreement, although the demand for dollars which the private sector debt generated was one of the major causes of the decline of the rupiah. In the preceding years, Indonesian companies had borrowed heavily overseas, and with the rupiah's fixed exchange rate looking stable for the foreseeable future, many borrowers did not bother to hedge their debts, that is, to protect them from currency fluctuations. Much of the debt was short-term, and when the value of the rupiah fell, many companies could no longer afford to service their dollar-denominated debts. Estimations of the value of total corporate sector foreign debt ranged from 45 billion dollars to 140 billion dollars, or between 40 and 120 per cent of Indonesia's GDP in 1997.[22]

In addition, the structural reform programme contained several ambiguities and conspicuous omissions. Tommy Suharto's controversial national car project, which was of great symbolic importance, was allowed to continue, as was the costly state-run

---

21. McLeod (1998: 40–41).
22. Indonesia's GDP was 624.3 trillion rupiah in 1997, and at an exchange rate of 5,450 to the dollar (at the end of the year), this equalled 114.6 billion dollars. For discussions and estimations of the size of the corporate sector debt, see *EIU Country Report Indonesia*, 1st quarter (1998: 32) and Soesastro and Basri (1998: 36–39).

aircraft maker IPTN (*Industri Pesawat Terbang Nusantara*).[23] The state monopoly on trade in wheat, soybeans and garlic was abolished, but it was retained on two other key foodstuffs, rice and sugar. Furthermore, the reforms did not contain any anti-trust legislation, which for example allowed Liem Sioe Liong's Salim group to continue to control over 95 per cent of wheat milling, a lucrative business in which Tutut also had a stake.[24] These omissions, together with some ambiguous statements by the president concerning the package, indicated to the market that Suharto, and thus in effect the Indonesian government, were hardly committed to its implementation.

As part of the financial sector reform programme laid down in the package, the government announced on 1 November that it would immediately close sixteen troubled banks. According to Finance Minister Mar'ie Muhammad, the banks were 'insolvent to the point of endangering business continuity and disturbing the whole banking system'.[25] However, it was not clear what criteria had been used for singling out the sixteen banks, and several other of the country's more than 200 banks appeared to be at least as troubled as the sixteen banks. The measure consequently backfired, and instead of restoring confidence in the financial sector, it triggered a loss of confidence in Indonesia's banking system as a whole. A large-scale flight of deposits from several private banks ensued, forcing the central bank to use large sums of money to prop up the private banks and keep them liquid.[26]

---

23. The IPTN was the flagship of Indonesia's so-called strategic industries under Minister of Technology and Research B. J. Habibie. Habibie's vision was that the IPTN and other high-tech projects would spearhead Indonesia's technological development, and create spin-off effects for other sectors of the economy. However, the IPTN and probably all the other strategic industries were unprofitable, and the government spent large sums covering their deficits. For the IPTN, see McKendrick (1992).
24. *Far Eastern Economic Review* (13 November 1997).
25. *The Economist* (8 November 1997).
26. McLeod (1998: 39–40); cf. also Muhammad (1998: 10).

It was conspicuous that several of the sixteen banks set for liquidation were owned by politically well-connected people. Two of the banks were owned by Suharto's children, Siti Hediati Hariyadi and Bambang Trihatmojo respectively, and one of them was owned by Suharto's half-brother Probosutejo. The latter two were furious over the decision to close their banks. In a rare display of public dispute between the government and the president's family, Bambang filed a lawsuit against Mar'ie Muhammad, claiming that the minister had closed the banks in order to discredit his family and, indirectly, to topple his father. It seemed that Bambang was upset mainly because of the prestige loss involved, but other reports said that he was angered by the fact that his brother Tommy's Bank Utama was not affected. A few days later President Suharto announced that the banks would remain closed, and Bambang ended the public row by withdrawing his lawsuit. Instead he transferred his bank's assets and reopened under a new name, but with the same staff and on the same premises. The affair once again demonstrated the favoured position of the first family's business interests, even in a time of crisis, and the public dispute together with the lack of transparent criteria for liquidating the banks caused a serious loss of confidence in the government's overall ability to deal with the crisis. The public row between Bambang and Mar'ie Muhammad also damaged President Suharto's personal prestige, as it gave the impression that the old man was losing control both of the economy and of his own family.[27]

Shortly after the affair of the bank closures, an anonymously written booklet entitled 'Conspiracy to destabilise Suharto'

---

27. *The Economist* (8 November 1997), *Far Eastern Economic Review* (20 November 1997), *Weekend Australian* (15/16 November 1997), and *Warta Ekonomi* (8 December 1997); cf. also Cole and Slade (1998: 63). The notion that Suharto had problems controlling the business activities of his children had had earlier precedents, most conspicuously when Tommy was awarded the national car licence in 1996 in competition with his siblings; see Kingsbury (1998: 211–213).

(*Konspirasi Menggoyang Soeharto*) appeared in Jakarta. It was written with the evident purpose of discrediting certain individuals and groups advocating political and economic reform. According to the booklet, Mar'ie Muhammad was the tool of a conspiracy aiming at toppling Suharto before the MPR session, in the context of which the liquidation of the banks was intended to discredit the president's family. The leaders of the conspiracy were said to be former commanders-in-chief of the military, General (retired) Benny Murdani and two ethnic Chinese businessmen, Sofyan [Sofjan] Wanandi and his brother Yusuf [Jusuf] Wanandi. The research institute CSIS (Centre for Strategic and International Studies), which was headed by Yusuf Wanandi, was also singled out as part of the conspiracy together with the Democratic People's Party, PRD, and a couple of student organisations. Internationally, the conspiracy allegedly received support from the Vatican, the CIA, the Israeli intelligence agency Mossad and overseas Chinese. The IMF, which was implicated as the extension of the CIA, was also said to be part of the conspiracy.[28]

The booklet looked like an elaboration of Bambang's assertion that the bank closures had been done with the intention of toppling his father. The thrust of the allegations suggests that the production was sponsored by elements of the Suharto family who were affected by the move to close the banks.[29] The booklet seemed to be part of an attempt to deflect attention from the first family's nepotism and the need for fundamental economic reform by shifting the focus to an alleged conspiracy theory with ethnic and religious dimensions. A national and international conspiracy of Jews, Catholics, Chinese, the United States and pro-democracy activists was accused of trying to destroy the Indonesian economy and topple Suharto. It implied that the

---

28. *Konspirasi Menggoyang Soeharto* (1997).
29. This was also the view of Mar'ie Muhammad; interview, Jakarta (16 November 1998).

conspiracy aimed at undermining the position of Indonesian Muslims as represented by the Suharto family by attacking their economic interests.

The economic crisis and the structural reforms proposed by the IMF agreement contributed to heightening the level of intra-elite economic competition towards the end of 1997. With the floating of the rupiah and the subsequent IMF negotiations, the influence of Indonesia's free-market economists, or technocrats, increased. The structural reforms which they advocated and which had been inserted into the IMF agreement directly threatened the economic interests of the Suharto family, as well as several of Suharto's business cronies and many senior politicians and bureaucrats who owed their economic fortunes to political favouritism or nepotism. In this context, it seems that the booklet was an attempt by parts of the Suharto family to fend off the attack on their interests by means of politicising ethnic and religious differences. The booklet also served to promote Suharto's re-election in March 1998, and thereby the preservation of the political economy which relied on his political power.

Renewed Opposition

In spite of the embarrassing affair of the bank closures, as of November 1997, the economic crisis had not yet started to have any thorough-going political implications in Indonesia. The economic problems caused a general atmosphere of uncertainty and drift, and the government's economic policies were criticised, but there was little expectation that the crisis would cause any major political change, including to threaten the paramount position of President Suharto. From December 1997, however, the Indonesian crisis started increasingly to take on political dimensions, primarily due to the deterioration of the economic situation and to worries over President Suharto's health.

In the last months of 1997 the Asian economic crisis deepened considerably because of its spreading to East Asia, particularly to South Korea, the world's eleventh biggest economy. Market worries that Korea would become a victim of the economic crisis had been present since the onset of the crisis, but became acute in October and early November as problems of the country's corporate sector debt and current account deficits increasingly became the focus of market concern. As the Korean currency, the won, came under speculative attack in November, the Korean government was forced to seek assistance from the IMF on 21 November.[30] The spread of the crisis to Korea set off a new round of devaluations in Southeast Asia, and for Indonesia it meant that the prospects for a swift recovery looked a good deal bleaker than just a few weeks earlier when the country's agreement with the IMF had been announced.

In this volatile situation, State-Secretary Murdiono announced on 5 December that Suharto would take a ten-day rest, cancelling his attendance at a meeting of the ASEAN Regional Forum as well as a scheduled visit to his wife's grave in Central Java. There was no mention of the president being ill, but appearing on television he looked frail. The year before, in July 1996, worries about Suharto's health had also been rife as he travelled to Germany for a medical check-up. Just as on that occasion, the lack of information sent the rumours spinning, serving as a forceful reminder of the political uncertainty around Indonesia's political succession. Suharto's ten-day rest in December 1997 triggered a twenty-per-cent decline for the rupiah, which at one point touched 6,000 to the US dollar. It is not clear what illness the president was suffering from; one rumour had it that he was suffering from a kidney ailment; another that he had had a light stroke.[31] On 16 December the president was back in

---

30. For the crisis in Korea, see Smith (1998) and Chang Ha-Joon (1998).
31. *Kompas* (6 and 13 December 1997) and *Asiaweek* (26 December 1997). For Suharto's medical check-up in Germany in 1996, see *EIU Country Report Indonesia*, 4th quarter (1996: 17–18).

office as scheduled, but with the inevitable image of being an ageing leader and his capability to lead the country increasingly in doubt.

To his opponents, Suharto's illness made him seem more vulnerable than he had in several years, and his ten-day rest became the trigger for a wave of open opposition against the president's leadership. Many of the regime critics who had been forced to take their opposition underground or to confine themselves to the university campuses as a result of the government's repression after the 27 July riot in 1996, now resurfaced and resumed or intensified their political activities. The university campuses, where the regime had tried to contain the opposition by allowing a limited political free-space, became the focus for the anti-Suharto movement. On 18 December, the students of the Gadjah Mada University in Yogyakarta held a referendum in which 83 per cent of the responding students rejected Suharto's candidacy for the presidential term 1998–2003. Around the same time, the students of the Diponegoro University in Semarang held a similar referendum in which 82 per cent rejected the president's renewed candidacy. Several other universities, mostly outside Jakarta, followed and held referendums in December 1997 and January 1998, all resulting in clear majorities for rejecting Suharto.[32]

As the year approached its end, Amien Rais, leader of the Muhammadiyah and a lecturer in political science at the Gadjah Mada University, emerged as Suharto's main challenger, declaring his willingness to stand as a presidential candidate in the upcoming presidential election. He had been the most popular candidate in the referendum among the students at his home university, receiving nineteen per cent of the votes. He also had the support of many modernist Muslims outside the universities. Earlier in the year a poll among the readers of the weekly

---

32. *Detektif & Romantika* (3 and 17 January 1998, and 21 February 1998).

Ummat had overwhelmingly elected him as the country's most popular Islamic leader. At a gathering in Jakarta on 28 December, close to a thousand Muslims, many of them leading intellectuals and ICMI activists, loudly expressed their support for the Islamic university lecturer's challenge to Suharto. At the same occasion, Amien Rais also received *Ummat*'s 'Man of the Year' award.[33] After Suharto earlier in the year had removed Amien Rais from ICMI for his outspokenness, Rais' popularity had surged. For the president, the demonstration of Muslim support for Amien Rais was a worrying indication that, in addition to the students' opposition, he was starting to lose his support from the urban middle-class Muslims which he had been courting in ICMI throughout the 1990s.

Environmental Crisis

While the economic crisis deepened and started to take on increasingly open political dimensions, another disaster raged in the plantations and forests of Sumatra and Kalimantan.[34] Thousands of fires in these areas covered large parts of Indonesia and its Southeast Asian neighbours in thick smoke, which in some places reduced daylight visibility to just a few metres. Not only were substantial areas of Indonesia affected by the smoke, but winds also carried the fumes north and west, causing severe smoke problems in Malaysia, Singapore, Brunei, Southern Thailand and parts of the Philippines. Tens of thousands of people had to be treated for respiratory and eye problems, and in the Malaysian state of Sarawak a state of emergency was declared after air pollution had reached levels considered as 'extremely hazardous'. Schools and businesses were closed, and people were told to stay indoors until the haze cleared.

---

33. *Detektif & Romantika* (3 January 1998), *Ummat* (5 January 1998) and *Far Eastern Economic Review* (8 January 1998).
34. For the fires, see Gellert (1998) and Cribb (1998b).

There were even suggestions to evacuate the whole population of Sarawak.

To a large extent, the disaster was man-made. Logging companies in Sumatra and Kalimantan burnt their waste and cleared the ground by setting the undergrowth on fire after having logged the areas concerned. The logging companies often worked closely with plantation companies, and clearing the ground of logged areas often served to make way for plantations, particularly palm oil plantations, which had grown rapidly in Indonesia since the 1980s. The use of fire by plantation entrepreneurs to clear ground seems to have been the single most important cause of the fires.[35] In addition, thousands of small-scale farmers used fire to clear ground for cash-crop plantations and for burning agricultural waste and garbage.

In 1997 the weather phenomenon El Niño caused a prolonged drought, causing the fires to rage out of control for several months, covering hundreds of thousands or even millions of hectares.[36] In the end of 1997 some rain fell in Sumatra and West Kalimantan, putting out some of the fires, and at about the same time the winds shifted, so the smoke cleared from Singapore and Malaysia. However, the drought continued in East Kalimantan, and as the winds started to shift again in February, the smoke problem returned in Singapore and Malaysia.[37]

The fires and the haze were by no means unexpected. Already in June 1997, Indonesia's Meteorological and Geophysical Agency, BMG (*Badan Meteorologi dan Geofisika*) had warned

---

35. Cribb (1998b: 9); see also Waluyo (1998).
36. Estimations of how large areas were destroyed by the fires ranged from the Indonesian government's estimation of 300,000 hectares to the World Wide Fund for Nature's (WWF) estimation of at least two million hectares; Cribb (1998b: 10) and Gellert (1998: 68–69).

El Niño is an irregularly occurring complex weather phenomenon affecting large parts of the southern hemisphere. For Indonesia, El Niños are usually associated with droughts.
37. Gellert (1998: 68, 71, 82–83).

that the predicted El Niño drought might cause haze problems.[38] As early as 1995, the practice of using fire to clear ground was outlawed in Indonesia after smoke problems the year before. However, the law was not implemented, as there was little political will on the part of the government to enforce it, especially against the often politically well-connected forest and plantation companies. Several businessmen close to Suharto had interests in the timber or plantation industries, such as Liem Sioe Liong and Mohammad 'Bob' Hasan, Indonesia's leading timber tycoon and a close friend and golfing partner of the president.

Both the government and the forest and plantation companies refused to acknowledge responsibility for the fires. President Suharto called it a natural disaster and blamed El Niño. Bob Hasan blamed slash-and-burn farmers, and rhetorically asked why timber companies would want to burn their raw material. Environment Minister Sarwono Kusumaatmaja and Forestry Minister Jamaludin [Djamaluddin] Suryohadikusumo seemed most concerned, but neither of them were able to take on the powerful timber and plantation companies. Sarwono also acknowledged that there was a lack of political will on behalf of the government to address the problem. In the early stages of the fire crisis, in September 1997, the government suspended the licences of 176 companies allegedly responsible for the fires, but by December most of the licences had been reinstated, in most cases without further action being taken against the companies. President Suharto gave no support to Jamaludin's effort to confront the logging companies, telling the minister that it was more important to fight the fires than to try to allocate the blame.[39]

---

38. Cribb (1998b: 4).
39. Gellert (1998: 82–84) and Cribb (1998b: 8–9); see also van Klinken (1998).

Internationally the fires were embarrassing to Indonesia, especially because they affected Indonesia's ASEAN partners, with which the country was keen to have good neighbourly relations. President Suharto also apologised twice to his neighbours for the smoke.[40] However, it was obvious that the Indonesian government lacked the political will to take action against the logging and plantation companies responsible for the fires, and that it was incapable of getting the fires under control. To the international community, the fires served to reinforce the perception of general government incompetence, as well as to highlight the precedence of private economic interests to national interest.

It is uncertain to what extent the fires and the smoke contributed to the general sense of crisis in Indonesia and to strengthening the image of government incompetence. According to Environment Minister Sarwono Kusumaatmaja, the smoke did not have any significant political impact in Jakarta, because the capital was not directly affected by the smoke problems, and the general public was little interested in environmental issues.[41] However, the government's lax attitude toward the logging and plantation companies once again highlighted the precedence of vested private interests over national interests. Suharto's refusal to let the companies share the responsibility for the fires also demonstrated his lack of will to sacrifice the interests of his close business cronies and associates. This attitude did nothing to improve the president's or the government's already uncertain credentials for dealing effectively with the crisis and implementing the economic reforms.

Social and Economic Aspects of the Crisis

In the last months of 1997, the effects of the economic crisis started to be felt massively throughout Indonesian society. The

---

40. Bird (1998: 175).
41. Interview, Jakarta (26 November 1998); cf. however Cribb (1998b: 13).

rupiah's exchange rate was 5,450 to the dollar at the end of the year, which represented a 58 per cent devaluation in less than six months, making it the worst performing currency in the world.[42] The rupiah's collapse meant that imported goods became prohibitively expensive, which both affected Indonesian consumers directly and Indonesian producers who used imported parts or raw materials in the production. While consumer prices increased steeply, salaries stayed flat, resulting in drastically reduced consumption and thus in aggregate demand. The fall in demand was further exacerbated by the fiscal and monetary austerity imposed by the IMF.

As mentioned before, one of the major problems for the corporate sector was the foreign debt burden. Many companies started to default on their debt repayments, which led to a downgrading of international credit ratings for Indonesian companies in general. Even those that did not default on their debts began to experience trouble in obtaining letters of credit from overseas banks for importing parts and raw material needed for production. These difficulties, together with the regional slow-down of the economy, hampered an export-led recovery which could have benefited from the weak rupiah.

The economic difficulties led many companies to lay off large numbers of their employees, or close down business altogether. On 30 December the Indonesian Chamber of Commerce and Industry, Kadin (*Kamar Dagang dan Industri*), estimated that one million jobs had already been lost as a result of the crisis. However, a few days later the head of Kadin's Jakarta branch estimated that 2.4 million workers had been laid off in the greater Jakarta region alone.[43] Initially, the crisis hit hardest in the big cities, especially in Java, where millions of people were forced into poverty. In June 1998, the ILO (International Labour Organisation) projected that some 5.4 million workers would be displaced by

---

42. *EIU Country Report Indonesia*, 1st quarter (1998: 29).
43. *EIU Country Report Indonesia*, 1st quarter (1998: 31).

the crisis in 1998. In addition, large numbers of Indonesian migrant workers, primarily in Malaysia, which also was affected by the regional crisis, lost their jobs and were forced to return home. Official projections by the Department of Manpower estimated that 13.4 million people, or 14.7 per cent of the work force, would be un-employed by the end of 1998.[44]

Many of the displaced workers sought alternative livelihoods in the already crowded informal sector, for example by selling food on the streets, driving pedicabs or providing various household services. However, the fall in demand also affected the informal sector, resulting in fiercer competition and less opportunity to make a living from such occupations.[45] Large numbers of poor urban migrants who were laid off simply returned to their villages of origin, trying to get by with help from friends and family. For many middle-class people, however, this was not an option, as they had severed their links to their home villages.[46]

In many rural areas the situation was difficult as the El Niño drought delayed or destroyed harvests. The total production of rice, the main staple food for most Indonesians, declined from 51.1 million tons in 1996 to 49.1 million tons in 1997, and the production of most other important food crops, such as maize, cassava and soybeans, declined as well.[47] The economic crisis also made it difficult for farmers to seek extra income from alternative employments in the formal and informal sectors.

---

44. ILO, Jakarta Office (1998: 2–3) and *EIU Country Report Indonesia*, 2nd quarter (1998: 33). The number of Indonesian migrant workers in Malaysia numbered hundreds of thousands. Between July 1992 and January 1997, 400,000 working permits were issued to Indonesian workers by Malaysian authorities, but the real number was probably significantly higher, since the number of illegal migrant workers in Malaysia in general exceeded the number of legal migrant workers; Muhamed (1998: 25).
45. ILO, Jakarta Office (1998: 2) estimated that half of the displaced workers in 1998 would be re-absorbed in the informal sector. See also Jellinek (1999) for a report from the grassroots level.
46. Johnson (1998: 39)
47. BPS (1998: 10–11).

One of the provinces which suffered most from the drought and the problems in its wake was Irian Jaya (New Guinea), where, by the end of 1997, more than a thousand people had died from starvation, malaria and other diseases. Many of the villages worst hit were situated in remote parts of the province, and a shortage of aircraft and pilots hindered rescue efforts. Local instances of acute food shortages also occurred in parts of Kalimantan and Java. Many people, both in urban and rural areas, could not afford to eat more than one or two meals per day, and were forced to shift from eating rice to cheaper food such as maize and cassava or various wild plants and insects.[48]

Even where rice was available, it was too expensive for many poor people. The inflation rate climbed steadily from the last months of 1997, and food prices were particularly affected. According to official statistics from 44 big cities, food prices rose by 10.1 per cent in January and 18.4 per cent in February 1998. In February 1998, one kilogram of rice cost on average 1,600 rupiah, compared with 970 rupiah a year earlier. At the same time, income opportunities decreased drastically for vast numbers of Indonesians, and for those who still had a job, salaries stayed the same or decreased due to shorter working hours. In several places around the country price increases on food and other basic goods led to rioting with looting and burning of shops. The riots mostly occurred in smaller towns in various parts of the country. Although they were limited in scope and few casualties were reported, the food riots gave some indication of the desperation felt by many poor people who became victims of the crisis. The spate of rioting peaked from mid-January to mid-February, and then abated.[49]

---

48. *Far Eastern Economic Review* (25 December 1997); see also Johnson (1998: 36–39).
49. For the figures, see *Bulletin Ringkas BPS* (November 1998) and *EIU Country Report Indonesia*, 1st quarter (1998: 31). For the riots, see *Digest* 52 (19 February 1998), *Tapol Bulletin* no. 146 (April 1998), Human Rights Watch/Asia (1998a) and the discussion in Chapter 6 below.

Overall, the result of the economic crisis was an enormous increase in the incidence of poverty. Using the official poverty line of 0.45 US dollars per capita per day, the ILO expected 100 million people, or 48 per cent of the population, to fall below the poverty line by the end of 1998. Other estimations expected the number of poor people to increase even more, approaching poverty levels similar to those which prevailed in Indonesia in the 1960s.[50] Regardless of what the correct figures are, the increase in poverty is bound to have tremendous social costs which will exhort their toll well into the next century.

From Economic to Political Crisis

The second half of 1997 saw a gradual but continuous erosion of public confidence in the government's and the president's capability. At first, the economic crisis did not seem insurmountable, and the measures taken by the Indonesian government in August and September were widely lauded internationally. However, the government's actions failed to win the confidence of the Indonesian business community. The corruption and nepotism which for many years had been a focus for popular resentment in Indonesia became the main obstacles for dealing effectively with the crisis, as they prevented the government from regaining the market's confidence in its policies and in the economy at large. Meanwhile, Suharto signalled that the business interests of his family and cronies would not be sacrificed, neither for the sake of the economy nor for the environment.

The IMF agreement, which was announced in late October, failed to break the downward spiral, in part because of the

---

50. ILO, Jakarta Office (1998: 4). Before the crisis, 22.5 million people, or 11.3 per cent of the population, lived below the poverty line according to official statistics; BPS (1998: 23). However, the official line of poverty was low by international comparison, and the real number of poor people may have been significantly higher even before the crisis; see Booth (1993) and (1998: 31–32).

market's distrust of the government's and President Suharto's commitment to the agreement, and in part because the economic policies and programmes contained in the package were inadequate and even counterproductive. The economic decline continued in November, exacerbated by the spread of the regional economic crisis to South Korea. Millions of Indonesians felt the effects of the crisis in the forms of unemployment, food shortages and other social and economic hardships.

Meanwhile, the political apparatus, carefully designed to support the status quo, continued to function. Golkar and a number of other official and semi-official organisations announced their support for Suharto's re-election, scheduled for March 1998. However, Suharto's ten-day rest in December caused much speculation about the president's health and served as a reminder of the political uncertainty around the presidential succession. Because Suharto looked weaker and more vulnerable than he had in a long time, oppositional groups and figures intensified their efforts to bring about a change in national leadership. Students, Muslim leaders and critics of the regime suddenly dared to voice their opposition against the president more openly than in the preceding years. By the end of 1997, with the economy in disarray and social discontent brewing within the society, it looked as if a big opportunity for the anti-Suharto opposition might be approaching.

CHAPTER 6

Towards a Seventh Term for Suharto

When Indonesia entered 1998 there was no end in sight to the economic crisis. Millions of Indonesians started to feel economic hardship, and the prospect of social and political turmoil began to look increasingly threatening. Meanwhile, a number of developments in early 1998 highlighted, as never before, the government's responsibility for the crisis and seriously damaged President Suharto's personal prestige. With an increasingly aggressive opposition demanding his resignation, it looked for a while in mid-January as if the president might be forced to step down. However, the counter attack from the regime came at the end of the month, when sections of the military leadership initiated a campaign to scapegoat the country's ethnic Chinese minority. The campaign served to deflect attention from the government's handling of the crisis and to achieve Suharto's smooth re-election as president in March.

Even though Suharto managed to survive the acute political crisis of early 1998, it left the image of a vulnerable president. The economic crisis deepened further, and the manipulative measures employed by the regime to maintain the political status quo exacerbated social, religious and ethnic conflicts among the elite, as well as in society at large. The price for keeping the ageing president in power started to look increasingly high.

The Second IMF Agreement

On 6 January 1998 Suharto appeared in parliament to present the government's budget proposals for the fiscal year 1998–99.

The president looked healthy, speaking untroubled for almost an hour. The budget, however, gave rise to some serious doubts. It was wildly optimistic, projecting a growth rate of four per cent, inflation at nine per cent and an exchange rate of 4,000 rupiah to the dollar, all of which deviated sharply from the projections of market analysts. It seemed that government spending would expand by a third, and the budget contained increases in subsidies on fuel and foodstuffs as well as the initiation of extensive labour programmes for the unemployed. The budget looked set to produce a deficit of around one per cent of GDP, which violated the IMF agreement from October. The budget was apparently designed to fend off the possibility of social and political unrest in the wake of the economic crisis, but it contained virtually no measures to implement the structural reforms stipulated in the IMF package. The budget strengthened the market's perception that the government lacked the will to implement the IMF agreement.[1]

On 8 January, the *Washington Post* cited an anonymous IMF official expressing unhappiness with the Indonesian government's implementation of the reform programme and with the budget proposition. The official also questioned Suharto's commitment to implementing the reforms. The report triggered a further

---

1. For the budget, see *Kompas* (7 January 1998) and *Asiaweek* (16 January 1998). The Indonesian government's way of presenting the budget differed somewhat from international practice, and to an extent it seems that the loss of confidence was triggered by the international media's misinterpretation of the budget. The figures of the 1998–99 budget were compared with the projections for the previous year which was misleading, because the realised figures for the fiscal year 1997–98 were far higher than projected. Consequently, the new budget was not as expansionist as represented in international media; Soesastro and Basri (1998: 21). Another source of confusion was that, in contrast to international standard methods of calculation, the Indonesian government treated foreign aid as a revenue and not as a means of funding a deficit, and therefore the budget showed a balance between revenues and expenditure instead of a deficit; *EIU Country Report Indonesia*, 1st quarter (1998: 20).

loss of confidence in the rupiah, which collapsed and fell below the psychological level of 10,000 to the dollar on the same day. In Jakarta, people panicked and started to stockpile food, as well as electronic goods and other consumer durables which were taken to represent a more stable value than the rupiah. People also rushed to the banks to try to change their rupiah savings to dollars.[2]

The government appeared to have lost control over the economy, and as it was the government's budget which had triggered the disastrous fall for the rupiah, the government's responsibility for the crisis was highlighted as never before. In response to the currency collapse, the government initiated a so-called 'Love the rupiah movement', Getar (*Gerakan Cinta Rupiah*), which encouraged people to change their dollar savings into rupiah. The campaign tried to strengthen the currency by appealing to nationalist sentiments, and Suharto's eldest daughter, Tutut, with her populist image, stood out as the main proponent of the campaign. It failed, however, to have any significant effect on the value of the currency, and cynics commented that no-one loved the rupiah more than Tutut.[3]

With serious social and economic, as well as political turmoil threatening Indonesia, the United States and the IMF jointly launched an emergency operation on 8 January. The IMF announced that its two top officials would travel to Jakarta shortly to negotiate a 'strengthening and acceleration' of the October agreement. The next day, US President Bill Clinton spoke to Suharto by telephone for almost half an hour, urging him to continue with the announced reforms and expressing his confidence in Suharto's leadership for overcoming the crisis.[4]

Within a week the new agreement was completed. Suharto insisted on personally signing the document, apparently in order to convince the world of his personal commitment to its imple-

---

2. *Washington Post* (8 and 9 January 1998), *Australian Financial Review* (9 January 1998) and *Gatra* (17 January 1998).
3. *The Economist* (17 January 1998) and Soesastro and Basri (1998: 20).
4. *Washington Post* (9 January 1998) and *Kompas* (10 January 1998).

mentation. On 15 January the president signed the agreement in a televised ceremony which showed the IMF's director Michael Camdessus standing imperiously over the president with his arms folded across his chest.[5]

The new agreement did not contain any pledges of additional support from the IMF or other donors, but rather focused on the commitments of the Indonesian government. The government would present a revised budget, which would ease the fiscal austerity somewhat. A budget deficit of one per cent of GDP was allowed, in order not to exacerbate the contraction of the economy. Meanwhile, funding to the state-run aircraft manufacturer IPTN was to be discontinued, and twelve major infrastructure projects, including a controversial power plant, were to be cancelled immediately. Subsidies on electricity and most fuels were gradually to be phased out, and all special privileges to the Timor car project were to be revoked immediately.[6]

The focus of the agreement, however, was on structural reform, and the package envisioned a complete deregulation of the Indonesian economy. Virtually all restrictive government regulations on the economy, in trade, production, and investment, were to be abolished. In practice, the reforms would mean taking on some of the most prominent vested interests of Suharto's relatives and close business associates, including several symbolically important arrangements, such as Liem Sioe Liong's wheat milling monopoly, a marketing board for the clove trade run by Tommy Suharto, and a plywood cartel controlled by timber tycoon Bob Hasan. The programme was indeed, in the words of Michael Camdessus, 'bold and far-reaching'.[7] If imple-

---

5. *Jakarta Post* (16 January1998). Camdessus's posture seems to have been unintentional; see *Asiaweek* (29 May 1998). However, it was widely interpreted in Indonesia and elsewhere in Asia as signalling an offensively superior and even neo-colonialist attitude.
6. IMF (1998a); in contrast to the first agreement, the second package was made public so as to increase transparency. *IMF Survey* (26 January1998) provides a summary of the agreement.
7. *IMF Survey* (26 January1998).

mented, the package would have thoroughly restructured the entire Indonesian economy.

Whereas the new agreement contained extensive structural reforms, it failed to address several of the weaknesses of the first IMF package two and a half months earlier. Like its predecessor, the new agreement contained no measures to solve the huge foreign debt problem of the private sector. The programme for the financial sector restructuring was still vague and wanting in detail. Furthermore, President Suharto's personal involvement was generally received with scepticism by the market. Immediately after signing the agreement, it was announced that the president would personally oversee the implementation of the reforms as head of a so-called Economic and Financial Resilience Council (*Dewan Pemantapan Ketahanan Ekonomi dan Keuangan*). The establishment of the council, which looked set to function as a type of economic super-government, indicated that Suharto had lost confidence in his economic ministers, whereas it was precisely these ministers who were most reputed by the market. Market analysts also had a widespread feeling that the president had accepted the agreement grudgingly, and therefore doubted his commitment to its implementation. Domestically, the agreement was widely seen as humiliating to national dignity, and Tommy Suharto called it a 'manifestation of neo-colonialism by developed countries'. The image of the signing ceremony with Michael Camdessus standing over the cowering president became a prime symbol of the perceived indignity, and also seriously damaged President Suharto's personal prestige.[8]

---

8. *Australian Financial Review* (17 January1998), Soesastro and Basri (1998: 23) and *EIU Country Report Indonesia*, 1st quarter (1998: 22). According to Finance Minister Mar'ie Muhammad, Suharto did not trust his economic ministers to negotiate with the IMF in the January agreement, and the president deliberately kept them out of the negotiation process. The president ordered that the drafts from the IMF be sent to him directly and they were translated by his long-time economic adviser Wijoyo [Widjojo] Nitisastro; interview with Mar'ie Muhammad, Jakarta (16 November 1998).

As a consequence of the shortcomings of the agreement and of the doubts about President Suharto's commitment to its implementation, the package failed to restore confidence in the rupiah, which continued to decline in the days after the announcement of the agreement. While Suharto, through his personal involvement in the dealings with the IMF, attempted to boost market confidence in his and the government's handling of the crisis, the effect seemed to be the opposite. One of the main consequences of the developments in mid-January was that market analysts started to regard Suharto as the main problem for the Indonesian government to deal effectively with the crisis and for restoring overall market confidence in the Indonesian economy.

Things got worse, however, when on 20 January Golkar announced fourteen criteria for its vice-presidential candidate in the upcoming March election. The criteria included an understanding for science and technology and the ability to assist the president internationally, two criteria which seemed to point to Minister of Research and Technology B. J. Habibie.[9] As a German-trained aeronautical engineer, Habibie no doubt fulfilled both these criteria. It was also widely understood that the minister was Suharto's preferred candidate for the vice-presidency, as he had been already in 1993. Habibie had a reputation for spending government money on large-scale technological projects, such as the IPTN, and for promoting protectionist and interventionist economic ideas. The indication that he might become vice-president and apparent successor to the ailing and weakened Suharto was received with great dismay by the market, and the rupiah tumbled, hitting a low of 17,000 to the dollar exactly a week after the president had signed the second IMF agreement. In Jakarta, the currency collapse once again caused panic buying of dollars and stockpiling. The revised state budget, which was

---

9. *Suara Karya* (21 January 1998).

released on 23 January, did nothing to restore market confidence and was widely seen as being out of touch with reality.[10]

At the end of January, several measures were announced for the banking sector reform as well as for the renegotiation of private foreign debt. The government also announced a voluntary three-month pause in all foreign debt servicing, which in effect meant a debt moratorium. To a large extent, the announcement only formalised the prevailing situation, in which many Indonesian companies had already stopped paying their debts. Meanwhile, the Economic and Financial Resilience Council, led by President Suharto, announced a number of measures to implement the structural reforms laid down in the IMF agreement, and a package of presidential instructions and decisions abolished, on paper, most major market distorting regulations and restrictions.[11] These concrete steps to try to resolve the crisis helped the rupiah to recover somewhat, but it still remained volatile, fluctuating between 7,000 and 11,000 to the dollar. Due to the size of their debts in foreign currency denominations, mostly dollars, such rates meant that the majority of Indonesia's large corporations and financial institutions were technically insolvent.

Pressure on Suharto

More than ever before, the rupiah's collapse in January highlighted the government's incompetence in managing the crisis. Whereas the first months of the crisis in 1997 had been largely driven by contagion from the Thai crisis and by the high demand for dollars by Indonesian companies, in January 1998

---

10. *Reuters* (22 January1998), *The Economist* (24 January1998) and *EIU Country Report Indonesia*, 1st quarter (1998: 24). For Habibie and his interests in research and development and Indonesia's state-run so-called strategic industries, see Shiraishi (1996).
11. *EIU Country Report Indonesia*, 1st quarter (1998: 25–26, 33), *The Economist* (21 January1998) and the Economic and Financial Resilience Council (1998).

it was the government's budget which triggered the currency collapse and subsequent panic. In this situation, the opposition to Suharto gathered new strength. On the day after the president's budget speech, on 7 January, Amien Rais publicly proposed the formation of a political alliance between Megawati, Abdurrahman Wahid and himself. Rais intended the alliance to be a platform for political reform and he called on the people not to nominate Suharto for another presidential term because of his failure to deal effectively with the crisis. Megawati immediately accepted the idea of an alliance, and a few days later she also announced her willingness to stand as a presidential candidate. Abdurrahman Wahid, however, was more cautious and only said that he agreed with the need for political reform.[12] Wahid was suspicious of and even adverse to Amien Rais, who had been one of the leading activists in ICMI until his removal in February the year before. Amien Rais had then been widely seen as a hard-line modernist Muslim, and he had previously stood out as hostile to Chinese Indonesians and Christians. From early 1998, however, Amien Rais started to tone down his previously rather intolerant image and acquire a more reconciliatory attitude towards non-Muslims and also to emphasise a more statesmanlike image.[13]

For Suharto, the proposed alliance was a potentially serious threat. Megawati, Amien Rais and Abdurrahman Wahid were his three most potent opponents, and for two years he had worked concertedly to remove them from any position of political influence. Megawati's ousting from the PDI chair, the co-optation

---

12. *The Age* (8 and 12 January 1998).
13. For Amien Rais' earlier hostile stance towards Christians and Chinese, see e.g. Ramage (1995: 98–99). When asked in an interview in September 1998 about his change in attitude towards Christians, Amien Rais said: 'Yes, it is a natural process. A stone never changes, I am not a stone. [...] I now have more appreciation of the plurality of the nation and feel the necessity of building a strong nation'; cited in Kato (1999: 22).

of Abdurrahman Wahid to support Golkar and the firing of Amien Rais from ICMI, all had served the purpose of preventing these outspoken and influential critics of Suharto from openly challenging the president. In a formal sense the scheme had succeeded, as all three had been excluded from the MPR line-up and had no chance of formally being nominated as contenders in the presidential election. However, the political engineering had not diminished the popularity of the three leaders; rather it had had the opposite effect for Megawati and Amien Rais. All three leaders had also very much managed to stay in the political limelight, and each could still count on millions of loyal followers. It was said that the three of them together could command the loyalty of around 90 million people, mostly in politically important Java.[14]

Students also continued to hold referendums in their campuses around the country, resulting in further calls for the president not to seek a seventh term in office. On 20 January, nineteen researchers at the Indonesian Academy of Sciences, LIPI, issued a statement which sharply criticised the government for its handling of the crisis and called for a change in national leadership. The prominent playwright and activist Ratna Sarumpaet tried to initiate a consolidation among the opposition movement and an umbrella organisation of students, artists, journalists and other activists, called Indonesian Solidarity for Amien and Mega, SIAGA (*Solidaritas Indonesia untuk Amien dan Mega*) was set up. The organisation was created to support Amien Rais and Megawati for their daring to declare themselves as presidential

---

14. The estimation was made on the somewhat dubious assumptions that all Muhammadiyah and NU members, each around 30 million, were loyal followers of Amien Rais and Abdurrahman Wahid respectively. Furthermore, it was assumed that the fifteen per cent of the votes which the PDI had collected in the 1992 election could be translated into 30 million Megawati supporters (i.e. fifteen per cent of Indonesia's population of 200 million). The latter reasoning was also supported by Abdurrahman Wahid; interview, Jakarta (7 October 1997).

candidates. SIAGA, as well as numerous other groups, staged a number of demonstrations in January and February, calling for economic and political reform and a change in national leadership.[15]

However, the anti-Suharto movement remained weak and uncoordinated, lacking a coherent strategy for achieving the desired change in national leadership. Neither Amien Rais nor Megawati was actively campaigning for the presidency, and neither of them seemed prepared to take the lead in the opposition movement. Although there were many demonstrations in Jakarta and elsewhere in the country calling for Suharto to step down, they were all very small, typically gathering just a few dozen participants. Abdurrahman Wahid, meanwhile, still refused to join hands with Amien Rais, and he failed to show up at a public meeting with Megawati, Amien Rais and twenty other prominent government critics on 15 January. In addition to his adverseness for Amien Rais, Wahid also probably feared that openly opposing Suharto or the military might lead to violence and general upheaval. On 19 January Wahid's political activities were abruptly cut short as he suffered a stroke and was hospitalised.[16]

Meanwhile, the arrangements for Suharto's re-election went ahead. On 20 January, after an audience in the presidential palace, Harmoko announced that Suharto had accepted Golkar's nomination to become president for the 1998–2003 period. Within a few weeks, all the other factions in the MPR also announced their nominations of Suharto, apparently making Suharto's unanimous re-election in March a foregone conclusion.[17]

---

15. *Detektif & Romantika* (21 February 1998), *Kompas* (21 January 1998), *Suara Pembaruan* (24 January 1998) and interview with Ratna Sarumpaet, Jakarta (5 November 1998).
16. *Kompas* (21 January 1998) and *Forum Keadilan* (9 January 1998).
17. *Jakarta Post* (21 January 1998) and *EIU Country Report Indonesia* 1st quarter (1998: 12).

With Suharto thus set to become re-elected, attention instead focused on the vice-presidency. Although Golkar's fourteen criteria for the coming vice-president seemed to point to Habibie, several other names were initially also mentioned by Golkar parliamentarians and cadres. Largely, the debate seemed superficial, as it was widely recognised that Suharto had already made up his mind in favour of Habibie. On 16 February, after most of Habibie's potential rivals, including Harmoko and the incumbent Try Sutrisno, had declared that they would not stand as candidates, Golkar formally announced that Habibie was the organisation's only candidate for the vice-presidency. The PPP and the PDI also declared their support for Habibie in mid-February, followed by the two remaining factions in the MPR, the Regional Representatives Faction *(Fraksi Utusan Daerah)* and ABRI later the same month.[18] Habibie's election thus looked as much a foregone conclusion as Suharto's election.

However, one of the names initially mentioned as fulfilling the fourteen criteria was Emil Salim, a former cabinet minister and technocrat who was widely respected as a competent and experienced politician untainted by corruption. To market analysts, he stood out as a far more acceptable candidate than Habibie, stressing his commitment to the IMF programme and urging the removal of market distorting arrangements such as cartels and monopolies. Emil Salim also initially received some support from within Golkar and at the end of January he declared himself willing to stand as a candidate for the vice-presidency. He also received the support of several leading figures, among them Sultan Hamengkubuwono X of Yogyakarta, Muslim intellectual Nurcholis Majid [Nurcholis Madjid], Environment Minister Sarwono Kusumaatmaja and prominent economist Sumitro Jojohadikusumo [Soemitro Djojohadikusumo]. In a campaign to have Emil Salim nominated, his supporters collected over 10,000 names in support for his candidacy and

---

18. *Detektif & Romantika* (21 February 1998 and 28 February 1998).

submitted them to the MPR in the end of February. Emil Salim seemed to have the support of some members of the MPR for Golkar, and the organisation's leadership, apparently wary of an open split in its ranks countered the campaign to have Emil Salim nominated by collecting declarations in support of Habibie from all their 588 MPs.[19]

Although Emil Salim's candidacy could not seriously threaten Habibie's election, the issue was apparently taken seriously by the Golkar leadership. The Emil Salim campaign was significant as an attempt to bring about a degree of political reform from within the existing system. The support from sections of the political elite, such as Golkar parliamentarians and cabinet ministers, showed that cracks in the regime were beginning to appear. If the campaign had succeeded in having Emil Salim nominated, it would have amounted to a highly symbolic challenge to Suharto's authority and to his prerogative of selecting the vice-president. However, with the five factions in the MPR all toeing the line, the campaign failed to achieve its goal.

With Suharto still controlling the political apparatus, as well as the military, at will, there was little the uncoordinated opposition movement could do seriously to threaten the president's position or the smooth running of the upcoming MPR session. However, the open expressions of opposition signalled a shift in Indonesia's political climate. After the worries about the president's health in December and the government's apparent problems in dealing with the economic crisis, the president's authority seemed to be declining. The opposition felt that it had the wind behind it, and consequently dared to be much more outspoken and bold than it had dared at any time in the past two decades.

---

19. *Jakarta Post* (25 February 1998), *Media Indonesia* (27 January 1998), *Australian Financial Review* (20 February 1998), *Detektif & Romantika* (28 February 1998) and *The Age* (26 February 1998).

Scapegoating the Chinese

On the evening of 18 January 1998 a home-made bomb exploded in a room of an apartment building in Central Jakarta. One person who was in the room was seriously injured, while two others were lightly injured and escaped from the place. According to the police, the bomb had exploded prematurely, and it was only one of several bombs which the police later claimed to have found in the room. The police also found a number of documents which linked the bombing to the PRD, and which laid out the plans for a revolution. According to the documents, the revolution would be accomplished with the support of four key groups: a well-known Jakarta research institute, a retired military officer who once wielded great power, the pro-Megawati masses, and the economic forces represented by Sofyan and Yusuf Wanandi. An e-mail message in a lap-top computer in the apartment allegedly said that Sofyan Wanandi had promised to support the movement financially.[20]

The alleged conspirators were essentially the same as the ones who had been blamed for the bank closures in November the year before. Through the link with the Wanandi brothers, the CSIS was easily identifiable as the implied research institute, and the reference to a retired general obviously pointed to Benny Murdani, who was also linked to the CSIS.

The bomb explosion signalled the beginning of a scapegoating campaign directed at Indonesia's Chinese minority, particularly parts of the Chinese business elite. The initiative

---

20. *Gatra* (31 January1998). It is uncertain who was responsible for making the bomb. The authorities blamed the PRD, but the party denied all involvement and stated that the party would never use violence as a political tool; interview with Ida Nasim Mh, secretary-general of the Central Leadership Committee of the PRD, Jakarta (26 November 1998). However, several journalists in Jakarta with connections in the PRD were convinced that the party in fact was responsible for making the bomb; confidential communication (November 1998).

for the campaign seems to have come from sections of the military. Senior officers, including the commander-in-chief, General Feisal Tanjung, advised the press to write stories critical of wealthy Chinese. A document, reportedly drafted by Kopassus, which laid out the conspiracy theory was circulated among the mass media, and most media followed the example of the official news agency Antara and started to use Sofyan Wanandi's Chinese name, Liem Bian Koen, in order to emphasise his ethnic identification.[21]

Major-General Prabowo, who nurtured close relationships with a number more or less radical Muslim organisations, seems to have played a key role in the campaign. On 23 January, he hosted a fast-breaking ceremony during the month of Ramadan at the Kopassus headquarters in Jakarta for 7,000 people, including several prominent Muslim leaders and activists. At the occasion, Prabowo's close associate, the Jakarta military commander Major-General Syafrie Syamsuddin [Sjafrie Sjamsoeddin], told the press that Sofyan Wanandi would be asked for clarification in connection with the bomb explosion. Prabowo also circulated copies of Sterling Seagrave's *Lords of the Rim* (1996), a popular book describing the economic activities of the overseas Chinese in Asia. The general reportedly also told the gathered Muslim leaders that he had met Sofyan Wanandi and that the latter had asked him to overthrow Suharto.[22]

The radical Muslim groups joined the campaign with great fervour. In its February issue, the militantly Islamic magazine *Media Dakwah* ran a cover story entitled 'Opposing the national traitors' *(Melawan Pengkhianat Bangsa)*, devoting nineteen pages to the fast-breaking ceremony and to hostile articles about Sofyan Wanandi and the CSIS. In several mosques around Jakarta meetings and discussions were held to discuss the alleged conspiracy. One of the larger meetings was held in the Al-Azhar

---

21. Human Rights Watch/Asia (1998a) and *The Age* (24 January 1998 and 16 February 1998).
22. *Media Dakwah* (February 1998), *EIU Country Report Indonesia*, 1st quarter (1998: 15) and *Tajuk* (23 July 1998).

Mosque in South Jakarta and had the theme 'Heart surgery for the CSIS' *(Membedah Jantung CSIS)*. At the meeting, Achmad Sumargono [Soemargono], executive chairman of one of the most active and radical Islamic organisations in Indonesia, the Indonesian Committee for Solidarity with the Islamic World, KISDI *(Komite Indonesia untuk Solidaritas Dunia Islam)*, read a paper entitled 'The lies of Liem Bian Koen' *(Kebohongan Liem Bian Koen)*.[23] Senior military officers also attended the talks. The chairman of ABRI's faction in parliament, Lieutenant-General Syarwan Hamid, spoke about the need to eradicate rats in Indonesia's economy, saying: 'These rats took away the fruits of our national development and work for their own self interest. [...] Don't think that the people do not know who these rats are. It's time to eliminate these rats.'[24] In February, President Suharto accused a conspiracy of domestic and international elements of trying to destroy the rupiah, and alluded to 'certain business people', a thinly veiled reference to the country's ethnic Chinese, supposedly responsible of triggering the crisis. Meanwhile, Aburizal Bakrie, chairman of the Indonesian chamber of commerce, Kadin, and the leader of one of Indonesia's largest non-Chinese business conglomerates, suggested that the economic crisis be used by the government to redistribute the property of the ethnic Chinese to indigenous Indonesians.[25]

---

23. *Media Dakwah* (February 1998). For the militancy of the magazine, see Liddle (1996b: 266–289). The discussion was arranged by KISDI together with three other Islamic groups; see *Republika* (9 February 1998).
24. *American Reporter* (February 1998). However, Amien Rais, who also was one of the speakers at the mosque meeting, countered Syarwan's rhetoric by saying that Indonesia has many kinds of rats, including the giant sewer rat *(tikus got)* living in its waterways – a clever, albeit thinly veiled, reference to President Suharto. The *American Reporter* translates tikus got as 'giant rodent', but sewer rat is a more precise translation, and seems more adequate in the context.
25. *The Age* (12 February 1998), *Far Eastern Economic Review* (5 March 1998) and *EIU Country Report Indonesia,* 1st quarter (1998: 15).

On 26 January, Sofyan Wanandi gave his clarification at the Jakarta headquarters of the Coordinating Agency for the Maintenance of National Stability, Bakorstanas *(Badan Kordinasi Pemantapan Stabilitas Nasional)*, a nominally civilian intelligence body. Feeling that he had been cleared of the allegations, and since there were no formal charges against him, Sofyan Wanandi shortly afterwards left the country for a long-planned business-cum-holiday trip to Australia. Rumours then spread that Sofyan Wanandi had fled the country, and he was scolded for being unpatriotic, for example by Feisal Tanjung, who said that Sofyan was not a good citizen. Shortly after his return to Jakarta on 8 February, Sofyan was questioned again by the police and military authorities.[26]

Several Muslim organisations, many of them apparently *ad hoc* groups linked to KISDI, also demonstrated outside the CSIS, demanding that the institute be closed down and that Sofyan Wanandi be brought to trial. It seems that some of the demonstrators were hired for the occasion. Certain media publications, such as *Detektif & Romantika*, which expressed scepticism about the story of the conspiracy, were also called upon by gangs of demonstrating youths. In an editorial, the magazine had implied that the alleged conspiracy was an attempt by the security forces to deflect the blame for the crisis from Suharto to the CSIS, and concluded that the story was not credible.[27]

---

26. *Detektif & Romantika* (14 February 1998) and Human Rights Watch/Asia (1998a).

27. *Detektif & Romantika* (7 February 1998). The magazine, in spite of its curious name, was a serious news magazine; see also p. 51 n. 2 above.

On the demonstrations against the CSIS and *Detektif & Romantika*, see *Republika* (27 January1998 and 28 January1998) and *Kompas* (7 February 1998). A staff member at the CSIS claimed that he saw that the demonstrators were paid at the end of the demonstrations, and several journalists in Jakarta also believed that the demonstrators consisted of rented crowds; confidential communications, October–November 1998.

The campaign against Sofyan Wanandi and the CSIS reflected a range of political and economic conflicts within Indonesia's elites. Sofyan Wanandi had on several instances criticised the government for its handling of the crisis. In December 1997, Sofyan Wanandi, together with a number of scholars from the CSIS, publicly criticised the government's inconsistency in implementing the economic reforms, and its lack of transparency. Sofyan Wanandi had also been critical of the 'Love the rupiah' campaign in early January, and had refused to repatriate his overseas assets, in spite of threatening phone calls from military officials.[28]

In addition, Sofyan Wanandi and the CSIS were critical of the prospect of Habibie becoming vice-president. A senior researcher at the CSIS, J. Kristiadi, was quoted as saying that the market would not accept Habibie as vice-president, and that the rupiah could fall to 20,000 to the dollar if he were elected. Instead of Habibie, Sofyan Wanandi wanted to see a military man as vice-president, in order to ensure political stability. He was rumoured to be campaigning behind the scenes for a re-election of the incumbent vice-president Try Sutrisno.[29]

The conflict also had deeper roots, on which the adversaries of Sofyan Wanandi and the CSIS could capitalise. The CSIS was associated with the late General Ali Murtopo [Moertopo], and the political intelligence organisation Opsus (*Operasi Khusus*, Special Operations), which engaged in various manipulative intelligence operations during the 1970s and 1980s. After Ali Murtopo's death in 1984, the *modus operandi* of Ali Murtopo and Opsus was continued by then commander-in-chief of ABRI, the Catholic General Benny Murdani. The operations of both Ali Murtopo and Benny Murdani were largely aimed at

---

28. *Panji Masyarakat* (9 February 1998) and *Far Eastern Economic Review* (19 February 1998).
29. *Panji Masyarakat* (9 February 1998) and *Tajuk* (23 July 1998). Sofyan Wanandi, however, denied that he had any preferred candidate from the military.

containing Islamic political aspirations, which in the 1970s and 1980s were seen as the biggest threat to the regime. Together with Try Sutrisno, who at the time was Jakarta military commander, Benny Murdani was also held responsible by many Muslims for the Tanjung Priok massacre in 1984 when security forces shot dead up to 200 demonstrating Muslims in a North Jakarta suburb. In the 1970s and 1980s the Chinese-Catholic dominated CSIS exercised great influence over government policy-making, and the institute was seen by many Muslims as anti-Islamic, having a history of working with the intelligence apparatus to contain Islamic political aspirations.[30]

Against this background, and against the background of the Chinese domination of much of the economy, allegations of various Chinese-Catholic conspiracies seemed easily to find resonance among many Indonesian Muslims. In the 1990s, the conspiracy theories were also able to draw on a wave of Islamic revival, strengthening the notion that Muslims were being marginalised in favour of Christians and Chinese. These sentiments were strong in radical Muslim circles, and perhaps among poor urban Muslims at large. At a time when the hardships of the economic crisis were being acutely felt by millions of Indonesians, the country's ethnic Chinese, especially the Chinese business tycoons, provided a convenient scapegoat to deflect the government's responsibility for the crisis.

Aside from the Wanandi brothers, Chinese Indonesian shop owners became the main victims of the scapegoating campaign, when their shops were attacked and looted in a spate of food rioting which occurred in different places around the country

---

30. For Ali Murtopo and Opsus, see Polomka (1971: 133–139) and MacDonald (1981), and on the association of the CSIS with the intelligence apparatus, see Anderson (1996b: 9 and *passim*). See also Ramage (1995: 99–100) about Muslim resentment against the CSIS. For the Tanjung Priok massacre, see Bresnan (1993: 219–244) and PSPI and Partai Bulan Bintang (1998) for an illustration of Muslim resentment over the massacre.

from around mid-January to mid-February. Small isolated instances of riots had begun to erupt already from December 1997, but by mid-January, the riots became much more frequent, and in contrast to earlier riots which had a multitude of causes, the riots from mid-January to mid-February were almost exclusively related to increases in food prices. As Chinese Indonesians dominated Indonesia's system of food distribution, they often, though not solely, became the victims of the riots. The direct and indirect verbal attacks by military officials on the Chinese contributed to the heightening of anti-Chinese sentiments and to exacerbate the unrest. The campaign against Sofyan Wanandi and the CSIS served to portray Indonesian Chinese in general as unpatriotic and greedy, refusing to repatriate their overseas assets to help the country overcome the crisis. Military officials also repeatedly stressed that hoarding amounted to subversion, an implicit accusation against mostly ethnic Chinese shop owners who raised their prices or closed down their shops because of fear of violence. The official anti-Chinese discourse and scapegoating thus endorsed racist sentiments and indicated that anti-Chinese violence might be tacitly approved of by the government as a way for venting popular frustrations in the wake of the economic crisis.[31]

The first riots directly related to rising food prices occurred in the adjoining districts of Jember and Banyuwangi, East Java, 12–16 January. After a demonstration of more than 1,000 people against rising food prices on 12 January, the next few days saw rioting flare up in several locations in the area. Crowds of people attacked and plundered shops, mainly owned by ethnic Chinese. In some cases, the shop owners were persuaded to sell their goods at old prices to avoid looting or destruction. The outnumbered security forces seem largely to have been unable

---

31. For the riots, see *Digest* 52 (19 February 1998) and Human Rights Watch/Asia (1998a). The related incidents in the following paragraphs are based on these reports.

to control the crowds, and reinforcements of riot police and troops from the Army's Strategic Reserve, Kostrad, had to be sent in. According to the police, 32 people were detained after the riots.

Java's strongly Islamic north coast was especially hit by the riots. In the evening of 26 January, in the small town of Kragan in northeast Central Java, fishermen protested against a 300-per cent increase in the price of kerosene, used for fishing lamps, by attacking two churches and destroying and looting fifteen shops owned by ethnic Chinese. In the next few days, rioting spread to several nearby towns on the highway along the north coast. On 28–30 January, three days of rioting took place in the Tuban district on East Java's north coast. The riots, which coincided with the *Idul Fitri* holiday marking the end of the fasting month Ramadan, saw the destruction of numerous Chinese-owned shops and the vandalising of a Pentecostal church. In mid-February, rioting in the area around the West Java town of Cirebon, also on the north coast, claimed the lives of two people, both suspected rioters who were shot by the security forces.

Riots also occurred in several provinces outside Java. On 1 February, in Donggala, Central Sulawesi, a group of youths began stoning Chinese-owned shops, after they found out that the price of brandy had increased. In Lombok, East Nusa Tenggara, two people were shot by police after a demonstration against the food prices had turned into a riot. In addition, isolated incidents of food riots, most of them involving attacks on shops and other property owned by Chinese Indonesians, occurred in South Sulawesi, Lampung, East Nusa Tenggara, North Sumatra, Irian Jaya, South Sumatra and Southeast Sulawesi.

Widespread as the rioting was, it was in most instances limited in scope, occurring primarily in smaller towns. The riots were typically unpredictable and spontaneous and directed at local Chinese shop owners. No shop owners were killed, and there were virtually no reports of bodily harm done to ethnic Chinese.

Altogether five people were killed in the riots, all of them rioters or bystanders who were shot by the security forces.

According to some media reports, the security forces allowed the rioting and looting to go ahead while standing aside watching, which led to speculation that the riots were engineered by sections of the military. However, the spontaneous nature of most riots together with the lack of concrete evidence or indication of military instigation makes such allegations seem implausible. The security forces were obviously overstretched in many instances, and local police and military often lacked training, experience and equipment for riot control. The passivity of the security forces was probably more attributable to insecurity on behalf of the troops about how to handle the situation and a fear of committing human rights abuses which might earn the military and the regime international and domestic criticism.[32]

Even if the riots in general were not caused by direct instigation, their occurrence was significantly attributable to the anti-Chinese rhetoric on behalf of sections of the military leadership and some Muslim activists who sought political, and perhaps economic, advantages from the effort to scapegoat the Indonesian Chinese. The anti-Chinese campaign served several different purposes for its different advocates. For the government in general, it deflected blame for the crisis and the rising food prices. It also paved the way for Habibie's election as vice-president by harassing and isolating Sofyan Wanandi, who seemed to be actively campaigning against Habibie's election. Furthermore, by playing off Muslims against non-Muslims, the government sought to diffuse opposition among the Muslims, particularly the opposition from Amien Rais and his supporters.[33]

---

32. Cf. Haseman (1997: 130) and the discussion around the 27 July riot in Chapter 2. See also *Digest* 52 (19 February 1998) and Human Rights Watch/Asia (1998a) for similar arguments.
33. Budiman (1998: 19).

For the radical Muslim activists who allied themselves with the military, the campaign signalled a chance to redress a long-standing grudge against the CSIS and Benny Murdani for their allegedly anti-Islamic activities in the 1970s and 1980s. Some Muslim activists may also have hoped for the campaign to increase their own popularity and political influence. Finally, Aburizal Bakrie's suggestion that the government initiate a programme of redistribution of Chinese-owned assets indicated that the campaign also may have had economic motives, with sections of Indonesia's non-Chinese business community hoping to take over businesses and other assets from the Indonesian Chinese.

For Indonesia's Chinese community, the campaign heightened the sense of insecurity. The concerted campaign by senior military leaders to scapegoat the Chinese indicated to many Chinese that the armed forces could not be trusted to help them in the event of more serious outbreaks of racist violence. This sense of insecurity precipitated a sharp rise in the number of applications for business migration visas to Australia submitted in Jakarta, mostly by ethnic Chinese. The increase was visible already from December 1997, and although the number of applications was still comparatively small, it demonstrated some of the insecurity that many Indonesian Chinese experienced in their home country because of the political and social volatility in the wake of the economic crisis.[34]

Stand-off with the IMF

The anti-Chinese violence around the country and the government's attitude towards the ethnic Chinese further exacerbated the economic crisis, as the prospect of serious social and political upheaval looked increasingly likely to market analysts. Meanwhile, neither the signing of the second IMF agreement,

---

34. *Far Eastern Economic Review* (19 February 1998). There were 130 applications in December 1997, compared with an average of 40 during the first eleven months of the year.

the revised state budget nor the reforms announced at the end of January had the desired effect on the exchange rate, which remained volatile, fluctuating between 7,000 and 11,000 rupiah to the dollar in the first weeks of February. It appeared that the IMF's medicine did not work, and the Fund came under fire, not only in Indonesia and other Asian countries, but also in the US congress and from leading international economists.[35] To Suharto, the costs of sticking to the IMF agreement seemed to exceed the benefits. At the same time, with his re-election coming up shortly, and with an increasingly vocal opposition, the president was hard-pressed to come up with a solution which could restore confidence in the economy and bring the rupiah back to a realistic exchange rate.

A possible solution was advised by Professor Steve Hanke, a US economist who apparently was introduced to Suharto on the initiative of two of his children, Tutut and Bambang, in early February. Steve Hanke was one of the world's leading proponents of the currency board system, an arrangement through which the rupiah would be pegged firmly against the US dollar and backed up with massive dollar reserves. Through a currency board system the exchange rate could be fixed at around 5,000–5,500 rupiah to the dollar, rates at which Indonesian companies would be able to resume debt payments and start to import production materials again.

On 11 February, Finance Minister Mar'ie Muhammad announced that the government was preparing regulations to implement a currency board system. Steve Hanke was appointed as special economic adviser to the president and they met several times to discuss the proposal. Shortly afterwards, the governor

---

35. *Detektif & Romantika* (7 February 1998). Jeffrey Sachs was the most vocal prominent economist criticising the IMF's programmes for solving the Asian crisis; see Soesastro and Basri (1998: 17) and Radelet and Sachs (1998: 23–32). One of Indonesia's most prominent economists and a long-time Suharto critic, Kwik Kian Gie, also questioned the IMF agreement, calling for swift measures to restore the rupiah's value; Mann (1998b: 115–116).

of the Bank of Indonesia, Sudrajad Jiwandono [Soedradjad Djiwandono] was 'honourably dismissed', reportedly because of his resistance to the currency board proposal. Market reactions to the proposal were sceptical, however, as most analysts doubted that Indonesia's foreign exchange reserves would be enough to back up the peg. Furthermore, signalling the tarnished image of the regime, many observers suspected that the currency board primarily was intended as a device to allow the Suharto family to move its assets overseas. The IMF reacted sharply to the suggestion, threatening to discontinue its bailout programme if Indonesia went ahead with the plan. On 21 February, US President Bill Clinton again telephoned Suharto, reportedly urging him to cancel the currency board proposal and continue with the IMF reform programme. However, in spite of the international pressure, Finance Minister Mar'ie Muhammad two days later said that Suharto would go ahead with the currency board system. Suharto then proposed an 'IMF plus' plan, which would include the currency board system, as well as a plan for restructuring private debt and a number of structural reforms.[36]

Meanwhile, it seemed that the government was sliding back on the structural reforms laid down in the second IMF agreement from January. A number of developments in February signalled that Suharto was no more committed to taking on the business interests of his friends and family than he had previously showed. In early February, contrary to the intention of the IMF agreement, Liem Sioe Liong and the president's grandson, Ari Sigit, were granted exclusive contracts over the water supply in the capital. By mid-February, it was reported that the plywood cartel run by Bob Hasan continued to operate

---

36. *The Age* (12 February 1998), *Jakarta Post* (18 February 1998), *Australian Financial Review* (12 and 20 February 1998), *Sydney Morning Herald* (20 February and 6 March 1998), *Asiaweek* (6 March 1998) and *Reuters* (28 February 1998). See also Soesastro and Basri (1998: 51–52) about the currency board proposal.

and impose levies on its members, in spite of a presidential decision in January abolishing the cartel. The state-run monopolies on trade and distribution of sugar and flour also continued to operate, as did the clove trading monopoly run by Tommy Suharto. Furthermore, at the end of the month, tax authorities announced that some tax exemptions for the national car project would be restored to allow Tommy's company, P.T. Timor, to sell already imported cars.[37]

All these developments signalled that Suharto was little committed to the implementation of the IMF agreement, and they did nothing to improve market confidence in the government's handling of the crisis. Meanwhile, the main problem with the currency board system was precisely that it needed confidence to function. The IMF strongly opposed the idea, and it was inconceivable that Indonesia would be able to sustain a fixed exchange rate without international support. Although Suharto was no doubt aware that he could not implement the proposal against the will of the IMF, his stand-off with the Fund served domestic political purposes. With his re-election coming up, Suharto tried to appeal to nationalist sentiments and undo some of the damage which his signing of the January IMF agreement had done to his personal prestige by taking a tough stance towards the IMF. As a consequence of the conflict and of the government's backtracking on the structural reforms, the IMF decided to delay its second disbursement of three billion dollars to Indonesia on 8 March. With only two days to the presidential election, Suharto responded by further escalating the stand-off, saying that the IMF package was not in line with Indonesia's constitution. His statement was followed up by Tutut, who expressed her resentment against

---

37. *EIU Country Report Indonesia,* 1st quarter (1998: 28–29) and *Australian Financial Review* (26 February 1998). For Bob Hasan and the plywood cartel, Apkindo (*Asosiasi Panel Kayu Indonesia,* Indonesian Panel Wood Association), see Barr (1998).

the conditions imposed by the IMF, saying 'We are a sovereign nation and we have our dignity'.[38]

The stand-off with the IMF together with the anti-Chinese campaign served to deflect the blame for the economic crisis from the government and President Suharto in order to achieve the president's re-election. The regime sought to counter the threats from the domestic opposition and the international community by drawing on nationalist sentiments and ethnic and religious divisions in its rhetoric. In the short term, the tactics were successful, in that they managed to mobilise support for the president and silence or isolate oppositional voices within the elite. In a little longer perspective, however, these tactics carried high costs in terms of increasing social and political polarisation and increasing levels of intra-elite competition and suspicion.

Securing Suharto's Re-election

As the opening of the MPR session on 1 March approached, there were few lines of division between the five factions in the assembly. All had declared their support for Suharto's re-election and for Habibie's election as vice-president. The rest of the MPR's agenda had been deliberated and meticulously prepared beforehand in committees and discussions since October, all to ensure a smooth general session, where no cracks in the façade of national consensus would appear.

What was more critical was the situation outside the assembly hall. Several student protests and smaller demonstrations in Jakarta and other cities occurred in February, and towards the end of the month the actions became more frequent and started to gather more people. On 26 February, a rally at the University of Indonesia, UI (*Universitas Indonesia*) in Depok outside Jakarta, reportedly drew 3,000 anti-Suharto protesters. While the police

---

38. *Jakarta Post* (9 and 10 March 1998).

and the military generally allowed demonstrations in the university campuses, they were determined not to allow street rallies which might disturb the MPR session. Throughout February, hundreds of activists were arrested for staging illegal demonstrations and other actions outside the university campuses. Some were released within a few hours or a day after their arrest, but many were detained and charged with various political offences.[39]

In addition, three pro-democracy activists, Pius Lustrilanang, Desmond Mahesa and Suyat, were kidnapped by the security forces in early February. Pius, who was active as secretary-general in SIAGA, was abducted at gun-point as he was waiting for a bus in Central Jakarta on 2 February. He was blindfolded and taken to a military detention centre, probably near Bogor outside Jakarta. Desmond was abducted the following day in the same manner. Suyat, an activist in the PRD's student organisation Indonesian Students' Solidarity for Democracy, SMID (*Solidaritas Mahasiswa Indonesia untuk Demokrasi*), was abducted from a friend's house in Solo, Central Java, also in the first week of February. At the time, it was not known what had happened to the three activists, but there were suspicions that the military was responsible for their abduction. The military, however, denied any knowledge of the whereabouts of the activists.[40]

A number of reshuffles in the military leadership were also announced ahead of the MPR session. Most important, the former army Chief of Staff, General Wiranto, replaced Feisal Tanjung as commander-in-chief, and Prabowo was promoted to three-star general. It was also announced that Prabowo would take over the command of Kostrad, which was a much more significant command with far more troops than his previous

---

39. Amnesty International (1998a) and *Tapol Bulletin* 146 (April 1998).
40. *Detektif & Romantika* (9 May 1998), Mahesa (1998) and Human Rights Watch/Asia (1998b). See further the discussion in Chapter 7 below about the abductions.

assignment as commander of Kopassus. It was also a politically important command, carrying considerable symbolic weight, because it was the same post that Suharto had held at the time of the abortive coup attempt in 1965 and from which he had acted to wrest power from Sukarno. Wiranto was immediately installed as commander-in-chief, and most other promoted officers also immediately took up their new commands, but Prabowo was scheduled to take up his new position only after the MPR session. The delay in Prabowo's instalment as Kostrad commander led to speculation that the military leadership, and perhaps even Suharto, was wary about Prabowo commanding large troop contingents in the capital at a politically critical moment. The promotion of both Wiranto and Prabowo also exacerbated the factionalism in the military, as the two generals were long known to have poor relations with each other. Whereas Prabowo was a key figure in the green (Islamic) group of officers, Wiranto was seen as the leader of the red and white (nationalist) group. In contrast to Prabowo, the new commander-in-chief was not close to Muslim leaders and activists, and he did not seem to be involved in the scapegoating campaign against the ethnic Chinese but instead expressed his concern over the racist violence.[41]

In order to demonstrate their capacity for quelling possible protests and unrest, the military staged several well-publicised street exercises in Jakarta in February. A week before the MPR session started, a ban on all political rallies went into effect, and as the delegates for the MPR session started to arrive in the capital, troops were deployed at strategic locations around the city to prevent any disturbances from occurring. According to the military, there were altogether 25,000 troops in Jakarta to maintain security during the MPR session.[42]

---

41. The Editors (1998), *Asiaweek* (20 March 1998) and *Sydney Morning Herald* (21 February 1998).
42. *Associated Press* (24 February 1998) and *Australian Financial Review* (20 February 1998).

On 1 March, the general session of the MPR opened, with Suharto reading his accountability speech to the assembly. The PPP and the PDI initially voiced some criticism about the speech being incomplete, in that it failed to mention the need for political reform and the need to redress the rampant corruption and collusion in government circles. Nevertheless both parties agreed with the other factions to approve the speech unanimously. The assembly also agreed to confer sweeping special powers on the president, instructing him to 'take necessary steps in order to safeguard the national unity and to prevent and deal with social unrest and other subversive threats'.[43] The decision in effect conferred unlimited powers on the president to deal with any possible future social and political disturbances by repressive means.

Meanwhile the anti-Suharto protests intensified during the twelve-day session. In several cities in Java, Sumatra and Sulawesi thousands of students protested against Suharto's candidacy and demanded political and economic reform. In Yogyakarta, thousands of students shouted 'hang Suharto' and burnt a three-metre effigy of the president. In Jakarta, however, the student protests were generally smaller in scope and not as openly confrontational towards the government and the military. The military also showed a conciliatory attitude toward the students when ABRI's faction in the MPR on 5 March received a delegation of twenty UI students, who presented their demands for political, judicial and economic reforms, including a change in national leadership.[44] Although the students failed to bring any of their demands into the agenda of the MPR, ABRI's willingness to allow them into the parliament building and to listen to

---

43. *Ketetapan-Ketetapan Majelis Permusyawaratan Rakyat Republik Indonesia 1998* (1998: 174). For reports from the MPR session, see *Tempo Interaktif* (7 March 1998) and *Asiaweek* (20 March 1998).
44. *Jakarta Post* (6 March 1998), *Associated Press* (4 March 1998), *Kabar dari PIJAR* (12 March 1998), Noegroho and Irawan (eds) (1998: 13) and *Suara Pembaruan* (6 March 1998).

their demands held considerable symbolic significance. For the students, it was a moral encouragement, which strengthened the legitimacy of their demands and demonstrated that the regime was responding to their actions, albeit in a limited way.

The security arrangements around the MPR session were carried out like clockwork, and no major disturbances occurred. The kidnappings of political activists continued, apparently as part of the military's operation to safeguard the MPR session. On the day after the assembly opened, one of Megawati's close aides, Haryanto Taslam, disappeared. Several student and labour activists were also arrested for trying to stage demonstrations or other activities during the session. Berar Fathia, a PDI politician who already in 1995 had declared herself as a presidential candidate, was arrested on 9 March for carrying leaflets in support of her candidacy. On 10 March, Ratna Sarumpaet and eight other pro-democracy activists were arrested in Ancol, North Jakarta, for trying to hold a 'People Summit', intended as an alternative gathering of pro-democracy activists.[45]

On the same day, 10 March, Suharto was elected by acclamation for another five-year term as president. The day after, his chosen vice-president, B. J. Habibie, was likewise elected by acclamation, and the MPR closed its 1998 general session. For Suharto, two years of preparations and manipulation of the political process had fulfilled its purpose.

Deepening Crisis and Political Isolation

The early months of 1998 saw a deepening of the economic crisis and a complete loss of market confidence in the government's ability to deal effectively with the crisis. President Suharto, in turn, lost his confidence in his economic ministers and signalled that he would take direct charge over economic policy and its

---

45. Amnesty International (1998a) and *Tapol Bulletin* 146 (April 1998).

implementation. He personally signed an agreement with the IMF, imposing a far-reaching economic reform programme on Indonesia. If implemented, the reforms would have dismantled the entire political economy which the president had carefully built up during three decades in power. However, market analysts concluded that the president's commitment to the programme was implausible, and the agreement failed to restore confidence in the Indonesian economy. Instead, the president's signing of the IMF agreement seriously damaged his personal prestige.

With the president looking weaker and more vulnerable than ever before, the anti-Suharto opposition stepped up its efforts to bring about political reforms and the president's resignation. Some of the most vocal opposition came from students around the country. In Jakarta, Amien Rais, and to a lesser extent Megawati, stood out as Suharto's most vocal and potent opponents. However, the opposition lacked coordination and consolidation, and Suharto retained the support and loyalty of the military and most of the political establishment. The anti-Suharto opposition therefore failed to bring about any political change or even constructive discussion with the regime.

To counter the opposition and to deflect the blame for the economic crisis, the regime initiated a campaign to scapegoat Indonesia's Chinese minority. Presumably with Suharto's approval, parts of the military leadership mobilised support among more or less radical Muslim groups for the campaign. The prime target of the campaign was Sofyan Wanandi, a prominent ethnic Chinese businessman who opposed Habibie's election to the vice-presidency and who had publicly criticised the government for its handling of the economic crisis. The wider message of the scapegoating campaign was that the economic crisis had been triggered by an anti-Islamic conspiracy of Indonesian Chinese, Christians and foreigners. The campaign endorsed anti-Chinese violence around the country, and in dozens of small towns, ethnic Chinese shop owners became the victims of riots protesting the rising food prices. At the same time,

Suharto also engaged in a stand-off with the IMF, trying to win domestic political support by evoking nationalist sentiments. Although the two campaigns largely achieved their purpose, to deflect public attention from the government's handling of the crisis and achieve the smooth election of Suharto and Habibie, they did so at the price of increasing ethnic tensions and exacerbating intra-elite conflict.

As the MPR session in early March approached, the level of military repression increased. Hundreds of demonstrators and activists were arrested for staging political activities, and three pro-democracy activists were kidnapped by the security forces. However, the military generally accepted political rallies in the university campuses, and around the country students began with increasing vigour as the MPR session approached to demand political and economic reforms and a change in national leadership.

In spite of the protests, Suharto was re-elected without a hitch as president on 10 March, and Habibie was duly elected vice-president the day after. The two elections demonstrated Suharto's continuing ability to control the political system at his will, but few people outside immediate government circles saw his re-election as a sign of renewed confidence in his leadership. In spite of widespread calls for reforms, the MPR failed to channel even moderate demands for political change. The contrast between the well-choreographed MPR session and the general political and social upheaval in the first two months of the year demonstrated the increasingly serious isolation of the regime from society at large.

CHAPTER 7

Student Opposition and Regime Repression

With Suharto smoothly re-elected for another term it looked as if a window of opportunity for the opposition definitely had passed. The president seemed to have regained the political initiative, and informed predictions had it that Suharto, long known as a political survivor, had overcome the crisis and that he now would go on leading the country through the coming years of painful economic recovery. Even Suharto's most prominent critic, Amien Rais, was despondent over the possibility of getting a change in political leadership. 'Suharto will never ever step down. He will die in office', he said in an interview immediately after the president was re-elected.[1]

However, the student demonstrations did not abate with Suharto's re-election; rather they gained strength from mid-March onwards. The military tried to contain the opposition with a combination of concealed repression and an official reconciliatory attitude. However, the military's double standards together with the lack of a clear official line towards the opposition seemed to indicate disunity within the government, and gave the impression that the Suharto regime might be starting to unravel.

The 'Crony Cabinet' and the Third IMF Agreement

On 14 March, only three days after he was sworn in as president, Suharto unveiled his new cabinet. It was unmistakably Suharto's

---

1. *Asiaweek* (20 March 1998).

cabinet, and above all it conveyed the impression of a lonely president appointing people around him for his trust in their personal loyalty rather than for their competence or capacity as individual decision makers. Fewer than one third of the new ministers had served in earlier cabinets. The influence of the technocrats declined, and some observers even doubted that the cabinet would have enough expertise to continue the negotiations with the IMF. Most ministers from the previous cabinet who had cooperated with the IMF and who were seen as proponents of the reform programme, among them Mar'ie Muhammad, were dropped. Instead, several of the new cabinet members had personal interests in preserving the regulations which the IMF reforms sought to abolish. Nearly all new ministers had private business interests, most of them a result of political connections. In the international media the new cabinet was soon dubbed the 'crony cabinet'.[2]

The most conspicuous 'crony' appointment was Suharto's golfing partner and timber tycoon Bob Hasan, who was appointed Minister of Trade and Industry. Most observers found it hard to imagine that he would willingly implement the IMF reforms, some of which directly affected his own business interests. The controversial plywood cartel which he controlled was of great symbolic importance, and its continued operation in spite of a presidential decision in January abolishing it had been one of the key indicators demonstrating Suharto's lack of commitment to the reform programme. Bob Hasan was the first cabinet member of Chinese descent to serve under Suharto, but his reputation as Suharto's crony by far overshadowed his ethnic identification, and he hardly stood out as a credible representative for Indonesia's Chinese community.

Suharto's eldest daughter, Tutut, became the first ever relative of Suharto in a cabinet, taking up the post as Social Affairs

---

2. Malley (1998: 156–158), *Digest* 53 (15 March 1998) and *EIU Country Report Indonesia*, 2nd quarter (1998: 15).

Minister. She had been active for several years in a wide range of social services and charity organisations. Tutut was widely believed to exercise great political influence through her father, and after her successful election campaign for Golkar the year before she looked set to take over as Golkar leader after Harmoko at the organisation's congress scheduled for October 1998.[3] The appointment of Tutut strengthened the perception that Suharto sought to establish his family as a dynasty which would continue to wield power after he himself was no longer in office. Several of the other new ministers, such as Minister of Home Affairs Hartono, Labour Minister Theo Sambuaga and Youth and Sports Minister Agung Laksono, were also close to the president's daughter, giving her a strong influential position in the cabinet.

The new Finance Minister Fuad Bawazier was also a friend of the Suharto family and held a position in Bambang's company Satelindo. As a director-general of taxation, he had announced a few weeks earlier that Tommy Suharto's national car project would have some of its tax exemptions restored. Fuad Bawazier was likely to be less averse to the first family's business interests than his predecessor, Mar'ie Muhammad. He was also one of the major proponents in Indonesia for the currency board system.[4]

There were fewer ministers with military backgrounds than in any of Suharto's previous cabinets, and most of them seemed to have been chosen primarily for their loyalty to the president, such as Minister of Home Affairs Hartono and the Coordinating Minister of Politics and Security, the former military commander-in-chief, Feisal Tanjung. General Wiranto, who was also widely seen as a Suharto loyalist, was appointed Defence and Security Minister. The appointment gave him a very strong position, as he retained his post as commander-in-chief of ABRI.

---

3. Malley (1998: 172–173).
4. *Digest* 53 (15 March 1998) and Malley (1998: 155); see also *Asiaweek* (27 March 1998).

In addition to the Suharto loyalists, some of the key ministers were also known to be close to Habibie, such as Coordinating Minister for Economics, Finance and Industry Ginanjar [Ginandjar] Kartasasmita and Minister of Research and Technology Rahardi Ramelan. All key ministers with military backgrounds, Feisal Tanjung, Hartono and Wiranto, were also friends of Habibie.[5] There were few people from ICMI in the cabinet, however, and on balance the cabinet was clearly more dominated by Tutut and her associates than by people close to Habibie.

With the presidential election secured and a new government in place, Suharto toned down his anti-IMF rhetoric. The new cabinet immediately started fresh negotiations with the Fund, and on 10 April a new agreement was announced, the third in less than six months. It was a review of the earlier agreements, and it restated most of Indonesia's previous commitments. There was no mention of the currency board system in the agreement. A list of more than a hundred concrete policy commitments of the Indonesian government was intended to give credibility to the package. Most of the intended reforms had specified target dates for their implementation, and the programme would be subject to continuous monitoring by an executive council reporting directly to the IMF and other major donors. The programme also announced measures for the restructuring of the private corporate sector debt and for bankruptcy and judicial reforms.[6]

The new agreement allowed the government to use budgetary funds to cushion the impact of the crisis for the poor. Subsidies on basic foodstuffs and fuels were only gradually to be phased out during the remainder of the fiscal year, and the complete elimination of several subsidies, particularly on fuel, was linked to the expected appreciation of the rupiah. The government was also allowed to introduce new subsidies on medicines and to initiate additional labour-intensive employment programmes for

---

5. Liddle (1995: 18) and *Forum Keadilan* (23 March 1998).
6. IMF (1998b).

the poor. These measures seemed designed not only to give relief to the millions of poor people in Indonesia, but also to reduce the risk of social unrest and political instability, all of which might disrupt the economic recovery.

The Student Movement

Suharto's re-election did not put an end to the student protests which had been staged around the country before and during the MPR session. On the contrary, over the two months following the closing of the assembly, the protests grew bolder and more intense in their demand for reform. The campuses became a political free space where long-suppressed demands for change could be vented openly by students and often by their lecturers and other academic staff as well. Before and during the MPR session, the military had tolerated actions in the university campuses in order to contain the protests and keep them off the streets. The security forces were obviously apprehensive that street protests might trigger rioting and general unrest, especially given the volatile social situation as a consequence of the economic crisis.

Initially, from December 1997 to around mid-February 1998, the protests were mainly isolated actions occurring in universities outside Jakarta, such as in Yogyakarta, Surabaya and Bandung. However, from the last week of February, with the MPR session approaching, the protests intensified, and they also became more frequent in Jakarta and surrounding areas. Starting on 25 February, the students of the University of Indonesia, UI, arranged a number of demonstrations on their main campus in Depok, as well as on their smaller Salemba campus in Central Jakarta. Although the UI students in general were not among the most radical or outspoken students, their actions were of great symbolic importance and received much coverage in the news media. The yellow jackets of the UI students were especially significant, symbolically linking the

1998 student movement to earlier student movements in Indonesian history, particularly the 1966 student movement which had helped to bring about the fall of President Sukarno and the transfer of power to Suharto.[7] In the history books of the New Order, the 1966 student movement was generally idealised and described as voicing the aspirations of the people. Much of the action at that time was focused on the UI's Salemba campus which was known as the 'Campus of the struggle of the New Order' (*Kampus Perjuangan Orde Baru*). In 1998, the UI students were able to draw on the historical parallel with their predecessors, and the Salemba campus was soon dubbed the 'Campus of the struggle of the people' (*Kampus Perjuangan Rakyat*) by the students.[8]

The students around the country were united by the similarity of their demands: lower prices, political reform, an end to corruption, collusion and nepotism, denoted by its Indonesian abbreviation KKN (*korupsi, kolusi dan nepotisme*), and the resignation of President Suharto. The latter demand, which from the start was rarely reported in the Indonesian media, was the most central. It was wittily integrated with the other demands in the slogan *Turunkan Harga*, which could either be interpreted literally, meaning 'Lower prices' or as an acronym for 'Bring down Suharto and his family' (*Turunkan Harto dan Keluarga*).[9]

After the closing of the MPR session on 11 March, the student protests spread in the second half of March and April to virtually every university campus in Indonesia. The movement was helped by the Indonesian media's extensive and generally sympathetic reporting on the students' actions, as well as by the campus press which had been allowed to operate for several years outside the normal restriction and self-censorship of the Indonesian media.

---

7. Interview with Lucky A. Lontoh, one of the leaders of the student organisation the Greater Family of the University of Indonesia, KBUI (*Keluarga Besar Universitas Indonesia*), Jakarta (6 November 1998).
8. *Tapol Bulletin* 146 (April 1998).
9. Ikrar Nusa Bhakti (1998: 176).

Particularly outside Jakarta, the Internet was another important channel for the students to disseminate and exchange information, with several alternative news services providing unofficial news coverage and political opinions.[10]

The students received the moral support of several leading government critics, particularly Amien Rais, who frequently addressed the students at their rallies and declared the movement to be the start of a 'people power' revolution. Former student activists from the 1966 student movement, including former Environment Minister Sarwono Kusumaatmaja and the unsuccessful candidate for the vice-presidency, Emil Salim, also expressed their support for the students' demands. Longstanding Suharto critics from the so-called 'generation of '45' (*angkatan '45*), senior retired officers who had participated in the war for independence 1945–49, also gave encouragement and support to the students.[11]

The protest movement lacked national coordination or central leadership. Various groups of students from different universities formed umbrella organisations and discussion forums, often

---

10. See Hill (1995: 114–118) and Stanley (1996) about the alternative press and Hill and Sen (1997) about information dissemination over the Internet in Indonesia. Student activists in Jakarta generally did not seem to think that the Internet was important as a medium of information for the student movement, because too few students had access to the Internet; personal communication, Jakarta (November 1998). However, as pointed out by Airlambang, an activist in the unofficial news agency the Information Centre of the Reformation Action Network, PIJAR (*Pusat Informasi Jaringan Aksi Reformasi*), the Internet was probably more important for information dissemination outside Jakarta. In several places, for example Surabaya, Internet material was printed, photocopied and circulated in large numbers among the students; interview, Jakarta (26 November 1998). It also seems that Internet access was more widespread in certain university towns outside Jakarta, particularly Yogyakarta; see Hill and Sen (1997: 69–70).
11. *Detektif & Romantika* (4 and 18 April 1998), *EIU Country Report Indonesia* 2nd quarter (1998: 18) and *Tajuk* (30 April 1998).

limited only to their own city or province. These efforts resulted in a multitude of organisations being set up in the university towns around the country in March and April. The organisations differed in their stance towards the regime, ranging from radical groups demanding of an immediate overhaul of the political system to more accommodative groups urging gradual reform and dialogue with the regime. The large number of organisations also reflected different field strategies and in some cases a degree of suspicion between the students from different universities or different social, religious and political backgrounds. In Jakarta, one of the largest and most radical organisations was the Greater Jakarta Students Communication Forum, Forkot (*Forum Komunikasi Mahasiswa se-Jabotabek*), which was set up in March and which claimed to represent students from 36 university campuses in the capital and surroundings. Like many of the other student organisations set up around the same time, Forkot lacked formal structures or leadership, which to an extent was a conscious strategy for avoiding the risk of government co-optation and infiltration.[12]

The military continued its policy of allowing political demonstrations and other activities in the university campuses, but as the students frequently tried to take their protests to the streets, they often clashed with the security forces who guarded the campus gates. In the week after the MPR session, dozens of students in Solo, Surabaya, Bandung and Bandar Lampung were wounded in such clashes. In the first days of April, clashes between students and the security forces in Yogyakarta resulted in hundreds of students getting wounded and requiring hospital treatment. The students often attacked the military and police with stones as they tried to break through their cordons, and

---

12. Interview with Roy Simanjuntak, spokesman for Forkot, Jakarta (23 November 1998). For attempts to map the various student organisations, see *Detektif & Romantika* (2 May 1998) and *Jakarta Post* (22 November 1998).

the troops answered by using their shields and batons, as well as water cannons and tear gas, to hold back the students.[13]

While the troops on the ground tried to contain the protests, the ABRI leadership suggested a national dialogue to discuss the students' demands. The commander-in-chief of the military, General Wiranto, said immediately after the MPR session that ABRI was prepared to confer with the students, but the invitation was generally received with scepticism among the students. Many student activists feared that a dialogue would be used by the military or the government to try to co-opt or splinter the student movement or force an ostensible consensus on its leaders. Furthermore, instead of holding a dialogue with ABRI, the students demanded direct talks with President Suharto, pointing out that the president had conferred with the students on several occasions during protests in the 1970s. On 30 March, Youth and Sports Minister Agung Laksono said that the president was prepared to talk with the students, and the minister invited them to send a letter to the president with their request for a meeting. However, no group of students took up the offer.[14]

Meanwhile, several meetings were held between students, rectors, local government representatives and the military on the local level, for example in Bandung, Yogyakarta, Surabaya and Bengkulu. ABRI's chief of social and political affairs, Lieutenant-General Susilo [Soesilo] Bambang Yudhoyono, called these talks very constructive, but the students were generally less enthusiastic. In Bengkulu, the students walked out on the dialogue; they felt that they had been allowed too few representatives. In Bandung, security personnel reportedly used the meeting to collect information about the student activists.[15]

---

13. *Detektif & Romantika* (28 March 1998 and 11 April 1998).
14. *Suara Pembaruan* (13 March 1998), *Detektif & Romantika* (28 March 1998 and 4 April 1998) and *Forum Keadilan* (20 April 1998).
15. *Republika* (30 March 1998) and *Detektif & Romantika* (4 April 1998).

Both Wiranto and Bambang Yudhoyono took an officially conciliatory attitude towards the students, expressing sympathy for their demands and for the need for gradual political reform. The ABRI leaders also continued their efforts to arrange a national dialogue, but the students were generally reluctant to accept the proposal. A scheduled meeting on 4 April had to be cancelled because most of the invited students rejected the invitation.[16]

While ABRI persisted in its attempts to hold talks with the students, other government officials were less sympathetic to the protests. Minister of Education and Culture Wiranto Arismunandar expressed his disapproval of the political activities in the universities and drew attention to a government ban from 1979 on all political activities in the university campuses. On 17 April, President Suharto said that the demonstrations disturbed the learning process in the campuses.[17]

On 18 April, the national dialogue proposed by Wiranto finally took place. Around 250 delegates, including representatives of the government, ABRI, students, rectors, various social organisations and intellectuals, took part in the meeting. Seventeen cabinet ministers attended, among them some of the most controversial ministers such as Tutut and Bob Hasan. The meeting was not primarily intended as a dialogue between ABRI and the students, but between the students and a wide range of government and non-government representatives. Thirty-nine universities and higher educational institutions were represented at the meeting. However, representatives of many of the leading and symbolically important universities were missing, among them the University of Indonesia, Yogyakarta's Gadjah Mada University, the Bandung Technological Institute (*Institut Teknologi Bandung*) and the Indonesian Christian University (*Universitas Kristen Indonesia*) in Jakarta. The student activists who did not attend the meeting claimed that the participating delegates were not representative of the students and charged that many

---

16. *Forum Keadilan* (20 April 1998).
17. *Suara Pembaruan* (15 April 1998) and *Kompas* (18 April 1998).

of them had been brought in from remote provinces. They also feared that the dialogue would be used by the government to legitimise repressive action against the students.[18]

The talks did not bring any concrete results, although this, according to General Wiranto, was not their purpose. The students brought their main demand, the resignation of President Suharto, to the fore, thus giving it unprecedented media attention. It also became clear that there were differences of opinion within the government about how to respond to the students' protests. Minister of Home Affairs Hartono was unsympathetic to the students' demands and questioned whether they really represented the people, and if so, which people. By contrast, ABRI's deputy chairman in parliament, Syarwan Hamid, expressed sympathy for the students' agenda, and claimed that they certainly could be said to represent the people.[19]

From the military's point of view, the initiative to arrange a dialogue between the students and the government represented a serious effort to seek a political solution which might end the increasingly loud protests and the violent clashes between the students and the security forces. ABRI tried to act in accordance with its prescribed socio-political role, taking active part in the national political life as a mediator and stabiliser. The students, however, were suspicious of the military's intentions and the almost daily clashes between the security forces and the students, together with widespread suspicions that the military was responsible for the continuing abductions of pro-democracy and student activists since February, served to further undermine the credibility of the military leaders' initiative. Many students also considered Wiranto's and other senior officers' expressions of sympathy for their demands as no more than an opportunistic strategy aimed at improving ABRI's popular image.[20]

---

18. *Detektif & Romantika* (25 April 1998).
19. *Aksi* (21 April 1998) and *Detektif & Romantika* (25 April 1998).
20. Interview with Roy Simanjuntak, spokesman for Forkot, Jakarta (23 November 1998).

The national dialogue failed to bring the political stand-off nearer to a solution and did nothing to stem the wave of student demonstrations around the country. Rather than becoming the starting point for a political process of co-opting the student movement to rescue the regime, it indicated that there were divisions within the government over how to deal with the students and their demands for political reform. If anything, the dialogue encouraged the students, indicating that the regime was becoming increasingly hard-pressed to find a way to end the protests.

Abductions of Political Activists

As the student protests intensified throughout March and April, the abductions of political activists, particularly student activists, by the security forces continued. As mentioned, one of Megawati's close aides, Haryanto Taslam, disappeared on 9 March, and on 12 March, one day after the closing of the MPR session, three student activists were abducted after attending a press conference at the Indonesian Legal Aid Foundation, YLBHI (*Yayasan Lembaga Bantuan Hukum Indonesia*), one of the largest NGOs in Jakarta. One of the activists, Faisol Riza, later testified about when he and his friend, Raharja Waluya Jati, were abducted:

> At 2.00 pm, Raharja Waluya Jati asked if I wanted to go and eat lunch with him. As we were walking down Jalan Diponegoro in the direction of Salemba we saw a red-metallic car of the brand Jimny (I am not completely sure about the brand) following behind us. We started to run while trying to catch a public transport which could take us from there, but we could not find one. We had to turn and enter the courtyard of the Cipto Mangunkusumo hospital and we ran to the second floor. Unfortunately, it was a dead end and we had to turn back. However, in front of us were already six sturdy men. They hit me in the solar plexus and captured me. My glasses fell off and broke to pieces (for one and a half months in custody I could not use them because they were taken from me). I did not know where Raharja Waluya Jati

was anymore. They dragged me downstairs and shoved me into a car [...].

In the car there were four men; two in the front and two in the back who guarded me. They forced me to bend my head and covered it with a jacket. In the car, I heard from their walkie-talkie that Raharja Waluya Jati had already 'been taken'.[21]

Three other student activists, all from the Gadjah Mada University, were abducted in similar ways on the same day in Jakarta, leaving a total of ten activists who had disappeared in February and the first half of March. It seems that all of the abducted activists were taken to an interrogation and torture centre run by the military close to Jakarta. One of the students abducted on 12 March, Mugianto, related in his written testimony of what happened to him and to his two friends, Nezar Patria and Aan Rusdianto, after they were kidnapped:

> After about an hour the car stopped. I was ordered to get out and to walk, led by them [the abductors]. I was ordered to take off my shoes and pants, leaving me wearing only my underpants. [...] After that I was hit repeatedly in the stomach and in my face until I fell down. They lay me stretched out on a camp-bed and tied my hands and feet to the bed. Then they started to interrogate me, giving me electric shocks with a device that sounded like a whip. They gave me electric shocks all over my feet and legs, especially around my knees. They first interrogated me about the identity of Nezar and then about Aan. Then they switched and started to interrogate Nezar and then Aan. At that time, when I heard the screams and voices of Nezar and Aan who were given electric shocks and being beaten, only then did I know that Nezar and Aan were there.[22]

In the third week of March, another student activist and a member of the PRD, Bimo Petrus, disappeared, and on 28 March, the chairman of the PRD's student organisation SMID, Andi Arief, was abducted by a group of armed men in Bandar Lampung.[23]

---

21. Riza (1998). For a list of the abducted activists up to and including March 1998, see Divisi Informasi and Dokumentasi YLBHI (1998).
22. Mugianto (1998).
23. *Detektif & Romantika* (4 April 1998).

From the end of March the disappearances increasingly became a focus of public attention. A coalition of human rights and pro-democracy NGOs and activists formed a Commission for the Disappeared and Victims of Violence, Kontras (*Komisi untuk Orang Hilang dan Tindak Kekerasan*), as a response to the wave of disappearances. The organisation sought to investigate and secure the release of missing activists, as well as to provide legal and psychological assistance to the victims and their families. Kontras also actively worked to bring the abductions to the public's attention, as well as to international attention, emphasising the political rather than the legal aspects of the problem and demanding that government and military authorities initiate serious investigations to find out what had happened to the abducted activists. International human rights organisations also drew attention to the disappearances, and many governments, including the US, several EU nations, Australia and Japan, expressed concern over the abductions. The suspicions that the government had sanctioned the military to conduct the disappearances contributed further to damage the international reputation of the regime. Kontras' deputy chairman Munir openly accused ABRI of being behind the abductions, but the military denied the accusations, claiming instead that the disappearances were part of a conspiracy to frame ABRI.[24]

In early April, two of the pro-democracy activists who had been abducted two months earlier, Pius Lustrilanang and Desmond Mahesa, resurfaced at their parents' houses in Palembang (South Sumatra) and Banjarmasin respectively. Both were physically in good condition, but they refused to say anything about what had happened to them since they disappeared, obviously because they had been threatened by their abductors. On 17 April, Haryanto Taslam, who was abducted on 9 March, suddenly

---

24. Kontras (1998), interview with Munir, Jakarta (9 November 1998), *EIU Country Report Indonesia*, 2nd quarter (1998: 18) and *Detektif & Romantika* (18 April 1998).

reappeared in a hotel in Surabaya. The week after, Andi Arief's family was informed that he was well and at the National Police Headquarters in Jakarta, where he was detained as a suspect in the case of the bomb explosion in Jakarta in January.[25]

On 27 April, Pius Lustrilanang defied the threats from his abductors and testified before the National Commission for Human Rights, Komnas HAM, and the press about what had happened to him. After he was abducted on 2 February, he was taken to a detention centre which he believed was located near Bogor outside Jakarta and locked up in a small cell. For three days he was interrogated and tortured, also with electric shocks. He was asked about his activities in the Indonesian Solidarity for Amien and Mega, SIAGA, and about an earlier meeting he had had with Megawati. He was also asked whether he knew Benny Murdani and Permadi, one of Indonesia's most politically controversial mystics who claimed to be the mouthpiece of Sukarno. After three days the interrogation stopped, and Pius was left in his cell with a radio outside turned on at high volume. However, at times when there was an interruption in the radio transmission, Pius could talk to the prisoners in the neighbouring cells in the detention centre. Pius claimed that he talked to Haryanto Taslam and three of the student activists who were abducted after the closing of the MPR session. After two months' detention, Pius was released. He was taken to the Soekarno-Hatta Airport in Jakarta and given a flight ticket to Palembang, where his family home was located. Before he was released, he was threatened that he would be killed if he revealed what had happened to him.[26]

Immediately after giving his testimony, Pius left Indonesia for the Netherlands, as he felt that he would not be safe if he remained in Indonesia. A few days later, the Komnas HAM released

---

25. *Detektif & Romantika* (18 April 1998, 25 April 1998 and 2 May 1998).
26. *Forum Keadilan* (18 May 1998).

a statement which concluded that the disappearances had been carried out with force and by an organised group. Although the commission did not openly accuse the military of the abductions, it observed that there were strong suspicions in society that elements of the security machine were involved in the disappearances.[27]

Even though ABRI vehemently denied all responsibility for the disappearances at the time, General Wiranto acknowledged two months later that members of the armed forces had been involved in the abductions.[28] It seems that the operation was part of a larger operation conducted by the military to counter oppositional threats from the students and pro-democracy activists around the MPR session. In particular, members of the PRD and its student organisation SMID, became victims of the abductions and torture, but there were also other student activists and Megawati supporters among the victims. It seems that a group from the special forces, Kopassus, had the main responsibility for the operation, but several other military units, including the Jakarta military district and the police, were involved as well.[29]

The kidnappings did little to silence the opposition or bring the student demonstrations to a stop. The operation was by no

---

27. Ibid.
28. *Kompas* (30 June 1998).
29. Cf. *Berita Kontras*, no. 1 (1998). A few months later, eleven members of Kopassus were arrested for their alleged involvement in the kidnappings, and in August the former Kopassus commander, Lieutenant-General Prabowo, was 'honourably discharged' from ABRI for his role in the abductions and torture of political activists; *Suara Pembaruan* (23 July 1998) and *Jakarta Post* (25 August 1998). However, the deputy chairman of Kontras, Munir, was convinced that since Kopassus was not the only group involved in the operation, ABRI should be held responsible for the abductions as an institution. Munir also believed that Prabowo's dismissal was related primarily to the conflict between Prabowo and Wiranto and to ABRI's internal consolidation. Prabowo would therefore have been dismissed even if he had not been involved in the abductions; interview, Jakarta (9 November 1998). Already in the beginning of May, there was speculation that the abductions would be used by Wiranto's group in the military to push aside Prabowo's group; *SiaR* (7 May 1998).

means the first of its kind under the New Order, but in 1998 the disappearances received unprecedented media attention in Indonesia, and led to much concern from the international community. In Indonesia, the political implications of the disappearances were amplified by the concerted efforts of human rights groups and activists, particularly Kontras, to draw attention to the issue and to the military's involvement in the abductions. The widespread and well-founded suspicions that the military was responsible for the disappearances, further damaged the image of the regime, particularly the image of the military, in the eyes of the students and most of Indonesia's political public. The disappearances also undermined the credibility of Wiranto's and the other ABRI leaders' initiative to arrange dialogues and to show a conciliatory attitude towards the students. As such, the operation contributed to rendering the attempts to start a meaningful dialogue between the regime and the students utterly unsuccessful.

Increasing Opposition

The student protests meanwhile continued to gain strength, and by the end of April, virtually all university campuses around the country held demonstrations, demanding economic and political reform. The students also increasingly began to voice demands for an extraordinary session of the MPR to elect a new president and vice-president and establish a political reform agenda. An extraordinary MPR session would theoretically allow for political reform and a change in national leadership within the existing constitutional framework, thus reducing the risk of serious social and political upheaval in connection with a regime transition.

In addition to support from the academic staff and university management, the students also received support from a wide spectrum of the urban middle-class. In a survey in April among urban dwellers with at least secondary education, an overwhelming majority, 88 per cent, responded that the students' demonstrations were in line with the people's aspirations. Many university-educated middle-class people as well as prominent leaders and commentators were members of the alumni organisations of their respective alma maters, and from the end of April these organisations started to join the students and arrange demonstrations demanding political reform. Both the alumni and many universities also helped the students financially and logistically, for example with transportation, food and medicines for the demonstrations.[30]

In the second half of April there was an escalation of the level of confrontation and violence between the students and the security forces. The students increasingly tried to take their protests to the streets. They felt that their actions were not effective if they were confined to the university campuses. In several places, such as Jakarta, Bandung, Malang (East Java) and Denpasar (Bali) the students clashed with the military and police who tried to prevent the demonstrations from going outside the campuses. In Medan, the students started to throw molotov cocktails, in addition to stones, at the security forces, and the troops responded by shooting tear gas and chasing the students with batons and rattan sticks. In a demonstration outside the North Sumatra University (*Universitas Sumatra Utara*) in Medan on 27 April, a student died accidentally as he tried to flee on his motorbike from a cloud of tear gas and fell, injuring his head on the ground. In Medan, the death triggered intensified demonstrations and more clashes with the security forces over the next few days, with the troops starting to use rubber bullets in their confrontation with the students.[31]

President Suharto, meanwhile, seemed unresponsive to the students' demands. On 1 May, he led a crisis meeting with the cabinet, the leaders of parliament and the military to discuss the situation after the MPR session. After the meeting, Minister of Home Affairs Hartono quoted the president as saying that the Indonesian people already had its policy guidelines until 2003,

---

30. *Tajuk* (30 April 1998) and *Detektif & Romantika* (2 May 1998).
31. *Detektif & Romantika* (2 May 1998) and *Forum Keadilan* (18 May 1998).

which had been decided by the MPR, and that political reform would have to wait until after that date. Suharto also said that the MPR already had chosen the president and vice-president, thus rejecting the demands for an extraordinary MPR session to elect a new national leadership. He furthermore said that he would not tolerate any disturbances to the national political stability, and he claimed that there were indications that the banned Communist party, PKI, was behind the attempts to create chaos before and after the MPR session in March. However, other leading establishment figures after the meeting showed a more conciliatory attitude to the students' demands. General Wiranto said that the government completely understood the essence of the students' demands and that the political and economic reforms had already been incorporated into the national agenda. He also called on the students to stop their protests. House speaker Harmoko, meanwhile, said that the parliament would initiate a review of the political laws governing the elections, the structure of the MPR and the parliament and the social and political organisations. The announcement was surprising, because it meant that the parliament for the first time during the New Order would use its constitutional right to initiate legislation.[32]

In spite of the sympathy expressed by Wiranto and Harmoko for the students' reform agenda, Suharto's uncompromising stand triggered an intensification of the students' demonstrations on the following day, 2 May, which coincidentally was the National Education Day *(Hari Pendidikan Nasional)*. At UI's Salemba Campus in Central Jakarta, thousands of students and workers gathered to demand Suharto's resignation. In Medan, student protests spilled over onto the streets and turned into small-scale rioting as bystanders joined the protests. Three cars were set on fire and a Timor auto showroom was destroyed by rioters before the security forces could get the situation under control.[33]

---

32. *Suara Pembaruan* (1 May 1998) and *Jakarta Post* (2 May 1998).
33. *Tempo Interaktif* (3 May 1998) and TGPF (seri 2) (1998: 6–7).

With the protests intensifying as a direct result of the president's statement the previous day, Minister of Home Affairs Hartono and Information Minister Alwi Dahlan were forced to give a clarification of the statement. Alwi Dahlan said that there had been a slight misunderstanding and that it was untrue that the president did not approve of reform. The minister furthermore said that the president had opened the door to reform, and said, as an example, that a revision of the election laws was underway.[34]

In the light of the more sympathetic stance of other regime representatives, such as General Wiranto and Harmoko, Suharto's erroneous attitude in the first days of May strengthened the students' conviction that the president was the main obstacle to political reform. His initial hard line and subsequent eagerness to explain that he was not opposed to reform also seemed to undermine his authority and indicated to the students that the president started to sway in the face of their protests against his leadership. From early May, the students began to air calls for Suharto's resignation with increasing vigour and openness in the demonstrations and on banners around the campuses, as well as along many roads outside the universities.[35] The actions also started increasingly to involve other groups, such as workers, housewives and high-school students. The prospect of general social and political upheaval as a result of the protests began to look increasingly likely.

A Regime under Pressure

After Suharto had been re-elected as president in March 1998, he endeavoured to take effective measures to deal with the economic crisis. He appointed a cabinet in which his daughter and a number of close friends and associates held prominent positions, thus taking a defensive stand towards the attacks on his position and the political economy which served to keep him in power.

---

34. *Kompas* (3 May 1998).
35. *Detektif & Romantika* (9 May 1998).

However, in spite of informed predictions to the opposite, the 'crony cabinet' initially showed itself to be serious in its efforts to solve the economic crisis. A third agreement with the IMF was negotiated less than a month after the cabinet was sworn in, and the government signalled a greater commitment to implementing its contents than it previously had.

However, the students around the country continued to demand economic and political reform and a change in national leadership. In March and April, the student movement snowballed and by the end of April it comprised virtually every university in the country. The students also received support from several prominent figures, as well as from a broader strata of the middle-class. The regime, meanwhile, responded with a double strategy. On the one hand, it sought to silence the opposition by repressive means, and several activists were kidnapped and tortured by the military. The other strategy, which was ABRI's official line, was to express a degree of sympathy for the students' demands and promise gradual reform. At the same time, the military tried to contain the protests by allowing them in the university campuses but not on the streets. However, towards the end of April, the situation was getting more violent and difficult to handle for the security forces.

The government as a whole lacked a coherent official line towards the increasingly vigorous opposition. While the military leaders tried to show a conciliatory attitude, certain government ministers and President Suharto himself showed less sympathy for the students' demands. The result of the regime's erroneous handling of the protests was an increasingly strong perception that the regime had started to crack under the pressure from the massive protests. The students felt that they were fighting a winning battle, and stepped up their actions to bring about political reform and the resignation of President Suharto.

CHAPTER 8

The End of Suharto

Although the student protests continued with unabated vigour, it seemed impossible to imagine in early May that they would force Suharto out of office before the end of the month. The economic situation seemed to have stabilised, and the 'crony cabinet' had shown a surprising vigour in tackling many of the reform measures and other requirements demanded by the IMF. It seemed that Indonesia had started the long and hard road to economic recovery, still under the leadership of President Suharto.

In the first weeks of May, however, the difficult economic and social situation in many of the big cities, combined with conspiratorial politicking among the elites, resulted in an explosion of violence which left over a thousand people dead and caused material destruction worth millions of dollars. With the impending threat of further upheaval as long as the anti-Suharto protests continued, elements within the regime also started openly to denounce the president and urge him to resign. By the third week of May, the pendulum had definitely swung to Suharto's disadvantage, and even his most loyal aides and sycophants scrambled to distance themselves from the president.

Riots and Continuing Opposition

On 4 May, the government announced large cuts in fuel and electricity subsidies. The decision, effective from 5 May, meant that the price of kerosene, the cooking fuel used by the poor, increased by 25 per cent, and diesel fuel, which was important for transportation costs and consequently for the price of a wide range of goods, increased by 60 per cent. Petrol, meanwhile, increased by 71 per cent. In the big cities, including Jakarta and Medan, motorists queued up to buy petrol before the price hike took effect.[1]

It seems that the decision was intended as a sweetener for the IMF's board meeting on 4 May, which was to decide about the release of the first of the Fund's monthly tranches of one billion dollars to Indonesia as laid down in the IMF agreement from April. Although the IMF defended the Indonesian government's decision to raise the prices, the increase was not dictated by the April agreement, which allowed for the gradual phasing out of the subsidies during the fiscal year 1998–99.[2]

On the same day as the government announced the fuel price hikes, some 500 students of the teachers' training college, IKIP (*Institut Keguruan Ilmu Pendidikan*) in Medan demonstrated outside their campus, again clashing with the security forces who blocked their way. At around five o'clock in the afternoon, the demonstration ended peacefully, with the students withdrawing to the campus and the security forces also agreeing to withdraw. According to the government-appointed Joint-Fact-Finding Team, TGPF (*Tim Gabungan Pencari Fakta*), which made a thorough investigation of the May riots in Indonesia, some female students tried to leave the campus after the evening prayer, but were stopped by a group of policemen outside one of the campus gates. The police started to assault the students, calling them 'whores' (*lonte*) and tore up their head scarves (*jilbab*). The students were also pawed by the police, and one of the officers exposed himself to the women. After having assaulted the students, the policemen left. Some students together with other

---

1. *Suara Pembaruan* (5 May 1998) and *Detektif & Romantika* (16 May 1998).
2. IMF (1998c) and *EIU Country Report Indonesia*, 2nd quarter (1998: 28). Later, after Suharto's resignation on 21 May, IMF officials admitted that they had been stunned by the government's decision to raise the prices so dramatically; ibid.

people who were in the neighbourhood started to look for the policemen. More people gathered on the streets, and a crowd assembled around a nearby police booth. The policemen who were on duty tried to disperse the crowd, which seemed to arouse the crowd. Some people set fire to a police vehicle which was parked outside the police booth, and the crowd then attacked and burnt the police booth itself. Rioting ensued with several shops and a shopping complex being attacked and looted, and at least fifteen vehicles being destroyed in the course of the evening. The security forces tried to disperse the crowds by shooting in the air, but it was not until two o'clock in the morning that the rioting abated.[3]

In the following four days, the rioting continued in Medan, and spread to several other towns to the south and west of the provincial capital. Dozens of cars parked on the streets were set

---

3. TGPF (seri 2) (1998: 7–9) and *Detektif & Romantika* (16 May 1998). To its greater extent, the source for the section on the riots Medan, Jakarta and Solo in May is the secret final report of the Joint Fact-Finding Team, TGPF (1998). The team was established by the government in July 1998 to 'find out and uncover the facts, the participants, and the background of the 13–15 1998 [sic] riot'; Joint-Fact-Finding Team (1998: 1). The team was headed by the chairman of Komnas HAM, Marzuki Darusman, and its members included representatives of the government, the military and several NGOs. The team, with the help of a twelve-man assistant team, conducted a thorough investigation and collection of data during its three months' work. It submitted its final report to the government on 23 October, but the full report was not made available to the public and some of the ministers who had commissioned the team, including Defence Minister and Commander-in-Chief Wiranto, were obviously upset with the findings of the team, which included a list of indications of military involvement in the riots. Wiranto said that the task of the team was only to find facts about the riots, and not to analyse them; *Gatra* (14 November 1998). At the end of its work, the team made only an executive summary available to the public; Joint-Fact-Finding Team (1998). However, parts of the report also leaked to the Indonesian media; e.g. *Tajuk* (1–15 October 1998). Cf. also the separate investigation in *Asiaweek* (24 July 1998), which in many parts gives a similar picture of the overall events in Jakarta as the TGPF report.

on fire and hundreds of shops, almost exclusively owned by ethnic Chinese, were looted or destroyed. Some, but not all, of the shops were set on fire after they had been looted, and in some cases, rioters took goods out from the shops to the middle of the street and set them on fire. There were no confirmed reports of casualties as a result of the riots, but many people were injured. The rioters were mostly young men or high-school students, but also women, older people and children took part in the looting.[4]

The riots in Medan and surrounding areas had their roots in the social and economic hardships which the economic crisis caused for many urban dwellers, and the large fuel price increases which the government announced on 4 May contributed to heighten the sense of frustration. However, the rioting was not a spontaneous outbreak of violence triggered by the fuel price hikes or the general social and economic situation. Several pieces of information collected by the government-appointed fact finding team, TGPF, indicate that the rioting was organised and deliberately planned and instigated. There were rumours that riots would occur as early as a week before they took place, and in the week before 4 May, several Chinese Indonesians who later became victims of the riots were terrorised and threatened, either by telephone or in person by gangs of hoodlums who were often known to the local people. Furthermore, the night before the rioting broke out, several shops – subsequently looted or destroyed – were marked with painted signs.[5]

The actual rioting was often instigated by gangs of provocateurs who started the looting and destruction and urged bystanders to join in. The typical provocateur wore a high-school student uniform, had a short haircut and well-trained body and acted as if he had been trained beforehand for the task. Some of the instigators were known to local residents as hoodlums, and

---

4. TGPF (seri 2) (1998: 9–18); see also *Detektif & Romantika* (16 May 1998).
5. TGPF (seri 2) (1998: 19, 22–23).

several of them were members of the Pancasila Youth (*Pemuda Pancasila*), officially a youth organisation close to Golkar and the military, but often accused of organising and mobilising criminal thugs for murky political purposes. When the rioting had started in one place, the instigators moved on and provoked people to start looting and destruction in another place.[6] Rioting consequently broke out in several places at the same time or with short intervals in between in Medan and other towns in the province, making it difficult for the security forces to contain and restrain the unrest.

In addition to several reports of the security forces being passive and allowing the looting to go ahead, there were also reports that military personnel were directly involved in looting and other illegal acts. According to an eyewitness, a group of army soldiers in uniform plundered a shop in the Simalungan district south of Medan, with three of their colleagues guarding the entrance. Two troop carriers reportedly took away the looted goods. The incident which initially sparked the unrest, the harassment of the female students, also led to suspicions that the policemen's behaviour was a deliberate attempt to aggravate the students and other members of the public. Furthermore, according to the commander of the North Sumatra riot police unit, Brimob (*Brigade Mobil*), his troops captured a Kopassus soldier from Jakarta, dressed as a hoodlum and with a concealed pistol and an M-16 automatic rifle, in the rioting. The soldier claimed that he had received his orders from the 'highest commander' (*pangti*), and that his presence must not be revealed to anyone, neither upward in the chain of command or to anyone else. The police sent the Kopassus soldier to the military district command (Kodim), from where he was subsequently released.[7]

---

6. TGPF (seri 2) (1998: 12–13, 18–19).
7. TGPF (seri 2) (1998: 16–17, 18, 23) and *ibid.* (seri 4) (1998: matrix 'Beberapa Indikasi Keterlibatan Aparat Keamanan dan Organisasi Pemuda dalam Kerusuhan Mei 1998' [Indications of the involvement of the security apparatus and youth organisations in the May 1998 riots], no. 6).

It is uncertain who might have been motivated to instigate the riots. If the military, or sections of the military, were involved, the purpose of the instigation may have been to create a chaotic situation as a pretext for cracking down on the student protests. On the other hand, the systematic anti-Chinese character of the unrest indicates that the Medan riots may have been part of a premeditated assault on the province's Chinese community, particularly the business community. In any case, the Medan riots had several features in common with the riots which occurred in Jakarta and a number of other big cities the week after, and it therefore seems that they were related, at least in part, to a larger scheme with national political motives.[8]

While Medan was shaken by racial riots, the confrontation between the students and the security forces became increasingly violent in several other cities, such as Jakarta, Yogyakarta and Ujung Pandang. To the students, the large fuel price rises demonstrated the government's economic incompetence and its insensitivity to the social and economic hardships suffered by large parts of the population. In several places, the students were joined in their demonstrations by masses of urban people, including formal and informal sector workers, people out of work and high-school students. The increasingly volatile social situation also affected the exchange rate and the stock market, both of which fell more than five per cent on 6 May over worries that the government would not be able to control the social and political unrest. Coordinating Minister of Politics and Security Feisal Tanjung called the Medan riots 'anarchy' and warned that the government would crack down on the rioters. However the scope for the regime to take repressive action was limited by its dependence on economic assistance from the outside, and the

---

8. The common features were mainly the involvement of military personnel, particularly from Kopassus, and the Pancasila Youth in the riots and the appearance and *modus operandi* of the instigators; see further the discussion below in this chapter about the riots in Jakarta and Solo.

US government openly warned the regime against the use of excessive force when handling the student protests.[9]

In Indonesia the dissenting voices gained strength on 6 May, when the leaders of the influential Muslim organisation ICMI said that the possibilities of a cabinet reshuffle and an extraordinary session of the MPR should be kept open. The organisation's executive chairman Achmad Tirtosudiro [Tirtosoediro], seconded by ICMI's secretary-general Adi Sasono, also said that only a government which was free from corruption, collusion and nepotism would have the commitment to implement political reforms. However, ICMI's former chairman and its main political patron, Vice-President Habibie, distanced himself from the statements of the ICMI leaders, saying that there was no need for a cabinet reshuffle or for an extraordinary MPR session. He also said, implausibly, that ICMI did not involve itself with political matters.[10]

Meanwhile, the student protests continued to gain strength, with students all over the country demanding immediate 'total reform' (*reformasi total*). The level of violence increased as the demonstrations grew in strength and size, and the confrontation started to claim fatalities. On 8 May a demonstrator was beaten to death by security personnel in Yogyakarta, and the day after a plain-clothes security officer died in a student demonstration in Bogor. Although it later turned out that the officer had died of a heart attack, he was initially reported to have been beaten to death by a group of students who discovered his identity.[11] The two deaths contributed to exacerbating the tension and animosity between the students and the security forces.

---

9. *Kompas* (7 May 1998), *Australian Financial Review* (7 May 1998), *Jakarta Post* (7 May 1998) and *The Australian* (7 May 1998).
10. *Suara Pembaruan* (7 and 9 May 1998). As mentioned above, in Chapter 7, the elimination of corruption, collusion and nepotism, commonly referred to as KKN, was one of the major demands of the students.
11. *Detektif & Romantika* (16 May 1998) and *Suara Pembaruan* (3 June 1998).

In this volatile situation, Suharto left Indonesia on 9 May for a week-long trip to Egypt to attend a summit of emerging world leaders. Before boarding his flight at the Halim airforce base in Jakarta, the president gave one of his rare press conferences, saying that he understood the people's suffering and that he had no worries about leaving the country in order to perform his duties. The president was accompanied to the airport by Vice-President Habibie, as well as by several senior military and government officials.[12] It was Suharto's first trip abroad since his ten-day rest in December the year before, and the president probably felt that cancelling the trip due to the political volatility would have made him look weak and would have amounted to admitting that he did not have full control over the situation. By contrast, the president's well-choreographed and widely published departure was meant to depict an image of stability and government cohesion, aimed at both the domestic public and the international community.

Jakarta in Upheaval

The situation remained calm in the days immediately following the president's departure. The eleventh of May was a national holiday, and in many places the student protests were temporarily suspended for the day. On the following day, 12 May, however, the confrontation between the students and the security forces came to a head, as troops shot dead four students in a demonstration at the Trisakti University in Jakarta. A foreign journalist who witnessed the event described it in the following way:

> At 5:10 p.m., without warning, shots rang out, and the police charged. The students ran: some retreated along the road, others bolted into Trisakti and the next-door campus of Tarumanegara University. Firing continuously into the air, most of the policemen pursued students back down the ramp

---

12. *Suara Pembaruan* (9 May 1998) and *Warta Ekonomi* (18 May 1998); see also Pour (1998: 1–30, 193–194).

to the highway, but dozens of others ran madly around the newly cleared stretch of road, attacking any lingering students with heavy rattan clubs. Even protesters watching from campus were targeted. [...]

Students started falling, and their colleagues realized live ammunition was being used. [...] Two policemen walked across Tarumanegara's courtyard, firing their rifles randomly. A third officer trailed behind, picking up spent shells as they fell to the asphalt. There were screams after police entered a building on the edge of campus. Four officers emerged moments later, dragging two frightened young women, one of whom had blood smeared over her neck and chest. [...] Nearby a Japanese cameraman, clinging desperately to his equipment, was savagely kicked and beaten.[13]

It was initially reported that six students had been killed and sixteen wounded, but it later turned out that the number killed was four. At first the military explained that the troops had opened fire because the students had attacked and beaten a plain-clothes security officer. However, this version contradicted eyewitness accounts by foreign journalists who said the shootings were unprovoked, and that the students were shot as they tried to flee from the security forces. Furthermore, the police who guarded the demonstration should only have been issued blanks and rubber bullets, but all four victims were killed by live bullets, apparently fired by snipers from a pedestrian overpass in front of the university.[14] The behaviour of the security forces at the Trisakti University contrasted sharply with the military's earlier way of handling the student protests, and it deviated from ABRI's policy of not entering the university campuses and of avoiding excessive violence when confronting the students.

The Trisakti shootings were widely covered in the media, and the four slain students were dubbed 'heroes of reform' (*pahlawan reformasi*). The next day a memorial ceremony was

---

13. David Liebhold in *Time* (Asian edition) (25 May 1998).
14. *Kompas* (13 May 1998, 14-15-1998) and *The Age* (14 May 1998). See also the eyewitness account in *Time* (Asian edition) (25 May 1998), part of which is cited above.

held at the Trisakti University, which was attended by thousands of students from different universities in Jakarta. Several of Suharto's most prominent critics in the previous six months came to speak to the students, such as Amien Rais, Megawati Sukarnoputri, Emil Salim and Sarwono Kusumaatmaja. The chairman of the government-sponsored faction of the PDI, Suryadi, also tried to address the students, but was met with verbal abuses and stone throwing and had to flee into one of the campus buildings.[15]

Meanwhile, a large crowd assembled outside the campus gates to watch the students' activities and the famous speakers who took part in the ceremony. Around noon the crowd started to become uneasy, and some of them called on the students to go out on the streets. When the students declined, the crowd continued to grow restive, and some street lamps were smashed. Shortly afterwards, a passing garbage truck was stopped and set on fire. Several cars, most of them belonging to students, which were parked behind the Citraland shopping mall across the road from the Trisakti University were vandalised, and two toll road booths were set on fire. The security forces present, meanwhile, did not attempt to quell the rioting, but guarded certain buildings in the area, such as the luxurious Citraland shopping mall and the nearby Grogol police station.[16]

From the area immediately around the Trisakti University, the rioting spread to nearby areas, mostly in West Jakarta, to the Grogol, Tanah Abang and Bendungan Hilir districts close to Jakarta's central business district, and in the direction of the airport and Tangerang, west of Jakarta. In Grogol, several shops, almost exclusively Chinese-owned, were looted, with rioters carrying away refrigerators, computers, TV sets and other electronic goods. Some of the goods were also taken out on the

---

15. *Far Eastern Economic Review* (28 May 1998) and *Detektif & Romantika* (23 May 1998).
16. *Detektif & Romantika* (23 May 1998).

streets and set on fire, together with numerous cars and some motorbikes which were parked on the streets. Many shops were smashed or set on fire after they had been looted. Several bank offices were attacked with stones, especially branches of the Bank Central Asia (BCA), Indonesia's largest private bank which was owned by Liem Sioe Liong and two of Suharto's children. The toll road to the airport was taken over by rioters who extorted money from the drivers and their passengers and looked for Chinese whose vehicles they could set on fire. The police were another prime target for the rioters: crowds attacked groups of policemen with stones and shouted 'police pigs' and 'police PKI'.[17]

The rioting continued throughout the night, and the next day, 14 May, it flared up all over Jakarta and in the neighbouring towns of Depok, Tangerang and Bekasi. Looting and destruction started in a number of different locations with no direct connection, but all during the same time-period – from around 9 a.m. till noon. According to the Joint Fact-Finding Team, TGPF, the riots started in most places after provocateurs had initiated the destruction and urged bystanders to join in. In general, the provocateurs came from outside the areas where they worked, and were thus not known to the local people. Most wore plain-clothes, such as jeans and T-shirt, but some provocateurs also wore high-school jackets without their school insignia. Most of the provocateurs in school uniforms seemed to be too old to be high-school students. The provocateurs mostly worked in groups of three to ten men and they used motor bikes or other motor vehicles to move between locations. Many were armed with clubs, and in some places they brought boxes or crates with stones and flammable liquids. Some of the provocateurs used mobile phones or walkie-talkies. They had apparently been trained beforehand for their tasks, such as

---

17. TGPF (seri 2) (1998: 25–29) and *Detektif & Romantika* (23 May 1998).

burning tyres and vehicles, destroying buildings and goods and urging the masses to join the rioting. The instigators tried to arouse the emotions of the masses by shouting anti-Suharto, anti-police and anti-Chinese slogans, as well as calling the students cowards and urging them to join the rioting. The provocateurs also appeared to have been trained beforehand in throwing stones and molotov cocktails, and some of them used the same body-swing technique generally employed by military forces for throwing hand grenades.[18]

The crowds who joined the rioting generally came from slum areas or poorer neighbourhoods than the one in which they rioted. After having been urged on by the provocateurs, the crowds joined the rioting and broke into shops and other buildings to loot them. Many electronics shops were looted, but also supermarkets, clothing stores and book stores were raided by the rioters. According to Jakarta's regional government, over 1,600 shops were looted or destroyed. Most of them were first looted and then set on fire. In addition, 40 shopping complexes were partly or completely destroyed, mostly by looting and fire. In several instances, there were still people in the buildings, and many of them were caught unawares by the fires. Several hundred people were killed in fires in shopping centres. In one incident, the Yogya Department Store in Klender, East Jakarta, over two hundred people died. Some of the people who were burnt to death were looters who could not get out in time, but among the victims were also many employees, shop owners and people who sought refuge from the rioting outside. In all, probably

---

18. TGPF (seri 2) (1998: 66–67, 69, 73–74). The TGPF's observation that military grenade-throwing techniques were used was partly based on the analysis of photos of rioters throwing stones and other objects; see TGPF (seri 3: photos 2, 3 and 4).

over 1,000 people died in the riots which by far were the worst seen by far in Jakarta.[19]

The looting and destruction were not confined to shops and shopping complexes. Hundreds of banks and offices were partly or completely destroyed and close to 2,000 motor vehicles were set on fire. An official estimate put the value of damaged property at almost 400 million US dollars. Rioters also attacked numerous police stations, hotels, restaurants and petrol stations, and over 1,000 private houses were looted or destroyed. Liem Sioe Liong's house in central Jakarta was looted and burned to the ground, and rioters took his portrait outside and symbolically cut it to pieces with their knives. Overall, most of the victims of the material destruction were Chinese Indonesians, particularly shop owners. The riots sent thousands of Chinese Indonesians fleeing out of the country, together with crowds of expatriate workers and their families who were evacuated by their employers. Many ethnic Chinese who could not get on a flight out of the country fled to other cities in the country or to the countryside.[20]

One of the most gruesome aspects of the riots was the rape and sexual assault of a large number of women, most of them of Chinese descent. The TGPF verified 64 cases of rape, several

---

19. TGPF (seri 2) (1998: 73, 77–79). The TGPF did not draw a firm conclusion regarding the number of casualties in the riot, but instead cited four different counts, varying from the Jakarta regional government's estimation of 288 dead to that of 1,190 dead by the Volunteers for Humanity's, TRuK (*Tim Relawan untuk Kemanusian*), an NGO. However, the TGPF noted that the 'different number found by the team [TRuK] compared to the official number occurred due to the huge number of victims being evacuated by people before the government's official evacuation took place'; Joint-Fact-Finding Team (1998: 9–10). Consequently, TRuK's figure of 1,190 seems to be the more reliable of the cited figures. The Komnas HAM, in an earlier report, also adopted TRuK's figure which at the time was 1,188 dead people; *Jakarta Post* (5 June 1998).
20. *Far Eastern Economic Review* (28 May 1998); for the official estimates of the material destruction, see TGPF (seri 2) (1998: 77–78, 80) and *EIU Country Report Indonesia*, 2nd quarter (1998: 20).

of them involving killing or mutilation of the victims, and nine cases of sexual violence or torture in the Jakarta riots. The numbers are probably underestimations, as the team also noted that the exact number was difficult to assess because of under-reporting. The rapes were generally gang rapes performed indoors in front of other people, but some also took place outside on the streets or in vehicles. In Bekasi, south of Jakarta, a group of unknown men raped a poor woman of Chinese descent as well as her two daughters aged six and nine in her own home. One family had their car stopped on the toll road going to the airport. Four men forced their way into the car, and on arriving at the airport, they robbed the family of their belongings and raped the mother and her nine-year-old daughter, before killing the mother. A seventeen-year-old woman who was waiting on a bus in Slipi, West Jakarta, was forced into a car where she was stripped naked and had her nipples cut off by six men. Several rape victims also had their vaginas and other body parts cut with broken bottles or other sharp objects.[21]

According to witnesses and victims of the riots, the security forces did little to quell the riots. In many locations, police and military were altogether absent, and in other places they stood by passively while the rioting went ahead. According to the TGPF, the failure of the security forces to quell the riots was partly due to the limitation of the troops' number and capacity and to the rapid escalation of the riots which could not be anticipated. The troops concentrated their efforts on safeguarding strategic objects, such as government buildings, embassies, large hotels and certain commercial buildings. In addition, however, there were weaknesses in the security forces' coordination and

---

21. TGPF (seri 4) (1998: 8–10 and matrix 'Data Korban Kekerasan dan Penyerangan Seksual Kerusuhan Mei 1998' [data over victims of sexual violence and aggression in the May 1998 riots] nos 13, 42 and 48). Using different verification methods, TRuK put the number of verified rape cases at 129; TGPF (seri 4) (1998: 5). For the rapes, see also Sumardi (1998).

communication which resulted in the troops on the ground receiving inconsistent, confusing and ambiguous orders. The lack of clear division of responsibilities even led to small-scale clashes between troops from different units. The TGPF concluded that the failure to maintain security was closely linked to the responsibility of the operational commander in Jakarta at the time for the riots, the Jakarta military commander Major-General Syafrie Syamsuddin, who did not perform his duty as he should have. According to *Asiaweek*, Syafrie even deliberately gave ineffective orders to his troops so that they could not be deployed efficiently to quell the riots.[22]

As in the case of Medan, there were indications of direct military involvement in instigating the riots in Jakarta. According to witnesses, a group of intelligence officers from the Jakarta military district command urged a crowd of people to destroy an auto showroom in Matraman, Central Jakarta. In Jalan Sudirman, also in Central Jakarta, a Kopassus soldier broke down the door to a residential house and urged a crowd of a hundred people outside to enter the house while he waved his gun at the occupants of the house. Ahead of the riots, soldiers also reportedly offered protection to the mainly ethnic Chinese shop owners in Glodok against payment, with one company of soldiers costing 40 million rupiah (*c.* 3,500 US dollars).[23]

Military Instigation?

Riots also flared in several other big cities, such as Surabaya, Bandar Lampung and Palembang (South Sumatra) on 13–15 May. The riots in these cities were on a smaller scale and

---

22. Joint-Fact-Finding Team (1998: 15, 17) and *Asiaweek* (24 July 1998). For the clashes between different troop units, see TGPF (seri 5) (1998: 249).
23. TGPF (seri 4) (1998: matrix 'Beberapa Indikasi Keterlibatan Aparat Keamanan dan Organisasi Pemuda dalam Kerusuhan Mei 1998', nos 30, 13, 27).

appear to have been less organised than the ones in Medan and Jakarta. However, the worst riots outside the capital occurred in Solo, Central Java, where the indications of military involvement in fanning the riots also are strongest. Four days before the riots broke out in Solo, on 10 May, a group of men in a green Land Rover with military licence plates reportedly offered money to people willing to take part in a demonstration on 14 May. According to the testimony of a man who met the men and received money and cigarettes from them, they wore red berets and striped shirts with their name labels on the right side of the chest taped over. The witness believed that the men were Kopassus soldiers, which the red berets also indicated, and as they spoke Indonesian rather than Javanese, he concluded, judging by their dialect, that they were not from Solo, but from Jakarta. He accepted 20,000 rupiah (c. two US dollars) from the men, as did four of his friends. When they asked what would happen on 14 May, they were told that there would be a crowd of people coming from the west and that they should just follow along. Later they would know what to do.[24]

In the morning on 14 May, the students of the Surakarta [Solo] Muhammadiyah University, UMS (*Universitas Muhammadiyah Surakarta*) held a demonstration at their campus a few kilometres to the west of Solo's city centre. The demonstration was heavily guarded by the security forces who blocked the roads out from the campus. As the students tried to break through the cordons, they clashed with the troops who released tear gas to keep the students inside the campus. Meanwhile, on the main road outside the cordon, a large crowd of people assembled to watch the confrontation. Shortly before noon, the security forces tried to disperse the crowd, which split in two and started to move in

---

24. TGPF (seri 2) (1998: 122) and *ibid.* (seri 6) (1998: 'Pengakuan Pelaku Perusakan dan Pembakaran Kerusuhan Solo 14–15 Mei 1998 [confession of a performer of destruction and burning in the Solo riots 14–15 May 1998]')

opposite directions, one to the west in the direction of Kartasura and the other to the east in the direction of Solo. At around 11.30, the crowd moving towards Solo started to become restive and set some tyres on fire in the middle of the road. Some people in a red jeep, thought to be military personnel, tried to provoke the crowd and urged them to destroy the city. As the crowd moved towards the city centre it grew to several thousand people. Many of them were high-school students on their way home from school, but provocateurs on motorbikes also went around town urging people to get out on the main street. Urged by the provocateurs, some people started to smash shop windows and set fire to vehicles on the street. The man cited above who had received 20,000 rupiah to take part in the demonstration, was ordered by a man in military uniform to throw stones which the uniformed man also provided for him. Vehicles arrived providing bottles of petrol as well as alcoholic drinks to the rioters. Some of the provocateurs were apparently members of the Pancasila Youth, and one member of the organisation was arrested carrying a list of buildings that were to be destroyed.[25]

In many respects the Solo riots looked more like a popular festival than a serious riot. Amateur video footage of the event shows crowds of cheering young men and teenagers waving and jumping in front of the camera, shouting 'Reform' (*Reformasi*) and 'Long live the people' (*Hidup rakyat*). There appears to have been little feeling of hatred or resentment and the atmosphere seems more cheerful than threatening or aggressive. The film shows few expressions of anti-Chinese sentiments, and members of the city's ethnic Chinese population joined other bystanders to watch the multitude of bonfires from burning vehicles and debris on the streets.[26] Although there were rumours before the riots that rapes would take place, the TGPF did not verify any

---

25. TGPF (seri 2) (1998: 109–111, 121–123).
26. 'Kerusuhan Mei '98/Solo [The May 1998 riot in Solo]' (1998); audio-visual material.

cases of rape or sexual violence in connection with the Solo riots.[27]

The burning, looting and celebration continued throughout the night between 14 and 15 May, and intensified in the morning. The security forces were absent in many locations where rioting occurred, and in other places they were seen passively standing by or resting at the side of the street. In all, 196 shops were looted or destroyed, most of them owned by ethnic Chinese. In addition, 50 bank offices, eight factories, 55 buses and hundreds of cars and motorbikes were partly or completely destroyed. Twenty-five private residences were destroyed, among them a house belonging to the speaker of the parliament and Golkar chairman Harmoko. Thirty-one people lost their lives in the riots, all of them in fires. Compared with Jakarta, this number was relatively small, probably partly because of the more benign character of the riots in Solo and partly because the security forces stopped people from entering the burning shopping complexes. However, in terms of material destruction and in relation to its size, Solo was probably the city worst hit by the May 1998 riots.[28]

As in Jakarta and Medan, the security forces in Solo were accused of not taking enough action to stop the rioting. A curious circumstance is also that the entire Kopassus contingent of 467 personnel permanently stationed in Solo was flown out from the city's Adisumarmo air base on the day of the riot. Most of the troops left at the same hour as the rioting started, at 2.00–2.15 pm on 14 May. It is not known where they were transported to.[29]

---

27. TGPF (seri 2) (1998: 126). It was also the view of Mulyanto Utomo, editor of Solo's leading newspaper, *Solopos*, that there were no indications whatsoever of rapes in connection with the riots in Solo; interview, Solo (2 November 1998).
28. For the figures, see TGPF (seri 2) (1998: 126–127). For a summary of the development of the Solo riots and an excellent photo documentation of the event, see Noegroho and Irwan (eds) (1998).
29. TGPF (seri 2) (1998: 131).

The TGPF stopped short of drawing the conclusion that the riots in Medan, Jakarta and Solo were deliberately organised and instigated as part of a national scenario. The team concluded that there were many different groups and individuals who 'played' in the riots to achieve benefits for themselves or for their own groups. Although ample evidence from the field indicated that the riots in Jakarta, Medan and Solo were systematically instigated, the team could not establish a positive connection between the unrest in the different cities. However, the TGPF noted in its analysis that the unclear circumstances around the Trisakti shootings and the findings from Solo seemed to strengthen suspicions that the riots were planned and organised on a national scale. Preparations for the Solo riots had taken place already on 10 May, two days before the Trisakti shootings which became the triggering factor for the riots in Jakarta, and to some extent in Solo. This circumstance, according to the team, raised suspicions that the Trisakti shootings were part of a larger scenario to instigate the riots.[30]

The team also identified a 'missing link' to establish a connection between the violence on the ground and the actions of certain 'key actors' suspected of being behind the unrest. The alleged missing link was a meeting which was held in the Kostrad headquarters in Jakarta on the evening of 14 May and which was attended by the Kostrad commander, Lieutenant-General Prabowo, the Jakarta military commander Major-General Syafrie Syamsuddin, the Kopassus commander Major-General Muchdi Purwopranjono and a number of civilian figures, including business leaders, Islamic leaders and NGO representatives. The TGPF recommended that the government further investigate the meeting to discover the role of Prabowo and other parties in the process which led to the riots. As this recommendation implicated a number of senior officers, prominent Muslim leaders and business people in the riots, the wording of it led to con-

---

30. TGPF (seri 2) (1998: 167–168, 155).

siderable controversy, and the TGPF was criticised for presenting slanderous accusations without evidence.[31]

However, the many reports of the dubious behaviour of military personnel before and during the unrest indicate that sections of the military were involved in instigating the riots. The involvement of personnel from the special forces, Kopassus, in all three cities, Jakarta, Medan and Solo, seems particularly incriminating, and strengthens suspicions that the group of senior officers around Lieutenant-General Prabowo was responsible for instigating at least parts of the unrest. Prabowo exercised strong influence in Kopassus, having commanded the special forces for over two years, from December 1995 to March 1998. His successor as Kopassus commander, Major-General Muchdi Purwopranjono, was a close ally of his and was reportedly promoted to the command on Prabowo's insistence. Furthermore, the failure to maintain order in Jakarta was largely due to inefficient orders to the troops given by the commanding officers in the area, most conspicuously the operational commander in the capital, Syafrie Syamsuddin. The seemingly deliberate lack of security operation in Jakarta strengthens suspicions against Prabowo and his allies, including Syafrie, because they controlled virtually all strategic upper and mid-echelon positions in and around Jakarta.[32]

---

31. Joint-Fact-Finding Team (1998: 16, 18) and *Gatra* (14 November 1998). Although General Wiranto initially said that the meeting was a normal occurrence, in February 1999 he said that he would call Prabowo immediately to ask for the latter's clarification of the meeting; *Jakarta Post* (24 February 1999). At that time, Prabowo was out of the country and had reportedly taken up residence in Jordan.
32. The Editors (1998: 184). Apart from the TGPF's recommendation that the role of Prabowo be further investigated, several prominent Indonesia watchers have also expressed suspicions that Prabowo's group instigated the riots; e.g. Booth (1998: 9), Bourchier (1998b: 22) and Gerry van Klinken in *Digest* 63 (29 May 1998). *Asiaweek* (24 July 1998) also throws its suspicions at Prabowo.

It is not completely clear what motive, or motives, Prabowo and the group around him would have had for instigating the riots. One possibility, which also was suggested by the TGPF, was that the riots were the culmination of an operation aimed at creating a chaotic situation which would require an extra-constitutional government. According to the TGPF, the preparations for this effort had started from the 'level of the highest decision-making people.'[33] This wording implies that President Suharto was involved and that he had ordered the operation in order to justify the use of the special powers which had been granted to him by the MPR two months earlier. At the height of the rioting, while the president was still in Cairo, he also reportedly asked the state secretariat to draw up decrees declaring martial law, but was eventually dissuaded by Wiranto from implementing them.[34] Although Suharto's scope for repressive action was limited by his dependence on goodwill and economic assistance from the international community, particularly the United States, the riots might have served to discredit the opposition and justify tougher action from the government against the opposition in the interest of national stability.

Another possibility which has been suggested is that Prabowo staged the riots in order to discredit the military commander-in-chief, General Wiranto.[35] The two officers were known to be averse to each other, and with Suharto out of the country, Prabowo may have staged the unrest to create the impression that Wiranto was incapable of commanding the security forces and upholding order. The chaotic situation would have occasioned a direct intervention by Prabowo to restore order, thus making him stand out as a national saviour. This scenario resembles the events of 1965–66, when Suharto used his position as Kostrad

---

33. Joint-Fact-Finding Team (1998: 17).
34. Vatikiotis (1998: 160). Vatikiotis does not give a source for this information.
35. Forrester (1998a: 20).

commander to wrest power from Sukarno. A senior military officer, quoted by *Asiaweek*, even suggested that it was Prabowo's plan to take power from Suharto in the same manner.[36]

A third possibility is that the riots were part of a concerted campaign against Indonesia's ethnic Chinese population, aiming at driving parts of the ethnic Chinese business community out of the country and thus facilitating a redistribution of their businesses and other assets to non-Chinese Indonesians. The rapes and sexual violence against Chinese Indonesian women, primarily in Jakarta, may in this context have been part of the campaign. Although there is no concrete evidence that either Prabowo himself or any group had organised such a campaign, the theory seemed to credible to many Chinese Indonesians, particularly against the background of the concerted campaign against Sofyan Wanandi and the Chinese business community in general in January and February.[37]

In spite of the extensive TGPF report, there is still a lack of information about what triggered the riots and who plotted them. Even if sections of the military helped to instigate the riots, for one or several of the possibilities mentioned above, a number of other factors also influenced the escalation of the violence. The possibility of a national conspiracy to create social unrest does not exclude the likely possibility that a number of local groups and individuals took the opportunity to instigate further rioting in their own interests. Pure gangsterism with groups of local hoodlums and petty criminals exploiting the occasion probably contributed significantly to the escalation and intensity of the violence. The deteriorating social and economic conditions in the big cities in the wake of the crisis was probably also an important part of the context, as was the ongoing politicisation and polarisation of ethnic and religious differences among the national elites. However, the generally jovial

---

36. *Asiaweek* (24 July 1998).
37. Informants in Jakarta (September and November 1998).

atmosphere in the Solo riots indicates that social and economic frustrations, as well as ethnic and religious hatred may have been less important than the deliberate instigation.

The Anti-Suharto Movement Gathers Momentum

On 14 May, as the riots raged in Jakarta and other big cities, Indonesian newspapers quoted Suharto from Egypt, saying that he was prepared to resign: 'If I am no longer trusted by the people, I will become a sage [*pandito*]. I will bring myself closer to God and bring up my children to become good people. [...] As for the country, I will guide from behind' [*tut wuri handayani.*].[38]

On the same day the president decided to cut short his visit to Egypt, and in the early morning of 15 May he returned to Jakarta. From around the same time, order was restored in Jakarta, with thousands of troops, including reinforcements from outside the capital, on guard at strategic locations and patrolling the streets. Suharto met Coordinating Minister of Politics and Security Feisal Tanjung to inform himself of the situation, and afterwards the president instructed the military to take tough measures to prevent criminal acts such as pillaging and plundering.[39]

Meanwhile, a rumour spread that the first family had fled the country in the wake of the upheaval, as the Marcos family had done from the Philippines in 1986. This rumour, together

---

38. *Republika* (14 May 1998). Suharto's use of the word *pandito* reflected back to a speech which he made in October 1997, and in which he expressed similar thoughts with reference to colonial and pre-colonial Javanese court philosophy. In the October speech, Suharto also used the term *lengser keprabon*, which can be translated as 'to abdicate,' thus indicating that the president regarded himself as a king rather than a constitutionally elected head of state. The Javanese expression *tut wuri handayani*, meaning 'to guide from behind', also had its origin in Javanese court philosophy. See further the analysis Nusantara *et al.* (1998: 80–86).
39. *Kompas* (16 May 1998).

with Suharto's quoted statement from Egypt that he was prepared to resign, gave an impression that his presidency might be nearing its very end. The violent upheaval in the wake of the Trisakti shootings also demonstrated the social and political volatility in the wake of the economic crisis, and strengthened the perception of government incompetence in handling the student protests as well as in maintaining general law and order. As a consequence, the calls for the president's resignation and political reform gained more strength and started to be aired more and more openly by important elements and figures within the regime. On 15 May, ICMI issued a statement saying that they welcomed the president's intention to resign, and on the same day, one of Golkar's main supporting mass organisations, the United All-purpose Mutual Self-help Organisation, Kosgoro (*Kesatuan Organisasi Serbaguna Gotong Royong*), called for an extraordinary MPR session to process a motion for the president's resignation. The NU also issued a formal statement welcoming the president's stance. In addition, fifteen prominent retired officers, most of them long-standing critics of Suharto, provided moral support to the opposition by issuing a statement signed the 'Officers of the Armed Forces' Generation of 1945' which called for Suharto's immediate resignation.[40]

With the anti-Suharto movement gathering strength, Amien Rais tried to resume his role as the leading spokesman for the anti-Suharto opposition. Shortly before the president's return from Egypt, he announced the formation of the Council of the People's Mandate, MAR (*Majelis Amanah Rakyat*), which claimed to gather 55 leading public figures, all calling for Suharto's resignation. According to Amien Rais, the council was intended to support the leadership of Suharto's successor, functioning as a kind of temporary collective leadership of various important components of society. The members consisted of leading

---

40. *Kabar dari PIJAR* (14 May 1998), *Digest* 55 (16 May 1998), *Forum Keadilan* (1 June 1998) and *Jakarta Post* (16 May 1998).

ICMI activists, including the organisation's secretary-general, Adi Sasono, as well as several former cabinet ministers, including Emil Salim, and representatives of various religious and social organisations and NGOs. However, the credibility of the initiative was reduced, as some of the figures listed as members claimed that they had not been contacted beforehand and asked whether they were prepared to be members. Moreover, it was rumoured that Prabowo had sponsored the formation of MAR, although this was denied by both Prabowo and Amien Rais. Neither Megawati or Abdurrahman Wahid were on the list of council members; Amien Rais, unconvincingly, explained this by saying that he had been unable to get in touch with them.[41]

After his return to Jakarta on 15 May, Suharto denied that he had ever said in Egypt that he was prepared to resign, and Minister of Information Alwi Dahlan instructed the TVRI to make a special broadcast from the Cairo meeting to clarify the president's statements. The next day Suharto met with the leaders of the MPR and parliament to discuss the political situation. After the meeting, House Speaker Harmoko announced that the president would take three steps. He would employ his special powers to ensure national security, he would continue the reforms, and he would reshuffle the cabinet. However, there were no concrete announcements concerning the cabinet reshuffle or the pace and content of the reform process. Widely regarded as 'too little, too late', the president's announced measures failed to stem the rising tide of opposition against him. As the president consulted with the faction leaders, some 5,000 Muslims gathered in Jakarta's Al-Azhar mosque to listen to ICMI's executive chairman Achmad Tirtosudiro calling for the president to resign for the good of the nation. Meanwhile, in Bandung 1,300 university lecturers and professors issued a statement calling for Suharto's resignation and for a return of his mandate to the MPR. Around the country, the students increas-

---

41. *Forum Keadilan* (1 June 1998).

ingly focused their demands on the holding of an extraordinary MPR session to replace Suharto, and the idea of occupying the parliament building to press for the session started to emerge.[42]

On 18 May in the morning, thousands of students arrived in cars and buses to the parliament to take part in a demonstration arranged by Forkot, one of the larger and more radical umbrella student organisations in Jakarta. Although the action clearly violated the military's restriction on out-of-campus protests, the troops, mostly from Kostrad, who guarded the gates to the parliament agreed to let the students into the premises. During the day yet thousands of students from various organisations and universities joined the action. Amien Rais, who in his capacity as chairman of the Muhammadiyah was at the parliament to attend a meeting with one of its commissions, called for massive demonstrations on 20 May, which symbolically was the Day of National Awakening (*Hari Kebangkitan Nasional*), commemorating the beginning of the independence struggle against the Dutch.[43]

In the afternoon of 18 May, House Speaker Harmoko held a press conference together with the four deputy speakers of the parliament, each representing one of the factions in parliament. At the meeting Harmoko read a joint statement from the house leadership, calling for Suharto to resign. Harmoko was seconded by ABRI's deputy speaker in the house and the chairman of ABRI's faction in parliament, Lieutenant-General Syarwan Hamid, who raised his fist in support of the declaration. The declaration was highly surprising, especially because it was read by Harmoko who was widely regarded as one of Suharto's firmest and even most sycophantic personal loyalists.[44]

---

42. *Jakarta Post* (16 May 1998 and 18 May 1998), *Kompas* (17 January 1998), *Republika* (17 May 1998, and *Detektif & Romantika* (23 May 1998).
43. *Panji Masyarakat* (1 June 1998) and Pour (1998: 105–106).
44. *Kompas* (19 May 1998); cf. also Young (1998: 104) about Harmoko's role.

After Harmoko had read the statement, most students who had demonstrated outside the parliament building began to leave the premises. However, a few dozen students from the Communication Forum of the Jakarta Student Senats, FKSMJ (*Forum Komunikasi Senat Mahasiswa Jakarta*), an umbrella organisation comprising the student senates of most large universities in Jakarta, decided to spend the night at the parliament. The students said that they would stay until Suharto had resigned and a date for the special MPR session had been settled. Syarwan Hamid welcomed their initiative and vowed to guarantee their safety. 'Please [spend the night]. If you need, bring a guitar,' he told the students.[45]

In just a few days after the riots between 13 and 15 May, the open calls for Suharto's resignation had gained unprecedented open support, with more and more establishment figures abandoning their support for the president. Although the students were sensing victory, not all of them were happy with the turn of events. Forkot's demonstration at the parliament on 18 May was not intended to continue as an occupation, and there were worries about logistics and security problems in connection with an occupation. Activists in Forkot also felt that the occupation was premature, as the student movement lacked consolidation and an articulated political programme beyond the demand for Suharto's resignation.[46] Furthermore, there was an apparent risk that the students would be exploited by groups and individuals in the political elite who were more interested in their own political survival than in any thorough political change. Neither Harmoko nor Syarwan Hamid was a credible proponent of political reform, and their call for Suharto to step down was probably more driven by opportunism than by political or ideological conviction. With Suharto's position looking increasingly untenable, many of his former allies and supporters strove to distance themselves from the president and

---

45. *Panji Masyarakat* (1 June 1998) and *Forum Keadilan* (15 June 1998).
46. Interview with Airlambang, activist in Forkot (26 November 1998).

jump on the train of reformation. Moreover, several of the most vocal newcomers calling for Suharto's resignation were people close to Vice-president Habibie, such as Harmoko, Syarwan Hamid and the ICMI leaders. If Suharto were to resign, the vice-president would, according to the constitution, automatically step in as president for the remainder of the five-year term. For opportunistic or ideological reasons, this prospect seemed to hold a considerable attraction for many of Habibie's associates.

Endgame

Harmoko's call for the president to resign triggered an immediate reaction from the military. After having met with Suharto in his home, General Wiranto summoned the military leadership to a meeting, and at eight o'clock in the evening of 18 May, less than five hours after Harmoko's statement, Wiranto gave a press conference accompanied by the whole line-up of senior leaders of ABRI, including the chiefs of staff of the army, navy and airforce, the chief of police and the Kostrad commander. Answering no questions, Wiranto only read a statement from the military:

> The armed forces of Indonesia declare that the declaration of the leaders of parliament that President Suharto should resign is the view of individuals although it was expressed collectively. [...] According to the constitution, such views do not have any legal status. [...] ABRI is still of the opinion that the most urgent task and duty of the government under President Suharto is to reshuffle the cabinet and to implement thorough reform to overcome the crisis.

Wiranto also announced ABRI's proposition that a reform committee be set up with both government and non-government members, especially critical groups and individuals. In addition, he called for the demonstrations on 20 May to be cancelled because of the risk of renewed violence and rioting.[47]

---

47. *Suara Pemabaruan* (19 May 1998) and Pour (1998: 113–115).

On the same evening, Suharto called the prominent Muslim intellectual Nurcholish Majid to his house for a consultation. Nurcholish had a few days earlier reportedly met some of the senior ABRI leaders, including the military chief of social and political affairs, Lieutenant-General Bambang Yudhoyono, to discuss a suggestion which Nurcholish had advocated in the media, for gradual political reform, including the setting up of a reform committee. Suharto's consultation with Nurcholish thus seems to have been a first step to implement ABRI's suggestion for political reform as announced by Wiranto the same evening. At the consultation, Suharto told Nurcholish that he was prepared to resign. 'In fact, I already wanted to resign since a long time ago. I've had it' (*Ya, dari dulu saya memang mau turun. Saya kapok.*) the president said according to Nurcholish. The president then asked to meet with a number of Muslim leaders, among them Abdurrahman Wahid and Nurcholish himself, the following morning.[48] Wahid had by this time largely recovered from his stroke in January.

Of the nine Muslim leaders who consulted with the president on morning of 19 May, four were from the NU, and only two from Muhammadiyah. Abdurrahman Wahid was there, but Amien Rais had not been invited. For two and a half hours, the president discussed the political situation and the meaning of political reform with the group. Nurcholish Majid, as well as at least one of the *ulama* from the NU, K. H. Ali Yafie, told the president that political reform meant nothing but his resignation.[49] According to Nurcholish the president said: 'I don't have any trouble with resigning. [...] But the trouble is, if I resign, is there any guarantee all this trouble will end? [...] You

---

48. *Detektif & Romantika* (30 May 1998) and *Panji Masyarakat* (1 June 1998).
49. Mietzner (1998b: 193–194) and *Detektif & Romantika* (30 May 1998).

know that if I resign now, Habibie will be the president and in my calculation the trouble will be even worse.'[50]

Immediately after the consultation, Suharto – accompanied by the group of *ulama* – went on national television to announce his measures for political reform. He would immediately appoint a new 'reform cabinet' (*Kabinet Reformasi*), which would oversee a revision of the election laws and other political laws, as well as the anti-corruption laws. The cabinet would be assisted by a reform council, led by the president personally, consisting of around 45 prominent figures from outside the government. Elections would be held as soon as possible, and after that the MPR would be assembled to elect a new president and vice-president. Suharto declared that he would not stand for re-election.[51]

For the students, Suharto's declaration that he would step down was a great moral victory. However, the president had not specified any time frame for the reform process or for when the elections could be held. The proposal would give Suharto considerable influence over the reform process and in shaping the political system after his resignation. Abdurrahman Wahid, who supported the president's plan, called on the students to stop demonstrating, but the partial victory rather strengthened their determination to continue their struggle until Suharto had actually resigned. A number of other prominent Suharto critics also rejected the plan and called on the president to step down immediately. Emil Salim said that Suharto should hand over power to Vice-president Habibie and allow for a presidential election within three months, and Achmad Tirtosudiro said that Suharto's resignation was a precondition of reform. Amien Rais accused the president of stalling and reiterated his threat to bring for one million of his followers to take to the streets on the following day. Meanwhile, Coordinating Minister of Economics, Finance and Industry Ginanjar Kartasasmita reportedly tele-

---

50. *International Herald Tribune* (25 May 1998).
51. *The Australian* (20 May 1998).

phoned State Secretary Saadilah Mursyid [Mursjid], saying that to hold elections earlier than scheduled was unconstitutional.[52]

Suharto's announcement that he would oversee gradual reforms and then resign has been interpreted both as the result of a plot by the military and as a ploy by Suharto to bypass the military and maintain his grip on power.[53] However, both these interpretations probably miss much of the dynamics of the intra-elite manoeuvring during Suharto's last days in power. The idea of the president leading the reforms, holding new elections and announcing his resignation seems to have originated from Nurcholish Majid, who had reportedly been called to the ABRI headquarters a few days earlier to discuss the idea with military leaders. The officers, at least Wiranto and his allies, apparently approved of the plan for the president's controlled and dignified exit, but left out one of Nurcholish's original provisions that Suharto place his wealth and those of his family at the disposal of the nation.[54] For the military, the plan held the attraction of thwarting Habibie's chances to become president, a prospect disliked by many senior officers, especially in the red and white (nationalist) group around Wiranto, because of the history of conflict between Habibie and the military.

On 18 May, with the president's civilian support crumbling, and with the prospect of massive protests and renewed upheaval as long as the protests continued, both the military and the

---

52. *The Australian* (20 May 1998), *Far Eastern Economic Review* (28 May 1998) and *Panji Masyarakat* (1 June 1998).
53. According to Mann (1998b: 233), Nurcholish Majid acted on behalf of Lieutenant-General Bambang Yudhoyono, who allegedly had encouraged Nurcholish to be blunt in asking Suharto to resign before the Muslim scholar's meeting with the president on the evening of 18 May. By contrast, Vatikiotis (1998: 162) interprets Suharto's attempt to gain support from the Islamic leaders, including Nurcholish, as an attempt to bypass the military and sees it as a sign that Wiranto was losing initiative on the political front.
54. *Panji Masyarakat* (1 June 1998) and *Detektif & Romantika* (30 May 1998).

president probably realised that he was unlikely to serve his full five-year term. On the evening of 18 May, already an hour before Wiranto held his press conference declaring ABRI's undivided support for the president in leading the reform process and proposing a reform committee, Suharto called Nurcholish to his house to discuss the proposal.[55] This sequence of events suggests that both the president and the military were involved in the initiative and that they had agreed on the plan beforehand.

Suharto's consultation with the nine Muslim leaders including Abdurrahman Wahid, was an attempt to shore up civilian support, mainly among the traditionalist Muslims represented by the NU, for his attempt to control the reform process and to arrange a dignified exit. The alternative to the president's plan seemed to be immediate resignation and a hand-over of power to Habibie. To Abdurrahman Wahid, the latter prospect was appalling. Not only had Habibie previously been involved in several attempts to damage Wahid's leadership of the NU, but Habibie's becoming president would also mean a greatly increased influence for Wahid's political adversaries in ICMI, many of whom Wahid regarded as sectarian and fundamentalist. By contrast, Suharto's effort to seek support from the NU for setting up the reform committee signalled that the president intended to give the NU greater influence during his last days in power.[56]

Meanwhile at the parliament, thousands of students from universities and colleges in Jakarta as well as from outside the capital arrived to take part in the occupation and demonstrations. The military who guarded the gates allowed the students to come into the premises, and to climb the roof of the main building where they put up banners with their demands for political reform and Suharto's resignation. There were even

---

55. Nurcholish received a phone call asking him to come to Suharto's house at 7 p.m. The press conference started shortly after 8 p.m.; *Panji Masyarakat* (1 June 1998).
56. Mietzner (1998b: 194–195).

reports that the military provided buses to transport the students to the parliament. The security forces who guarded the parliament and the surrounding areas seem mostly to have come from Kostrad and the marines, with the former controlling the main entrances to the complex.[57] The deployment of Kostrad troops suggests that Prabowo directly controlled at least parts of the security arrangements in and around the parliament. With Prabowo's allies also controlling most of the other troops in the capital, Wiranto was presumably not in full control over the situation around the parliament.

On the morning of 19 May, a number of vigilantes from various youth organisations, among them the Pancasila Youth, came to the parliament to express their support for Suharto and for Wiranto's declaration the evening before, including the formation of a reform committee. Although the situation was tense and almost resulted in a physical clash between the students and the vigilantes, the latter eventually left peacefully after having presented their demands to Golkar's faction in parliament. The next day, a group of Pancasila Youth members in university jackets destroyed a tape recorder and set fire to an archive in one of the office buildings at the parliament, apparently in an attempt to discredit the student movement. There were also several rumours and considerable fear among the students that they would be attacked by thugs from the youth organisations or by the military. In the early morning of 20 May, the arrival of hundreds of Kostrad troops and marines triggered an alert among the students who believed that the troops would attack and try to oust them from the premises. However, it turned out that the troops had come to protect the students from attacks from the outside.[58] In general, the Kostrad troops who guarded the parliament seemed to enjoy a good relationship with the students.

---

57. *Kompas* (20 May 1998); see also Forrester (1998b: 42–43). According to Mann (1998b: 236) the marines provided buses to the students after Syarwan Hamid had granted permission for the protests.
58. *Kompas* (20 May 1998) and *Panji Masyarakat* (1 June 1998).

It has been suggested that the Pancasila Youth members were sent by Prabowo to the parliament to create disturbances.[59] However, the thrust of their demands, supporting Wiranto and his initiative that a reform committee be set up, rather suggests that the commander-in-chief or his allies had commissioned their demonstration. It seems less clear why Prabowo would have wanted to create disturbances by sending in the hoodlums. It has also been suggested that, contrary to trying to disturb the anti-Suharto protesters at the parliament, Prabowo worked with Habibie to encourage the president to resign.[60] Prabowo entertained close links with several Islamic organisations and activists, many of whom were close to or active in ICMI.[61] Many of these groups and activists probably expected to gain greater influence and stature if Suharto were to resign in favour of Habibie. In addition, Prabowo may have expected that if Habibie were to become president he would favour the group of green (Islamic) officers around Prabowo in their competition with the red and white group around Wiranto. Although there is no evidence that Habibie conspired with Prabowo to overthrow Suharto, the Kostrad commander seems to have had an interest in the vice-president's ascendancy, and the situation around the parliament suggests that Prabowo used his influence there covertly to put pressure on Suharto by permitting the students' actions.

In spite of the uncertainty of the security situation in Jakarta as a result of the split in the military, the ABRI leaders were determined not to allow Amien Rais or anyone else to lead a 'people power' revolution on the streets of Jakarta. During the night between 19 and 20 May, troops from all four branch services, including the police and units from both Kostrad and Kopassus, erected barricades throughout Jakarta. Seventeen

---

59. Forrester (1998b: 40).
60. *Asiaweek* (24 July 1998).
61. For Prabowo's connections with different Islamic groups, see *Panji Masyarakat* (1 June 1998) and Media Dakwah (February 1998).

thousand troops were deployed around the city to forestall the prospect of massive demonstrations and unrest. The Jakarta military commander, Syafrie Syamsuddin, had the operational command over the troops. At dawn on 20 May, the Day of National Awakening, an apparently shaken Amien Rais went on television calling for his supporters to cancel the demonstration. Later he said to the media: 'Somebody told me, who happens to be an army general, that he doesn't care at all if [...] an accident like Tiananmen will take place today.' Although the streets of Jakarta were calm, large demonstrations against Suharto and for political reform took place in a number of other big cities around the country. The biggest demonstration took place in Yogyakarta, where Sultan Hamengkubuwono X expressed his support for the reform movement before hundreds of thousands of people in the square in front of his palace.[62]

Amien Rais instead joined the students demonstrating at the parliament, as did numerous other prominent Suharto critics. There were also leading members of NGOs and other sociopolitical organisations there, and members of Jakarta's middle-class showed their sympathy for the students by providing them with food, water and other essentials. The women's organisation the Voice of Concerned Mothers (*Suara Ibu Peduli*), led by activist Karlina Leksono, coordinated and distributed the logistic support to the students. On 20 May the students' action at the parliament had increased substantially from two days earlier, and tens of thousands of students arrived during the day to demand Suharto's resignation.[63] With thousands of students swarming the parliament building, climbing on its roof and staging all sorts of political demonstrations and free-speech forums, the students' occupation of the parliament became a prime symbol of people power in Indonesia.

---

62. *Kompas* (21 May 1998) and *The Age* (20 May 1998).
63. *Panji Masyarakat* (1 June 1998).

On the same day, Golkar's faction in parliament held a meeting and afterwards announced its decision to call for an extraordinary MPR session to elect a new president and vice-president. However, the MPR would not call the president to account for the completed part of his presidential term, a provision apparently designed to save the face of Suharto. Separately, Harmoko, pressured by the students, declared that if the president had not resigned within two days, the faction leaders of the MPR would meet to discuss the possibility of calling a special session to impeach the president. On the same day, US Secretary of State Madeleine Albright urged Suharto to engage in a 'historic act of statesmanship,' implying that the president should resign.[64]

Meanwhile, in the presidential palace the attempt to put together a reform committee was failing. Immediately after Suharto's consultation with the nine Muslim leaders on 19 May, a list of the 45 proposed members of the committee had been drawn up and approved by the president. Among the figures were several of Suharto's most prominent critics, including Amien Rais, Abdurrahman Wahid, Megawati Sukarnoputri and Nurcholish Majid. The task to contact the 45 people was assigned to State Secretary Saadilah Mursyid and Yusril Ihza Mahendra, a Muslim intellectual and professor of political science at the University of Indonesia. However, almost all of the people contacted declined to sit on the committee. Even Nurcholish Majid and Abdurrahman Wahid rejected their invitations, in spite of their public expressions of support for the president's plan.[65]

On the evening of 20 May, Suharto received the final blow which seemed to have made him make up his mind and resign the following day. In a letter to the president, fourteen cabinet ministers said that they disagreed with the president's plan to reshuffle the cabinet and that they were not prepared to sit on

---

64. *Detektif & Romantika* (30 May 1998), *Forum Keadilan* (15 June 1998) and *Wall Street Journal Interactive Edition* (21 May 1998).
65. *Forum Keadilan* (15 June 1998).

a reshuffled cabinet.[66] Among the signatories were most key economic ministers, including Coordinating Minister of Economics, Finance and Industry Ginanjar Kartasasmita. Ginanjar, as well as several of the other fourteen ministers were close to Habibie, such as Transportation Minister Giri Suseno, Minister of Mines and Energy Kuntoro Mangkusubroto and Minister of Research and Technology Rahardi Ramelan. When he received the letter, Suharto instructed Habibie to persuade the ministers to change their minds, but, deliberately or not, Habibie failed in his mission.[67] Instead Habibie, who was reportedly very hurt by Suharto's comment the day before that things would be worse if he became president, advised Suharto to step down. The vice-president is also said to have promised Suharto a dignified retirement, warning that others might not be so reasonable.[68] According to a close associate of Habibie, Suharto agreed to step down, but the president wanted to appoint a new cabinet and then resign in a few days or weeks. As Habibie left Suharto's house later in the evening, he did not know that the president was about to hand over power to him the following morning.[69]

The declaration of the fourteen ministers that they were not prepared to sit on a reshuffled cabinet together with the failure to set up a reform committee left Suharto with little choice but to resign. For the president, not being able to present either of them would mean a complete loss of face. At around 10.30 p.m., the leaders of the parliament were contacted by Suharto's staff and asked to be at the state palace at 8.30 the following morning.

---

66. *Forum Keadilan* (15 June 1998).
67. *Detektif & Romantika* (30 May 1998) and *Far Eastern Economic Review* (4 June 1998). According to the latter, Habibie, instead of persuading the ministers to change their minds, asked them to give their support to himself.
68. *International Herald Tribune* (25 May 1998) and *Asiaweek* (24 July 1998).
69. Dewi Fortuna Anwar, key note address, 'The Habibie Presidency' at the 1998 Indonesia Update Conference, Canberra (25 September 1998).

Although at the time they were only told that the president wanted to meet them for a consultation, it seems that the president had already made up his mind to resign. From around this time, a rumour also started to spread in political circles about the president's imminent resignation.[70]

Later that night, General Wiranto visited Suharto in his house to discuss the president's resignation. According to several analysts, as well as reports in many Western news media, Wiranto told the president at their meeting that it was time for him to resign, which allegedly triggered the president's decision to do so.[71] However, it is uncertain where this piece of information comes from; there seem to be no accounts of what was discussed at the meeting, and virtually none of Wiranto's close associates seem to believe that Wiranto persuaded the president to resign.[72] Other reports say that Wiranto told the president either that the military could no longer guarantee security in Jakarta, or that the military was not prepared to go any further than it already had to keep him in power.[73] Regardless of what Wiranto told Suharto, it seems, against the background of the events earlier in the evening, that Suharto had already made up his mind to resign the following morning before his late-night meeting with the commander-in-chief. It is thus more likely that the president used the meeting to reassure himself of ABRI's

---

70. *Forum Keadilan* (15 June 1998) and *Gatra* (30 May 1998).
71. For media reports that Suharto decided to resign after Wiranto's visit, see e.g. *Sydney Morning Herald* (22 May 1998), *International Herald Tribune* (25 February 1998), *Time* (Asian edition) (1 June 1998) and *Asiaweek* (5 June 1998). Mann (1998b: 248), Suryadinata (1998: 230) and Forrester (1998b: 46) also subscribe to this version.
72. John McBeth, Jakarta correspondent for the *Far Eastern Economic Review*, key note address, 'Political Update' at the 1998 Indonesia Update Conference, Canberra (25 September 1998). Michael Vatikiotis (1998: 159–160) also disbelieves reports that Wiranto presented Suharto with a military ultimatum.
73. *Far Eastern Economic Review* (4 June 1998) and *EIU Country Report Indonesia*, 2nd quarter (1998: 22) respectively.

support for the hand-over of power to Habibie and to obtain guarantees for his own security. According to *Asiaweek*, Wiranto made three demands at the meeting in exchange for his and ABRI's support to Habibie: Wiranto would remain commander-in-chief, Habibie would commit to reform and Prabowo would be transferred.[74]

Suharto Resigns

At nine o'clock in the morning of 21 May Suharto went on national television and read his resignation speech. Referring to the failure to set up the reform committee, Suharto said that it was no longer necessary to reshuffle the cabinet and that he believed that it would be very difficult for him to implement his duties as president in a good manner.

> Therefore, in line with article eight of the 1945 constitution and after earnestly taking into consideration the views of the leadership of the parliament and the leadership of its factions, I have decided to declare that I resign from my office as president of the Republic of Indonesia as of the time I read this declaration today, Thursday 21 May 1998. [...] In line with article eight of the 1945 constitution, the vice-president of the Republic of Indonesia, Professor Doctor Engineer B. J. Habibie, will conclude the remainder of the presidential term and mandate from the MPR 1998–2003. For the help and support of the people while I led the state and nation of Indonesia, I express my thanks, and I seek forgiveness if there were any mistakes and shortcomings.[75]

---

74. *Asiaweek* (24 July 1998).
75. *Media Indonesia* (22 May 1998); for an English translation of the full text of the speech, see Forrester and May (eds) (1998: 246–247). Engineer is an academic title in Indonesia, and it is custom on formal occasions to list all main titles in front of a person's name. Article eight of the 1945 constitution reads: 'If the president dies, resigns or is unable to perform his duties during his term, he is replaced by the vice-president until the end of his term.' *UUD 1945* (undated: bab III, pasal 8).

After the president had read his speech, Habibie stepped forward and took the presidential oath before the members of the supreme court. When he had finished, Suharto shook his hand, and the two men left the room, without Habibie making any further statement or declaration as newly installed president. Wiranto immediately stepped up to the microphone and read a declaration of support from the military for Habibie as president, saying that ABRI was still united and urged the people to respect Suharto's personal wish to resign in accordance with the constitution. He furthermore said that ABRI vowed to guarantee the safety and honour of Suharto and his family.[76]

At the parliament, Suharto's resignation triggered a joyous celebration, and the students, joined by thousands of other people, sang the national anthem and waved their flags and banners. Some gave thanks to God, shouting out 'God is great' (*Allahu Akbar*), while others danced in the fountain in front of the parliament building. On television, students were seen exchanging high-fives with the Kostrad troops deployed to guard and protect them.[77]

However, the students were generally unhappy with the transfer of power to Habibie. He was widely seen among the students as being too close to Suharto and too tied up in the former president's web of corruption and cronyism. Although most of the students decided to discontinue the occupation, several of them, mainly from Forkot, stayed at the parliament, rejecting the transfer of power from Suharto to Habibie and demanding that a special session of the MPR be called to demand that Suharto account for his actions as president.[78]

Meanwhile, Prabowo apparently suspected that Wiranto had struck a deal with Habibie involving his transfer from the Kostrad

---

76. *Kompas* (22 May 1998).
77. See *Panji Masyarakat* (1 June 1998) and *Time* (Asian edition) (5 June 1998).
78. *Panji Masyarakat* (1 June 1998) and Pour (1998: 163–164).

command. He reportedly appealed to Suharto immediately after the latter's resignation to obstruct the transfer, but was instead admonished by Suharto as well as by other family members, for making trouble.[79] In the afternoon, news spread that the presidential palace was surrounded by troops, believed to have been ordered there by Prabowo. According to intelligence reports, the troops were from Kopassus.[80] Coordinating Minister of Politics and Security Feisal Tanjung ordered a troop reduction, but the order was not followed, and instead the number of troops in the city centre increased.[81] In the evening of 21 May, Prabowo, accompanied by the Kopassus commander, Major-General Muchdi Purwopranjono, showed up in full battle gear at the presidential palace and demanded to see Habibie. A scuffle occurred between Prabowo and the presidential guard, as the Kostrad commander initially refused to hand over his pistol before entering the palace. Eventually Prabowo conceded and was allowed to see Habibie unarmed.[82] According to one of Habibie's close associates, Prabowo presented the president with a list people whom he wanted to sit on the cabinet. Wiranto would retain his position as defence minister, but Prabowo demanded that he be replaced as commander-in-chief by the army chief of staff, General Subagyo Hadisiswoyo. Prabowo himself was to be promoted to a new post as deputy commander-in-

---

79. *Far Eastern Economic Review* (4 June 1998).
80. *Panji Masyarakat* (1 June 1998).
81. Dewi Fortuna Anwar, key note address, 'The Habibie Presidency' at the 1998 Indonesia Update Conference, Canberra (25 September 1998).
82. There is some uncertainty as to the time and place for the incident. According to the *Far Eastern Economic Review* (4 June 1998) it occurred at the presidential palace on 22 May. Forrester (1998b: 59), meanwhile, sets the date to 21 May and the place to Habibie's home. *Asiaweek* (24 July 1998) sets the place to the presidential palace, and the date to 21 May. The latter version accords with that of Habibie's aide, Dewi Fortuna Anwar, key note address, 'The Habibie Presidency' at the 1998 Indonesia Update Conference, Canberra (25 September 1998).

chief.[83] Prabowo also reportedly told Habibie that he had already made arrangements to assemble a gathering of Muslims to retake the parliament building and restore order the following morning, and he demanded to be rewarded for this and other services. However, Prabowo eventually left the palace without having had his demands granted by the president. Meanwhile, Habibie, fearing for his life, moved to the state guest house (*Wisma Negara*) where he remained overnight, but no further disturbances occurred.[84] The obvious threat of a coup d'état triggered an alert among the other military units in Jakarta, and military presence in Central Jakarta remained heavy for the following 24 hours.[85]

In the morning of 22 May, thousands of Habibie supporters arrived at the parliament and tried to take over the free-speech area where the students who still occupied the parliament were rallying against Habibie. The pro-Habibie demonstrators arrived in buses and claimed to represent different Islamic groups, including some groups known to have close links with Prabowo. Some activists who led the demonstration were also close to Prabowo, such as KISDI's executive chairman Achmad Sumargono and Muslim activist Fadli Zon. A verbal stand-off occurred between the two groups, but a physical clash was hindered by the security forces. The Habibie supporters, some of whom apparently had been hired for the occasion, left in the late afternoon.[86]

---

83. Dewi Fortuna Anwar, key note address, 'The Habibie Presidency' at the 1998 Indonesia Update Conference, Canberra (25 September 1998).
84. Forrester (1998b: 59).
85. *Suara Pembaruan* (23 May 1998); see also Habibie's comment on the incident in *Jakarta Post* (16 February 1999) and *Tempo* (23 February 1999).
86. *Jakarta Post* (23 May 1998), *Gatra* (30 May 1998) and *Panji Masyarakat* (1 June 1998). The latter observed that the pro-Habibie masses 'apparently were coordinated by a certain party', while *Time* (Asian edition) (5 June 1998) described them as a 'rent-a-crowd of Habibie-ites [sic]'. For a more favourable evaluation of the pro-Habibie demonstrators, see *Media Dakwah* (June 1998).

At around the same time, Prabowo was officially relieved of his command over Kostrad at a closed ceremony. He was to be transferred to Bandung where he was assigned as chief of the Army's Staff and Command School, Seskoad (*Sekolah Staff dan Komando Angkatan Darat*), a position out of the capital and with no combat troops under his command. His associate, Kopassus commander Major-General Muchdi Purwopranjono, was also immediately removed from his position. The two replacements marked the beginning of a process, led by Wiranto, to consolidate ABRI and to remove Prabowo's associates from strategic positions.[87]

Shortly before midnight the same evening, troops under the command of the chief of staff of the Jakarta military command, Brigadier-General Sudi Silalahi, entered the premises of the parliament and turned the remaining students out of the area. The students left without resistance, and the operation seems to have gone off without incident or physical violence. The students were transported in buses to the nearby campus of the Atmajaya University, where they spent the rest of the night.[88] Five days of 'people power' at the parliament had come to an end.

---

87. *Kompas* (23 May 1998). Further reshuffles in the military occurred in the weeks that followed, and at the end of June, Syafrie Syamsuddin was deprived of the Jakarta military command; see *Jakarta Post* (25 and 26 June 1998). On 24 August, Prabowo was 'honourably discharged' from ABRI for his involvement in the abductions and torture of political activists around the MPR session in March; *Jakarta Post* (25 August 1998). He subsequently left the country, and in December it was reported that he would take up residence in Jordan, where he would be granted an honorary citizenship; *Suara Pembaruan* (22 December 1998). In February 1999, however, General Wiranto said that he would call Prabowo to give a clarification of his role in the May riots, and the general also said that Prabowo could be brought to trial for his involvement in the abductions; *Jakarta Post* (24 February 1999).
88. *Panji Masyarakat* (1 June 1998).

A Soft Coup?

Apart from Suharto's family and immediate close associates, few people in Indonesia regretted the president's resignation. For several years, there had been a widespread feeling among the political elites as well as among the general public that the succession was long overdue. However, many of the students who had fought for several months to bring down Suharto felt that there was still a long way to go in the reform process. Although Habibie immediately signalled his commitment to political reform and more openness, most students were disappointed that they had failed to bring about a more thorough regime change. Even though Suharto was gone, the political framework of the New Order remained intact.

There was also a widespread feeling that the students had been exploited as pawns in the political manoeuvring among the elites. In its final stages, the fall of Suharto was more due to intra-elite manoeuvring than to 'people power.' As the president's position started to look increasingly untenable in the wake of the riots and the continuing student protests, more and more of his associates in various social and political organisations as well as the parliament and finally in the cabinet, abandoned their support for the president. Among the establishment figures who towards the end most vocally denounced the president were several of Habibie's associates, who apparently favoured the prospect of Suharto stepping down and handing over power to the vice-president.

In his last days, Suharto failed to shore up support, even among ICMI's and Habibie's long-standing political adversaries in the military and the NU, because no-one was prepared to risk their political fortunes by associating themselves with the out-going president. When finally, on 20 May, fourteen of his key cabinet ministers declared that they opposed the president's plan for reform, Suharto was left with little choice but to resign and hand over power to Habibie.

Habibie's own role in the succession process is unclear. Although there is no evidence that he actively conspired to depose Suharto, the latter possibly believed that Habibie had done so, and after the transfer of power the relationship between the two men became markedly cooler. Another question mark regards Prabowo's role. If the relationship between Suharto and Habibie became cooler, it seems that Suharto after his resignation completely broke with his son-in-law. There are indications that Prabowo and his associates were involved in instigating parts of the riots in Medan, Jakarta and Solo, and it has been suggested that the Kostrad commander worked with Habibie to encourage Suharto to resign. Prabowo seems to have counted on benefiting from Habibie's ascendancy, but his plans backfired as Suharto, on the night before his resignation, reassured himself of Wiranto's support for the hand-over of power to Habibie. In the new power constellation, there was no room for Prabowo.

CHAPTER 9

Conclusion

This book has been a study of the decline and fall of the Suharto regime. For three decades, from 1966 to 1996, the president and his New Order regime ruled Indonesia with considerable success, maintaining political stability and overseeing unprecedented economic development and modernisation. However, as this development occurred, the authoritarian regime did not envisage any substantial political or social change, which led to an increasing gap between the regime and a range of new social and political aspirations that had emerged in the wake of the economic development. From the late 1980s and throughout the 1990s, a wide range of dissidents, including students, intellectuals, pro-democracy activists and the members of various NGOs, started to criticise and challenge the regime with increasing openness and boldness. The failure of the regime to accommodate these new aspirations together with Suharto's advanced age led to a widespread feeling in society that the time was ripe for political change. However, the exclusionary political system of the New Order had no functioning political channels for bringing about such change. Instead, quasi-democratic political institutions were employed to create a superficial impression of national political consensus around the president's and the government's overall objectives and policies. The political apparatus combined with the regime's repressive controls and the president's distribution of material favours in exchange for political loyalty to maintain the political status quo, particularly the paramount and unchallengeable position of President Suharto. In 1996, these arrangements were challenged by an emerging coalition of oppositional forces, and the regime's handling of this challenge signalled the start of the political crisis which eventually, in combination with the regional economic crisis, led to the fall of Suharto two years later.

Political Engineering

With the political system designed to maintain the status quo, the political parties under the New Order were not supposed to be opposition parties, but rather to demonstrate broad support for the government and the president's national leadership. In early 1996, however, it seemed that the smaller of the two legal parties, the Indonesian Democratic Party, PDI, under its popular leader Megawati Sukarnoputri might try to defy these arrangements by seizing a substantial share of the votes from Golkar in the May 1997 election and by then challenging Suharto for the presidency in 1998. Even though the political system could be relied upon to ensure that Suharto's re-election was not at risk, the PDI's initiatives threatened the legitimacy of the regime as they would demonstrate the waning popularity of the government and expose a crack in the façade of national consensus around Suharto's leadership. The regime responded to this challenge, as it had on several earlier occasions, by trying covertly to manipulate the political process. A party congress was engineered which ousted Megawati and reinstated the more compliant Suryadi as chairman, thus barring Megawati and her supporters from taking part in the election. However, Megawati did not accept her removal silently. She openly accused elements within the government and the military of engineering the congress and of interfering with the party's internal affairs, and indeed the vast majority of politically educated Indonesians could see that her accusations were largely true.

Megawati's defiance created a sense of opportunity for several groups outside the PDI that were critical of Suharto and the regime. A loose coalition of pro-democracy groups and NGOs on the political left, many with connections to the Democratic People's Party, PRD, emerged in response to the government's heavy-handedness towards Megawati. At the PDI's headquarters in Central Jakarta, her supporters together with hundreds of students and NGO representatives set up a free speech forum, demanding political reforms and an end to corruption and nepotism. Many of them called for total reform involving a complete overhaul of the political system and the reinstatement of full political and civil freedoms.

The regime responded to the emerging reform coalition with more manipulation and repression. In cooperation with the Suryadi faction of the PDI and with the help of hired thugs, the military staged a violent attack on the party headquarters on 27 July 1996, ousting the troublesome Megawati supporters and activists. The clash was supposed to look like an internal showdown between the Megawati and Suryadi factions of the PDI, but the involvement of the military was obvious. After the take-over, rioting broke out spontaneously in the area around the party headquarters. Thousands of poor urban people vented their frustrations and anger in an uncontrolled protest which lacked a politically coherent direction, but which nevertheless gave an indication of the social and economic grievances brewing among parts of the urban masses.

For the government the riots provided a pretext for cracking down on the oppositional left, especially the PRD, which was blamed for having masterminded the unrest. A number of activists and vocal political opponents were brought to trial and sentenced to long prison terms for various political offences. The sweeping-up action, like the operation which removed Megawati, was undertaken in anticipation of the general election in May 1997 and the subsequent MPR session and presidential election in March 1998. The objective was to ensure that no political forces opposed to the status quo would be able to disturb the national political rituals. However, the heavy-handedness of the government and the military drew attention to the undemocratic nature of the regime and fed political cynicism among Indonesia's political public.

Communal Violence and Its Political Implications

In addition to the 27 July riots in Jakarta, a number of riots occurred in various places in Indonesia in the second half of 1996 and early 1997, many of which seem to have been related to a perceived general increase in social and economic disparities. Available figures suggest that income disparities in Indonesia increased in the 1990s, and there was plenty of visible evidence of a wide gap between rich and poor, especially in the bigger cities, which reinforced the perception of widespread social and economic injustice. Meanwhile, social tolerance towards income disparities seems to have decreased, resulting in widespread resentment among groups who felt comparatively disadvantaged by the economic development. As indicated by the riots in Jakarta and other big cities, the resulting discontent might readily spill over into violence.

However, several of the riots also had evident ethnic and religious undertones, which led to worries among many analysts and social commentators that ethnic and religious tensions were intensifying and that they might lead to more extensive violence and general social upheaval. The worst instance of communal violence in Indonesia in over 30 years occurred in early 1997 in West Kalimantan, where probably around 500 people were killed in fighting between indigenous Dayaks and transmigrated Madurese.

In other places, ethnic resentment mainly focused on Indonesia's ethnic Chinese, who on average were better off than the rest of the population. Anti-Chinese sentiments drew on long-standing tensions between indigenous Muslim groups and the mainly non-Muslim Chinese Indonesians, but also fed on widespread resentment against the government's economic policies which greatly favoured a small number of ethnic Chinese tycoons, many of whom had personal links to President Suharto.

There are also indications that two of the most serious riots in 1996, those in Situbondo and Tasikmalaya in East and West Java respectively, were instigated in order to destabilise Abdurrahman Wahid's leadership of Indonesia's largest Muslim organisation, the traditionalist NU. Suspicions concentrated on groups within the mainly modernist Muslim intellectual organisation ICMI together with elements of the military which were sympathetic to ICMI. Wahid himself fanned the suspicions by publicly accusing ICMI's secretary-general Adi Sasono of instigating the riots.

The outcome of the unrest and the intra-elite manoeuvring in its wake was to bring Abdurrahman Wahid closer to the government. The previously hostile relationship between Suharto and the NU leader improved, and Wahid agreed to help Suharto's daughter Tutut in the election campaign for Golkar. From this perspective, it seems that the religious and ethnic violence in the NU areas was linked to the upcoming election. However, there is no evidence of the conspiracy theories implicating ICMI and the military, and the abundance of conspiracy allegations in Indonesian political life should serve as a warning to be sceptical of accusations which are not backed up by concrete evidence. Regardless of their possible veracity, more than anything else the allegations in the wake of the riots gave an indication of the deep-seated mistrust and mutual suspicions among Indonesia's political elite as the Suharto era was nearing its end.

The General Elections and the Onset of the Economic Crisis

The May 1997 election failed to restore the crumbling legitimacy of the regime. Megawati's ousting and the crack-down against the pro-democracy movement in the wake of riots of 27 July the year before had already tainted the image of the election and the democratic credentials of the regime. The PDI's disastrous election result was widely, and probably correctly, interpreted as a result of voter distaste with the government's meddling in the party's affairs. Although Golkar did its best election ever, collecting three quarters of the votes, it was obvious that the figure to a large extent was due to the government's and the military's extensive manipulation before and around the election. Consequently, few people outside immediate government circles imagined that the election result reflected public opinion. In addition, the election campaign was the most violent ever under the New Order, with numerous clashes between supporters of Golkar and the PPP and between supporters of Megawati and Suryadi. Altogether, hundreds of people were killed, mostly in traffic accidents, but also in a big fire in Banjarmasin and as a direct result of political violence.

From August 1997, the regional economic downturn which had started in Thailand the previous month began to affect Indonesia, and the central bank abandoned the rupiah's fixed exchange rate against the US dollar. At first it looked as though Indonesia would ride out the storm relatively unscathed. The government immediately tightened fiscal and monetary policies and in early September it announced a deregulation package designed to boost confidence in the currency. Although these measures were widely lauded by the international financial community, they failed to break the rupiah's downward slide, which was largely driven by a high demand for dollars due to the huge short-term dollar-denominated debts held by many Indonesian companies. Furthermore, many Indonesian businessmen were distrustful of the government's and President Suharto's commitment and ability to deal effectively with the crisis. They believed that the prevalence of corruption, nepotism and cronyism, especially in government circles, prevented effective action, and many companies and wealthy private individuals moved their capital off-shore, thus contributing further to the rupiah's decline.

In October, Indonesia decided to seek assistance from the IMF. The announcement of the IMF agreement at the end of

October initially restored some confidence in the rupiah, but within a few weeks the currency resumed its downward slide. Several of the policies contained in the agreement, including the prescribed fiscal and monetary austerity, were widely seen by market analysts as insufficient or even damaging to the Indonesian economy. The agreement lacked a clear strategy for strengthening the rupiah as well as a strategy for how the foreign exchange funds provided should be used. Unlike previous similar agreements signed by the IMF, the package also contained a structural reform programme, including deregulation measures and a programme for the privatisation of government enterprises. However, partly because of the flaws in the agreement and partly because President Suharto appeared to be little committed to the implementation of the agreement, it failed to have the desired effect on the economy. A public dispute between Finance Minister Mar'ie Muhammad and two members of the Suharto family over the closure of their banks directly damaged market confidence in the agreement, and also damaged President Suharto's personal prestige. Meanwhile, the government failed to take effective action to put out the large forest fires which raged in Sumatra and Kalimantan, and this failure further fuelled the image of government incompetence, especially among the international community.

In the last month of the year, Suharto took a ten-day rest, which sparked worries about the president's health and served as a reminder of the country's uncertain political future. Apart from triggering a further decline for the rupiah and exacerbating the economic crisis, the president's rest period signalled the start of a wave of intensified opposition against Suharto. As he looked weaker and more vulnerable than in a long time, students, as well as leading Muslims and other regime critics started to voice their criticism against the president boldly and more openly than before, thus signalling a significant change in the political climate.

Increasing Tensions

In early January 1998 President Suharto presented a wildly optimistic state budget which seemed to violate parts of the agreement with the IMF. The budget triggered a collapse in the value of the rupiah and panic buying in Jakarta. A renegotiation of the IMF agreement, signed by President Suharto personally in mid-January, failed to restore confidence in the Indonesian economy, and was widely seen as an insult to national dignity which consequently damaged Suharto's personal prestige further. A week later, signals came that Suharto wanted to see his close aide and Minister of Research and Technology B. J. Habibie as vice-president, which triggered a further decline for the rupiah.

Largely as a result of these developments, the president began to be seen widely as the main block to economic recovery, and in January the calls for his resignation intensified. Amien Rais, leader of Indonesia's second largest Muslim organisation, the modernist Muhammadiyah, proposed an alliance between Megawati, Abdurrahman Wahid and himself to challenge Suharto's re-election in March. The popularity of the three leaders made such an alliance a potentially serious threat to the president. However, because of Wahid's suspicion of and aversion towards Amien Rais, the initiative stalled, and on 19 January it definitely lost momentum when Abdurrahman Wahid suffered a stroke and was hospitalised.

Meanwhile, to counter the threat from the opposition, the regime as represented by sections of the military leadership with the assistance of a number of radical Muslim groups, staged a campaign which concertedly tried to scapegoat the country's ethnic Chinese population for the economic troubles. The campaign served to deflect attention from the government's and President Suharto's responsibility for the economic crisis and to shore up support for Suharto's and Habibie's election. A main target for the campaign was Sofyan Wanandi, a prominent ethnic Chinese businessman who was critical of the government's handling of the crisis and who opposed Habibie's election as vice-president. The anti-Chinese rhetoric of government and military officials endorsed anti-Chinese sentiments and combined with the economic hardships suffered by millions of Indonesians to provoke a wave of food riots around the country in January and February. In the short term, the campaign achieved its political objectives, but it did so at the considerable price of exacerbating ethnic tensions and intra-elite conflict.

The MPR session in early March was a well-choreographed event which demonstrated Suharto's continuing control over the political apparatus, in spite of the economic problems and the widespread and vocal opposition against his rule. Most of the assembly's members were appointees of Suharto, and all potentially troublesome figures had been excluded from its line-up. With security tight around the eleven-day session, no major disturbances or protests occurred on the streets of the capital. The 76-year-old president was duly re-elected for his seventh consecutive five-year term, and his chosen candidate for the vice-presidency, B. J. Habibie, was also elected without dramatics. A few days after he was sworn in on 11 March 1998, Suharto unveiled his new cabinet, dominated by personal loyalists and the group around his daughter Tutut, who became Minister of Social Affairs. The cabinet conveyed the impression of an increasingly isolated president relying on the advice and loyalty of his close friends and family. Although many analysts doubted that Suharto, because of his age and the gravity of the economic problems, would serve his full five-year term, the anti-climax of the MPR session conveyed the impression that the momentum for the opposition had passed, and even the president's most prominent critics seemed despondent about the chance of bringing about any significant political change in the near future.

In order to keep the anti-Suharto protests off the streets before and during the MPR session, the military allowed demonstrations and other political activities to be held in the university campuses. However, the student protests did not end after the MPR session. Instead they gained strength throughout March and April, and the security forces became increasingly stretched in their efforts to contain the protests. With the military's scope for repressive action limited by Indonesia's dependence on international economic assistance, the military leaders tried to initiate a dialogue with the students, and some senior officers, including the commander-in-chief, General Wiranto, expressed sympathy for their demands for political reform. However, the students were generally distrustful of the military's initiative to hold dialogues. A number of student and pro-democracy activists were kidnapped around the time for the MPR session and it was widely, and correctly, suspected that the military was responsible for the abductions. In April some of the kidnapped activists resurfaced and one of them, Pius Lustrilanang, publicly told his story, which strengthened suspicions towards the military, thus further damaging its tarnished image in the eyes of the students and the general political public. Although the commander of the strategic reserve, Kostrad, and Suharto's son-in-law, Lieutenant-General Prabowo Subianto, later admitted his involvement and the involvement of personnel from the special forces, Kopassus, in the abductions, a number of other military units also took part in the operation.

Towards the end of April, the level of confrontation between the students and the security forces intensified as the protesters increasingly tried to take their demonstrations outside the university campuses. Suharto, meanwhile, showed little sympathy for the demands for political reform, saying that such could not be implemented before 2003 and expressing the suspicions that the banned Communist Party, PKI, was trying to instigate unrest. However, the military's more conciliatory attitude, as well as a limited positive response from the leaders of parliament to the students' demands, signalled in early May that the regime was unsure of itself, and strengthened the students' confidence and feeling that they were fighting a winning battle. Their demands increasingly came to focus on the holding of an extraordinary MPR session to recall the president's mandate and elect a new national leadership.

With the student protests showing no sign of abating and with the prospect of general upheaval and violence looking threatening, the price for keeping Suharto in power started to look increasingly high. There was already a widespread feeling that his resignation was long overdue, and the opposition once again started to gather momentum, now with the support of a broader stratum of the middle-class, as well as an increasing number of Suharto's former supporters among the political elite.

The Fall of Suharto

On 12 May, while Suharto was on an official visit to Egypt, security forces shot dead four students at a demonstration at Jakarta's Trisakti University. The incident triggered two days of widespread rioting and looting in Jakarta which left over 1,000 people dead. The rioting was mainly, but not exclusively, directed at the Chinese Indonesian population and their property. The security forces often did little to stop the rioting, and there were several reports that military personnel instigated and encouraged the unrest. Apart from Jakarta, riots also occurred simultaneously in four other big cities, including Solo, where there were particularly strong indications that members of Kopassus actively instigated the riots. Suspicions of military involvement focused on Prabowo and the group around him in the military. Prabowo exercised great influence over Kopassus, and together with his allies in the military he controlled the security arrangements in the capital where the rioting was most extensive. Several motives have been suggested for Prabowo's instigation of the riots. He may have tried to discredit his rival, the military commander-in-chief General Wiranto, or he may have tried to create a chaotic situation which would justify a proclamation of martial law and a crackdown on the student movement. It has also been suggested that Prabowo planned to wrest power from his father-in-law in much the same way as Suharto had done from Sukarno in the mid-1960s. Another possible motive is that the instigation was part of a conspiracy involving Prabowo's group in the military and certain radical Muslim groups and activists close to the Kostrad commander. The conspiracy would have aimed at driving Chinese Indonesian businessmen and entrepreneurs out of the country, in order for non-Chinese Indonesian business people to fill their place. The latter theory would explain the seemingly systematic rapes and sexual assaults on a large number of ethnic Chinese women in the Jakarta riots.

In the short term, the main political consequence of the upheaval was to reinforce the perception that the Suharto presidency was nearing its end and to demonstrate that the president no longer was a guarantor of order and stability. Meanwhile, a rumour spread that Suharto had said in Egypt that he was prepared to resign. Although the president immediately denied the statement on his return to Jakarta on 15 May, the rumour, combined with the general atmosphere of upheaval in the wake of the riots, triggered a wave of calls from various social and political organisations and leading figures welcoming the president's alleged intention to step down. These calls signalled a growing opposition from establishment groups previously loyal to the president.

On 18 May, a number of students decided to occupy the parliament to press for Suharto's resignation and the holding of an extraordinary MPR session. On the same day, the leaders of the parliament, led by House Speaker Harmoko and the chairman of the military's faction in parliament, Lieutenant-General Syarwan Hamid, called for the president to resign. However, neither Harmoko or Syarwan Hamid were credible proponents of political reform, and many student activists worried that the decision to occupy the parliament was premature and might result in the students being used as a pawn in intra-elite political manoeuvring. Many of the new calls for Suharto's resignation came from groups and individuals close to Vice-President Habibie, who had an interest in the latter taking over the presidency. The troops guarding the parliament who allowed the students to enter the premises were largely Kostrad troops under Prabowo's control, raising the possibility that the Kostrad commander may have favoured and actively worked to bring about Suharto's resignation in favour of Habibie.

With Suharto's intra-elite support crumbling and with the economy in disarray due to the social upheaval and political uncertainty, the president realised that he had no other option but to resign. With the full backing of the military leadership under Wiranto, he announced his intention to reshuffle the cabinet, appoint a reform committee of leading oppositional figures, oversee reforms and resign after having held new elections. The president sought support from Abdurrahman Wahid and the NU for his plan, which would have provided him with a dignified retreat, while granting him control over the reform process. Although Wahid was eager to prevent Habibie from becoming president, which would mean a greatly increased influence for Wahid's political adversaries in ICMI, the NU leader rejected the invitation to sit on the reform committee, as did almost all of the other proposed members. With Suharto's presidency already doomed and with former associates scrambling to distance themselves from the president, virtually no-one was prepared to risk their political future by associating themselves with Suharto. In the afternoon of 20 May, Suharto received the coup de grâce when fourteen cabinet ministers, many of whom were key economic ministers and associates of Habibie, collectively informed the president that they were not prepared to sit on a reshuffled cabinet. With the president's plan for gradual withdrawal thus thwarted, he was left with no choice but to resign immediately, handing over power to Vice-president Habibie. Having reassured himself of the military's support for the transition and for his own safety, Suharto announced his immediate resignation in the morning of 21 May.

Prabowo, who had close links with several Muslim activists and organisations, including sections of ICMI, probably expected to benefit from Habibie's ascendancy. The Kostrad commander seems to have hoped that Habibie would support him in his competition with the red and white (nationalist) group of senior officers around Wiranto and allow him and his allies to strengthen their influence over the military. It has even been suggested that Prabowo aspired to take over the national leadership himself. However, his hopes were thwarted as Wiranto agreed to support Habibie in exchange for free hands to consolidate the military and remove Prabowo and his allies from any strategic positions. Prabowo reportedly tried to threaten Habibie in order to have the decision reversed, and there are even indications that he considered attempting a coup d'état. However, Prabowo seems to have realised that he had lost the battle, and the day after Suharto resigned he was deprived of the Kostrad command. Three months later, Prabowo was discharged from active military service and he was subsequently allowed to leave the country without having to answer for his involvement in the abductions and torture of a number of political activists, several of whom were still missing and feared dead more than six months after the fall of Suharto.

The Legacies of Suharto's Fall

The military was, apart from the presidency, the most influential institution in the New Order. Against this background, it could have been expected that the military would take a leading role in the Indonesian post-Suharto political landscape. However, the military came out of the transition with a severely tarnished public reputation. The exposure of its involvement in the abductions of political activists was very embarrassing, although the military leadership tried to prevent the affair from reflecting badly on the military as a whole by blaming the entire operation on the demoted Prabowo and his associates. In addition, the widely reported passivity of the security forces in the riots and the suspicions of direct military instigation further served to discredit the military and to cast doubt on its professional competence. The general discrediting of the military in the months following Suharto's fall also made possible the revelation of numerous atrocities committed by the security forces during the Suharto era, especially in Aceh and East Timor where the military for decades had waged bloody wars against independence guerrillas. The uncovering of several mass graves and other incriminating evidence against the military gained widespread media attention, and further contributed to tarnishing ABRI's public image and to strengthen calls for the military to withdraw altogether from its involvement in politics.

Suharto had based his main claims to legitimacy on the positive economic development which he oversaw during most of his more than three decades in power. However, the 1997 economic crisis and the government's obvious incompetence in dealing effectively with the problems cast severe doubts on this claim. Since Suharto, from early 1998, increasingly came to be seen as the main obstacle to economic recovery, his earlier achievements in the economic field also came under fire. The prevalence of corruption, collusion and nepotism was widely seen as damaging to economic development, and critics argued that the problems were at the root of the economic crisis. As the economic crisis deepened, Suharto and his family came to personify many of the ills which plagued the Indonesian economy. This circumstance all but eliminated the president's previous claim to legitimacy based on the New Order's economic success. After more than three decades in power, Suharto could claim the credit for numerous achievements in the economic field, but his desire to go down in Indonesian history as the 'Father of Development' was thwarted by the economic crisis and the sharp rise of poverty in its wake.

Indonesian politics during the 1990s were heavily dominated by Suharto. Most other political actors depended for their fortune and influence on their proximity to the president, who controlled virtually all major political institutions. Towards his final days, he increasingly filled them with political loyalists to maintain his grip on power. Against this background, it was astonishing how quickly his support from inside the regime unravelled in the last days of his presidency. Around mid-May, when the pendulum appeared to have swung against Suharto, most of the political establishment which until then loyally had supported the president, scrambled to distance themselves from him and to join the chorus of opposition calling for his resignation. For many of Suharto's former supporters, such moves were mainly driven by opportunism, although some of Habibie's associates, such as many ICMI activists, probably felt that their political aspirations were better met if Suharto resigned and handed over power to the vice-president.

To a large extent, the swift unravelling of intra-elite support for the president can be explained by the widespread feeling that his resignation already was long overdue. Throughout the 1990s, Indonesian politics had been a waiting game with political actors trying to win short-term political benefits while simultaneously positioning themselves for the succession. The unsettling social, political and economic developments in the two years leading up to Suharto's fall further contributed to the general mood that the time was ripe for a political change, and this mood also affected many members of the political elite, including several of Suharto's aides. When the tide turned against Suharto and there were no longer any rewards for supporting the president, many actors swiftly abandoned their support for him. Instead they tried to avoid to be brought down themselves by Suharto's fall and ensure that they would come out on the winning side. As the former Suharto supporters in the elite distanced themselves from the president, they simultaneously detached Suharto from the system which he for several years had manipulated and controlled at his will in order to maintain his power.

The outcome was that the New Order's major political institutions and the overall system remained intact, and consequently the fall of Suharto did not constitute a regime transition proper. Most of the political establishment remained intact, and most politicians who benefited from the presidential succession, including President Habibie himself, owed their positions to Suharto in the first instance. The change of president led to a significantly more open political climate, but at the time of writing it remains to be seen whether Suharto's resignation signalled the beginning of a gradual democratic transition or merely an adaptation of the authoritarian regime to shifting circumstances with no more than a broadening of elite support.

The Suharto era left little in terms of democratic culture or any tradition of a wider political participation. The New Order under Suharto strove concertedly to exclude Indonesia's broad masses from taking active part in the nation's political life. Consequently, national politics was almost exclusively an elite affair, and whenever mass mobilisation occurred it mostly served the interests of members of the elite.

Throughout Suharto's and the regime's tenure in power, manipulation and political engineering were widely employed to defend the political status quo. These tactics continued, and perhaps even intensified, during Suharto's last years in power, but they seemed less effective than before, probably because of the higher levels of education among Indonesians in general and because of the increasing difficulties for the government to control the flow of information. During Suharto's last days in power, sections within the regime, including the military, apparently acting with Suharto's approval, actively tried to politicise ethnic and religious divisions in order to achieve political and possibly economic objectives. Such strategies exacerbated ethnic and religious tensions and led to a sharp increase in the number of instances of communal violence around the country. The ensuing social volatility combined with the economic crisis and a general feeling of upheaval and dissolution of authority to increase the risk for further outbreaks of violence in the immediate post-Suharto era. Suharto's resignation took place in the wake of the biggest riots ever in Jakarta, which left over 1,000 people dead and left widespread fear of renewed violence, particularly among the Chinese Indonesian population. Although the transition was peaceful in comparison with Indonesia's only previous presidential succession, the one in 1965–66, many Indonesians were depressed by the outbreak of uncontrolled violence and the conspiratorial and manipulative character of intra-elite political manoeuvring around the succession.

The politicisation of ethnic and religious issues led to increasing suspicion and aversion between different groups and individuals at the elite level. The religious riots in late 1996 and their aftermath increased long-standing tensions between the leaders of traditionalist and modernist Islam. The anti-Chinese rhetoric on behalf of sections of the military and their allies in radical Muslim circles in early 1998 exacerbated suspicions between Muslim leaders and members of the predominantly ethnic Chinese business elite. The economic crisis, moreover, exacerbated the competition for material benefits and resources among these groups and thus further contributed to the deterioration of intra-elite relations and the general atmosphere of distrust and suspicion. These immediate legacies of the late Suharto era, together with the lack of democratic tradition after his more than 30 years in power, are probably some of the most serious obstacles that need to be overcome in order to build a more democratic and open political system in Indonesia in the near future.

Bibliography

Abimanyu, Anggito and Rob Goodfellow (1997) 'The Culture of Economic Change in Indonesia: From Rapid Growth to the National Car Policy', in Rob Goodfellow (ed.), *Indonesian Business Culture*, Oxford: Butterworth-Heinemann, pp. 115–139.

Aditjondro, George Junus (1998) *Guru Kencing Berdiri, Murid Kencing Berlari: Kedua puncak korupsi, kolusi, dan nepotisme rezim Orde Baru dari Soeharto ke Habibie* [The teacher urinates standing, the student urinates running: the two peaks of corruption, collusion and nepotism under the New Order regime], Jakarta: Masyarakat Indonesia untuk Kemanusian (MIK) and Pusat Informasi Jaringan Aksi Reformasi (PIJAR) Indonesia.

—— (1997) 'Indonesia: The Anti–Subversion Law: A Briefing', Amnesty International Report ASA 21/03/97.

—— (1998a) 'Arrests of activists in connection with the March 1998 Presidential Election', Amnesty International Report ASA 21/20/98.

—— (1998b) 'Indonesia: Paying the price for "stability"', Amnesty International Report ASA 21/12/98.

Anderson, Benedict R.O'G. (1972) 'The Idea of Power in Javanese Culture', in Claire Holt (ed.), *Culture and Politics in Indonesia*, Ithaca (New York) and London: Cornell University Press, pp. 1–69.

—— (1996) 'Ben Anderson tentang demo PDI' [Ben Anderson about the PDI demonstration], Internet posting on the INDONESIA-L list (11 July 1996).[1]

---

1. INDONESIA-L (e-mail: apakabar@clark.net) is an e-mail list with information, news and debates about current affairs in Indonesia. All previous postings from the list are available from the searchable REG-INDONESIA database; internet gopher page, at the URL: <gopher://gopher.igc.apc.org:2998/7REG-INDONESIA> (version current at 25 February 1999).

Andersson, Bo, Lena Bang-Dryselius, Ingrid Olsson and Thommy Svensson (1977) 'Kupphändelserna i Indonesien 1965. En källkritisk analys' [The coup events in Indonesia 1965. A source critical analysis], *Historisk tidskrift*, vol. 97, no. 3, pp. 289–320.

Antlöv, Hans (1995) *Exemplary Centre, Administrative Periphery. Rural Leadership and the New Order in Java*, Richmond (Surrey): Curzon Press.

—— (1996) 'Revolution or Peaceful Evolution in Indonesia?', *NIAS nytt*, no. 3, pp. 9–10.

Anwar, M. Syafi'i (1992) 'Islam, Negara, dan Formasi Sosial dalam Orde Baru: Menguak Dimensi Sosio-Historis Kelahiran dan Perkembangan ICMI' [Islam, state and social formation under the New Order: widening the socio-historic dimensions of the founding and development of ICMI], *Ulumul Qur'an* vol. 3, no. 3: Supplement, pp. 1–28.

Aspinall, Ed (1996) 'What happened before the riots?', *Inside Indonesia*, no. 48, pp. 4–8.

Bahar, Ahmad (1996) *Biografi Politik Megawati Soekarnoputri 1993–1996* [Political biography of Megawati Soekarnoputri 1993–1996], Yogyakarta: Pena Cendekia.

Baroto, Al (1992) 'Indonesia's 1992 general election: changes and continuity', *The Indonesian Quarterly*, vol. 20, no. 3, pp. 244–256.

Barr, Christopher M. (1998) 'Bob Hasan, the Rise of Apkindo, and the Shifting Dynamics of Control in Indonesia's Timber Sector', *Indonesia*, no. 65, pp. 1–36.

Barton, Greg (1994) 'The Impact of neo-Modernism on Indonesian Islamic Thought: the Emergence of a New Pluralism', in David Bourchier and John Legge (eds), *Democracy in Indonesia: 1950s and 1990s*, Monash Papers on Southeast Asia; no. 31, Clayton (Victoria): Centre of Southeast Asian Studies, Monash University, pp. 143–150.

—— (1996) 'The Liberal, Progressive Roots of Abdurrahman Wahid's Thought', in Greg Barton and Greg Fealy (eds), *Nahdlatul Ulama, Traditional Islam and Modernity in Indonesia*, Monash Papers on Southeast Asia; no. 39, Clayton (Victoria): Monash Asia Institute, Monash University, pp. 190–226.

—— (1997) 'Indonesia's Nurcholish Madjid and Abdurrahman Wahid as intellectual "Ulamâ": the meeting of Islamic Traditionalism and Modernism in neo-Modernist thought' in *Studia Islamika*, vol. 4, no. 1, pp. 29–81.

Barton, Greg and Greg Fealy (eds), (1996) *Nahdlatul Ulama, Traditional Islam and Modernity in Indonesia*, Monash Papers on Southeast Asia; no. 39, Clayton (Victoria): Monash Asia Institute, Monash University.

Bastaman, Syarif (1995) 'Kemelut dalam PDI dan NU: Melumpuhkan Kemandirian Masyarakat' [Crisis in the PDI and the NU: Paralysing the autonomy of society] in A.B. Nasution *et al.*, *Catatan Keadaan Hak Asasi Manusia 1994*, Jakarta: Yayasan Lembaga Bantuan Hukum Indonesia (YLBHI) pp. 15–34.

Bertrand, Jacques (1996) 'False Starts, Succession Crises, and Regime Transition: Flirting with Openness in Indonesia', *Pacific Affairs*, vol. 69, no. 3, pp. 319–340.

—— (1997) '"Business as Usual" in Suharto's Indonesia', *Asian Survey*, vol. 37, no. 5, pp. 441–452.

Biers, Dan (ed.), (1998) *Crash of '97*, Hong Kong: Far Eastern Economic Review.

Bird, Judith (1998) 'Indonesia in 1997. The Tinderbox Year', *Asian Survey*, vol. 38, no. 2, pp. 168–176.

Booth, Anne (1993) 'Counting the Poor in Indonesia', *Bulletin of Indonesian Economic Studies*, vol. 29, no. 1, pp. 53–83.

—— (1994) 'Repelita VI and the Second Long-term Development Plan', *Bulletin of Indonesian Economic Studies*, vol. 30, no. 3, pp. 1–40.

—— (1998) 'Economic Development, National Security and Political Accommodation in Indonesia in the New Order Era', Revised paper prepared for the ESRC (Economic and Social Research Council) Pacific Asia Programme Project on Security, Development and Political Accommodation in Pacific Asia, London (July 1998): Workshop, Institute of Commonwealth Studies (unpublished).

Bourchier, David (1984) *The Dynamics of Dissent in Indonesia: Sawito and the Phantom Coup*, Modern Indonesia Project Publications, no. 63, Interim Report, Ithaca (New York): Cornell University, Southeast Asia Program, Cornell Modern Indonesia Project.

—— (1990) 'Crime, Law and State Authority in Indonesia', in Arief Budiman (ed.), *State and Civil Society in Indonesia*, Monash Papers on Southeast Asia; no. 22, Clayton (Victoria): Centre of Southeast Asian Studies, Monash University, pp. 177–214.

—— (1998a) 'More educated, more ruthless', *Inside Indonesia*, no. 53, pp. 14–15.

—— (1998b) 'The Shaming of the Indonesian Military', *Asia-Pacific Magazine*, no. 13, pp. 22–24.

BPS (*Biro Pusat Statistik* [Central Bureau of Statistics]) (1998) *Indonesia dalam Angka 1997. Indonesia in Figures*, Jakarta: Biro Pusat Statistik.

Bresnan, John (1993) *Managing Indonesia: The Modern Political Economy*, New York: Columbia University Press.

Brooks, Karen (1995) 'The Rustle of Ghosts: Bung Karno in the New Order', *Indonesia*, no. 60, pp. 61–99.

Budiman, Arief (1998) 'Friend or foe?', *Inside Indonesia*, no. 54, pp. 18–19.

Cala, Kristne (1988) 'The "Sawito Affair" of 1976–1978: the role of the Pancasila', *Review of Indonesian and Malaysian Affairs*, vol. 22, no. 2, pp. 180–186.

Caldwell, Malcolm (ed.) (1975) *Ten Years' Military Terror in Indonesia*, Nottingham: Spokesman Books.

Cederroth, Sven (1994) 'New Order Modernization and Islam', in Hans Antlöv and Sven Cederroth (eds), *Leadership on Java*, Richmond (Surrey): Curzon Press, pp. 137–162.

Chang Ha-Joon (1998) 'South Korea: The Misunderstood Crisis', in Jomo K.S. (ed.), *Tigers in Trouble: Financial Governance, Liberalisation and Crisis in East Asia*, London etc.: Zed Books Ltd, pp. 222–231.

Cole, David C. and Betty F. Slade (1998) 'Why has Indonesia's Financial Crisis Been so Bad?', *Bulletin of Indonesian Economic Studies*, vol. 34, no. 2, pp. 61–66.

Coppel, Charles A. (1983) *Indonesian Chinese in Crisis*, Kuala Lumpur and New York: Oxford University Press.

Cribb, Robert (1990) 'Indonesian Political Developments, 1989–90', in Hal Hill and Terry Hull (eds), *Indonesia Assessment 1990*, Canberra: Department of Political and Social Change, Research School of Pacific and Asian Studies, Australian National University, pp. 24–42.

—— (1991) *Gangsters and Revolutionaries. The Jakarta People's Militia and the Indonesian Revolution 1945–1949*, Honolulu: University of Hawaii Press.

—— (1996) 'Megawati and the PDI Affair: Implications for Indonesian Politics', *NIAS nytt*, no. 3, 1996, pp. 7–8.

—— (1998a) 'Indonesien idag – framgångar och dilemman' [Contemporary Indonesia – achievements and dilemmas] in *Asiatiska vägval. Delstudier för en svensk Asienstrategi*, Ds (Departementsserien [Departmental series]) 1998: 34, Stockholm: Regeringskansliet, pp. 203–266.

—— (1998b) 'More Smoke than Fire: The 1997 "Haze" Crisis and other Environmental Issues in Indonesia', in Annamari Antikainen-Kokko (ed.), *Ecological Change in Southeast Asia*, Åbo: Centre for Southeast Asian Studies, Åbo Akademi University, pp. 1–13.

—— (ed.), (1990) *The Indonesian Killings 1965–1966. Studies from Java and Bali*, Monash Papers on Southeast Asia; no. 21, Clayton (Victoria): Centre of Southeast Asian Studies, Monash University.

Crouch, Harold (1979) 'Patrimonialism and Military Rule in Indonesia', *World Politics*, vol. 31, no. 4.

—— (1980) 'The New Order: The Prospect for Political Stability', in Jamie Mackie (ed.), *Indonesia – the Making of a Nation*, Canberra: Research School of Pacific Studies, Australian National University, pp. 657–667.

—— (1992) 'An Ageing President, An Ageing Regime', in Harold Crouch and Hal Hill (eds), *Indonesia Assessment 1992: Political Perspectives on the 1990s*, Canberra: Department of Political and Social Change, Research School of Pacific Studies, Australian National University, pp. 43–62.

—— (1993) *The Army and Politics in Indonesia*, Ithaca (New York): Cornell University Press.

Desmond, Junaidi Mahesa (1998) 'Berita Acara Pemeriksaan (Saksi)' [Record of Hearing (Witness)], Jakarta (25 May 1998): Markas Besar Tentara Nasional Indonesia, Angkatan Darat, Pusat Polisi Militer [Headquarters of the Indonesian National Armed Forces, Army, Centre of Military Police], (unpublished).

Divisi Informasi and Dokumentasi YLBHI [Division of information and documentation, YLBHI] (1998) 'Daftar Orang-orang Hilang/Pernah Hilang Berdasarkan Waktu Dinyatakan Hilang' [List of disappeared/previously disappeared people based on the time of disappearance], Jakarta: Kontras documentation, (unpublished).

DPP/PDI (Dewan Pimpinan Pusat/PDI [PDI central board]) (1993) *Bahan–Bahan Kongres iv PDI Tahun 1993* [Material for the fourth PDI congress 1993], Jakarta: DPP/PDI.

Economic and Financial Resilience Council (1998) 'Press Release by the Economic and Financial Resilience Council', (21 January 1998), KITLV (Koninklijk Instituut voor de Taal-, Land- en Volkenkunde) Daily Report (26 January 1998) [internet WWW page, at the URL <gopher://oasis.leidenuniv.nl:71/00/kitlv/daily-report/980126.TXT> (version current at 2 February 1998)].

Editors (1993) 'Current Data on the Indonesian Military Elite: January 1, 1992–August 31, 1993', *Indonesia*, no. 56, pp. 119–152.

—— (1994) 'Current Data on the Indonesian Military Elite: September 1, 1993–August 31, 1994', *Indonesia*, no. 58, pp. 83–101.

—— (1995) 'Current Data on the Indonesian Military Elite: September 1, 1993– September 30, 1995', *Indonesia*, no. 60, pp. 101–146.

—— (1997) 'The Indonesian Military in the Mid-1990s: Political Maneuvering or Structural Change?', *Indonesia*, no. 63, pp. 91–105.

—— (1998) 'Current Data on the Indonesian Military Elite: October 1, 1995–December 31, 1997', *Indonesia*, no. 65, pp. 179–194.

Eklöf, Stefan (1997) 'The 1997 General Election in Indonesia', *Asian Survey*, vol. 37, no. 12, pp. 1181–1196.

Eldridge, Philip (1995) *Non-Government Organizations and Democratic Participation in Indonesia*, Kuala Lumpur: Oxford University Press.

Fealy, Greg (1996) 'The 1994 NU Congress and Aftermath: Abdurrahman Wahid, Suksesi and the Battle for Control of NU', in Greg Barton and Greg Fealy (eds), *Nahdlatul Ulama, Traditional Islam and Modernity in Indonesia,* Monash Papers on Southeast Asia; no. 39, Clayton (Victoria): Monash Asia Institute, Monash University, pp. 257–277.

—— (1997) 'Indonesian Politics, 1995–96: The Makings of a Crisis', in Gavin W. Jones and Terence H. Hull (eds), *Indonesia Assessment: Population and Human Resources*, Canberra: Research School of Pacific Studies, Australian National University, pp. 19–38.

Feith, Herb (1992) 'East Timor: The Opening Up, the Crackdown and the Possibility of Durable Settlement', in Harold Crouch and Hal Hill (eds), *Indonesia Assessment 1992: Political Perspectives on the 1990s*, Canberra: Department of Political and Social Change, Research School of Pacific Studies, Australian National University, pp. 63–80.

Forrester, Geoffrey (1998a) 'Introduction', in Geoff Forrester and R.J. May (eds), *The Fall of Soeharto*, Bathurst (New South Wales): Crawford House Publishing, pp. 1-23.

—— (1998b) 'A Jakarta diary, May 1998', in Geoff Forrester and R.J. May (eds), *The Fall of Soeharto*, Bathurst (New South Wales): Crawford House Publishing, pp. 24-69.

Forrester, Geoffrey and R J May (eds), (1998) *The Fall of Soeharto*, Bathurst (New South Wales): Crawford House Publishing.

Frederick, William H. (1982) 'Rhoma Irama and the Dangdut Style: Aspects of Contemporary Indonesian Popular Culture', *Indonesia*, no. 34, pp. 102–130.

Gaffar, Afan (1992) *Javanese Voters. A Case Study of Election Under a Hegemonic Party System*, Yogyakarta: Gadjah Mada University Press.

Garnaut, Ross (1998) 'The East Asian crisis', in Ross H. McLeod and Ross Garnaut (eds), *East Asia in Crisis: From being a miracle to needing one?*, London and New York: Routledge, pp. 3–27.

Gellert, Paul K. (1998) 'A Brief History and Analysis of Indonesia's Forest Fire Crisis', *Indonesia*, no. 65, pp. 63–85.

Goodfellow, Rob (1995) 'Api Dalam Sekam: the New Order and the ideology of anti-communism', Working Paper; no. 95, Clayton (Victoria): Centre of Southeast Asian Studies, Monash University.

Grant, Ronald M. (1979) 'Indonesia 1978: A Third Term for President Suharto', *Asian Survey*, vol. 19, no. 2, pp. 141–146.

Guinness Flight (1997) 'The 21st Century belongs to Asia', *Investment Research Series* (July 1997) Pasadena (California): Guinness Flight.

Hadad, Toriz (ed.), (1998) *Amarah Tasikmalaya: Konflik di Basis Islam* [The wrath of Tasikmalaya: conflict based on Islam], Jakarta: Penerbit Institut Studi Arus Informasi (ISAI).

Halawa, Ohiao (1993) *Membangun Citra Partai: Profil Drs. Soerjadi, Ketua Umum DPP PDI periode 1986–1993* [Developing the party image: profile of Doktorandus Soerjadi, general chairman of the PDI central board 1986–1993], Jakarta: Nyiur Indah Alam Sejati.

Halldorsson, Jon O. (1998) 'Suharto's End Game', paper presented at the Nordic Institute of Asian Studies (NIAS), Copenhagen (31 March 1998) (unpublished).

Hanazaki, Yasuo (1998) *Pers Terjebak* [Framed press], Jakarta: Institut Studi Arus Informasi (ISAI).

Haribuan, Irwan (ed.), (1996) *Megawati Soekarnoputri: Pantang Surut Langkah* [Megawati Soekarnoputri: Never give up], Jakarta: Tim Institut Studi Arus Informasi (ISAI).

Hariyanto, I. (ed.) (1998) *Melangkah dari Keruntuhan Tragedi Situbondo* [Going forward from the debacle of the Situbondo tragedy], Jakarta: Penerbit Gramedia Widiasarana Indonesia (Grasindo).

Harsono, Andreas (ed.), (1998) *Huru-hara Rengasdengklok* [The Rengasdengklok riots], Jakarta: Institut Studi Arus Informasi (ISAI).

Haseman, John B. (1997) 'Indonesia and ABRI. Challenges for the Future', *Southeast Asian Affairs 1997*, Singapore: Institute of Southeast Asian Studies (ISEAS) pp. 125–140.

Hefner, Robert (1993) 'Islam, State, and Civil Society: ICMI and the Struggle for the Indonesian Middle Class', *Indonesia*, no. 56, pp. 1–35.

Henderson, Callum (1998) *Asia Falling? Making Sense of the Asian Currency Crisis and its Aftermath*, Singapore: McGraw-Hill Book Co.

Hill, David T. (1995) *The Press in New Order Indonesia*, Jakarta: Sinar Harapan.

Hill, David T. and Krishna Sen (1997) 'Wiring the Warung to Global Gateways: The Internet in Indonesia', *Indonesia*, no. 63, pp. 67–90.

Hill, Hal (1996) *The Indonesian Economy Since 1966: Southeast Asia's Emerging Giant*, Cambridge: Cambridge University Press.

—— (1997) *Indonesia's Industrial Transformation*, Singapore: Institute of Southeast Asian Studies (ISEAS).

—— (1998) 'The Indonesian economy: the strange and sudden death of a tiger', in Geoff Forrester and R.J. May (eds), *The Fall of Soeharto*, Bathurst (New South Wales): Crawford House Publishing, pp. 93–103.

Hughes, John (1968) *The End of Sukarno*, London: Angus and Robertson.

Human Rights Watch/Asia (1994) *The Limits of Openness. Human Rights in Indonesia and East Timor*, New York: Human Rights Watch.

—— (1996) 'Indonesia: Election monitoring and human rights', *Human Rights Watch/Asia*, vol. 8, no. 5.

—— (1997) 'Communal Violence in West Kalimantan', *Human Rights Watch/Asia*, vol. 9, no. 10.

—— (1998a) 'Indonesia Alert: Economic Crisis leads to Scapegoating of Ethnic Chinese', internet WWW page at the URL: <http//:www.hrw.org/hrw/press98/feb/indo-al2.htm> (version current at 22 February 1999).

—— (1998b) 'Indonesia: More Pressure Needed on Disappearances', internet WWW page, at the URL <http://www.hrw.org/hrw/press98/june/indo0622.htm> (version current at 19 February 1999).

Ikrar Nusa Bhakti (1998) 'Trends in Indonesian student movements in 1998', in Geoff Forrester and R.J. May (eds), *The Fall of Soeharto*, Bathurst (New South Wales): Crawford House Publishing, pp. 167–178.

ILO (International Labour Organisation), Jakarta Office (1998) *Employment Challenges of the Indonesian Economic Crisis*. Jakarta: ILO, Jakarta Office and UNDP.

Imawan, Riswanda (1996) 'Kata Pengantar' [Preface] in Ahmad Bahar, *Biografi Politik Megawati Soekarnoputri 1993–1996*, Yogyakarta: Pena Cendekia, pp. 1–9.

IMF (International Monetary Fund) (1998a) 'Indonesia Memorandum of Economic and Financial Policies', (15 January 1998) internet WWW page at the URL: <http://www.imf.org/external/np/LOI/011598.htm> (version current at 22 February 1999).

—— (1998b) 'Indonesia Memorandum of Economic and Financial Policies', (10 April 1998) internet WWW page at the URL: <http://www.imf.org/external/np/LOI/041098.htm> (version current at 22 February 1999).

—— (1998c) 'International Monetary Fund Press Briefing', (4 May 1998) internet WWW page at the URL: <http://www.imf.org/external/np/tr/1998/TR980504.HTM> (version current at 22 February 1999).

Indonesian Legal Aid Foundation (1997) 'YLBHI Human Rights Report 1996', Jakarta: Yayasan Lembaga Bantuan Hukum Indonesia (YLBHI) [unpublished].

Indonesian National Commission on Human Rights (1997) *Annual Report 1996*, Jakarta: Komnas HAM.

IRIP (Indonesia Resources and Information Programme) News Service (1997) 'Making an ass of the law', *Inside Indonesia*, no. 50, pp. 2–4.

Irwan, Alexander and Edriana (1995) *Pemilu: Pelanggaran Asas Luber* [Election: Violations of the principles of direct, general, free and secret], Jakarta: Pustaka Sinar Harapan.

Jannisa, Gudmund (1997) *The Crocodile's Tears. East Timor in the Making*, Lund Dissertations in Sociology; no. 14, Lund: Department of Sociology, Lund University.

Jellinek, Lea (1999) 'The new poor', *Inside Indonesia*, no. 57, pp. 4–6.

Jenkins, David (1983) 'The Evolution of Indonesian Army Doctrinal Thinking: the Concept of *Dwifungsi*', *Southeast Asian Journal of Social Science*, vol. 11, no. 2, pp. 15–30.

—— (1984) *Suharto and His Generals. Indonesian Military Politics 1975–1983*, Ithaca (New York): Cornell Modern Indonesia Project, Southeast Asia Program, Cornell University.

Johnson, Colin (1998) 'Survey of Recent Developments', *Bulletin of Indonesian Economic Studies*, vol. 34, no. 2, pp. 3–60.

Joint-Fact-Finding Team (1998) 'Final Report of the Joint-Fact-Finding Team on 13–15 May 1998 Riot. Executive Summary', Jakarta (23 October 1998): TGPF (unpublished).

Jomo K.S. (ed.) (1998) *Tigers in Trouble. Financial Governance, Liberalisation and Crises in East Asia*, London: Zed Books.

Jones, Sidney (1996) 'Human Rights in Indonesia. Testimony before the Senate Foreign Relations Committee, Subcommittee on East Asia and Pacific Affairs', (18 September 1996) Washington DC: US Congress, (unpublished).

Jones, Sidney and Mike Jendrzejczyk (1997) 'Indonesia puts more critics on trial', [internet posting on the INDONESIA-L list (8 February 1997) – see p. 238, n. 1].

Kato, Hisanori (1999) 'Islamic conversations', *Inside Indonesia*, no. 57, pp. 22–23.

Kerusuhan Situbondo. Draft Buku Putih [The Situbondo riot. White book draft] (1996) n. p.: Gerakan Pemuda Ansor.

Ketetapan-Ketetapan Majelis Permusyawaratan Rakyat Republik Indonesia 1998 [Decisions of the 1998 People's Consultative Assembly of the Republic of Indonesia] (1998) Jakarta: Eko Jaya.

Kingsbury, Damien (1998) *The Politics of Indonesia*, Oxford: Oxford University Press.

Kitley, Philip (1997) 'New Order Television Rituals', in Michael Hitchcock and Victor T. King (eds), *Images of Malay–Indonesian Identity*, Kuala Lumpur: Oxford University Press, pp. 236–262.

Konspirasi menggoyang Soeharto [Conspiracy to destabilise Soeharto] (1997) Jakarta: publisher unknown.

Kontras (1998) 'Kontras: Organizational Summary', Jakarta: Kontras documentation (unpublished).

Labrousse, Pierre (1993) 'Chronique d'élections annoncées', *Archipel*, vol. 46, pp. 25–40.

Labrousse, Pierre (1994) 'The Second Life of Bung Karno. Analysis of the Myth (1978–1981)', *Indonesia*, no. 57, pp. 175–196.

Lane, Max (1991) *'Openness', Political Discontent and Succession in Indonesia: Political Developments in Indonesia 1989–1991*, Australia-Asia Paper; no. 56, Brisbane: Centre for the Study of Australia-Asia Relations, Division of Asian and International Studies, Griffith University.

Lauridsen, Laurids S. (1998) 'Thailand: Causes, Conduct, Consequences', in Jomo K.S. (ed.), *Tigers in Trouble. Financial Governance, Liberalisation and Crises in East Asia*, London: Zed Books, pp. 137–161.

Liddle, R. William (1985) 'Soeharto's Indonesia: Personal Rule and Political Institutions', *Pacific Affairs*, vol. 58, no. 1, pp. 68–90.

—— (1987) 'The Politics of Shared Growth. Some Indonesian Cases', *Comparative Politics*, vol. 19, no. 2, pp. 127–146.

—— (1988) 'Indonesia in 1987: The New Order at the Height of its Power', *Asian Survey*, vol. 28, no. 2, pp. 180–191.

—— (1992) 'Indonesia's Democratic Past and Future', *Comparative Politics*, vol. 24, pp. 443–461.

—— (1993) 'Politics 1992–1993: Sixth Term Adjustments in the Ruling Formula', in Chris Manning and Joan Hardjono (eds), *Indonesia Assessment 1993. Labour: Sharing in the Benefits of Growth?*, Canberra: Department of Political and Social Change, Research School of Pacific and Asian Studies, Australian National University, pp. 26–42.

—— (1995) 'Islam and politics in late new order Indonesia' (Paper presented at the conference on Islam and Society in Southeast Asia, Jakarta, May 29–31, 1995) (unpublished).

—— (1996a) 'A useful fiction: Democratic legitimation in New Order Indonesia', in R.H. Taylor (ed.), *The Politics of Elections in Southeast Asia*, New York etc.: Woodrow Wilson Center and Cambridge University Press, pp. 34–60.

—— (1996b) *Leadership and Culture in Indonesian Politics*, Sydney: Asian Studies Association of Australia, and Allen and Unwin.

Lindblad, Thomas (1997) 'Survey of Recent Developments', *Bulletin of Indonesian Economic Studies*, vol. 33, no. 3, pp. 3–33.

Lowry, Robert (1996) *The Armed Forces of Indonesia*, St Leonards (New South Wales): Allen and Unwin.

Lucas, Anton (1997) 'Land Disputes, the Bureaucracy, and Local Resistance in Indonesia', in Jim Schiller and Barbara Martin-Schiller (eds), *Imagining Indonesia: Cultural Politics and Political Culture*, Ohio University Center for International Studies, Monograph in International Studies, Southeast Asian Series; no. 97, Athens (Ohio): Center for International Studies, Ohio University, pp. 229–260.

Luwarso, Lukas (ed.), (1997) *Jakarta Crackdown*, Jakarta: Alliance of Independent Journalists (AJI).

Lyon, Margot L. (1993) 'Mystical Biography: Soeharto and Kejawen in the Political Domain', in Angus MacIntyre (ed.), *Indonesian Political Biography. In Search of Cross-Cultural Understanding*, Monash Paper on Southeast Asia; no. 28, Clayton (Victoria): Centre of Southeast Asian Studies, Monash University, pp. 211–238.

MacDonald, Hamish (1981) *Suharto's Indonesia*, Blackburn: Fontana.

MacFarling, Ian (1996) *The Dual Function of the Indonesian Armed Forces: Military Politics in Indonesia*, Canberra: Defence Studies Centre.

MacIntyre, Andrew (1991) *Business and Politics in Indonesia*, Sydney: Allen and Unwin.

—— (1994) 'Organising Interests: Corporatism in Indonesian Politics', Working Paper; no. 43, Clayton (Victoria): Asia Research Centre on Social, Political and Economic Change, Monash University.

Mackie, Jamie and Andrew MacIntyre (1994) 'Politics', in Hal Hill (ed.), *Indonesia's New Order: The Dynamics of Socio–Economic Transformation*, Sydney: Allen and Unwin, pp. 1–53.

Malik, Dedy Djamluddin (ed.), (1998) *Gejolak Reformasi Menolak Anarki. Kontroversi Seputar Aksi Mahasiswa Menuntut Reformasi Politik Orde Baru* [The flame of reform rejects anarchy. The controversy around the students actions demanding political reform of the New Order], Bandung: Zaman Wacana Mulia.

Mallarangeng, Rizal and R. William Liddle (1996) 'Indonesia in 1995: The Struggle for Power and Policy', *Asian Survey*, vol. 36, no. 2, pp. 109–122.

Mallarangeng, Rizal and R. William Liddle (1997) 'Indonesia in 1996: Pressures from Above and Below', *Asian Survey*, vol. 37, no. 2, pp. 167–174.

Malley, Michael (1998) 'The 7th Development Cabinet: Loyal to a Fault?', *Indonesia*, no. 65, pp. 155–178.

Mann, Richard (1998a) *Economic Crisis in Indonesia. The Full Story*, Singapore: Gateway Books.

—— (1998b) *Plots and Schemes That Brought Down Soeharto*, Singapore: Gateway Books.

Manning, Chris and Sisira Jayasuriya (1996) 'Survey of Recent Developments', *Bulletin of Indonesian Economic Studies*, vol. 32, no. 2, pp. 3–43.

Maurer, Jean-Luc (1997) 'A New Order Sketchpad of Indonesian History', in Michael Hitchcock and Victor T. King (eds), *Images of Malay-Indonesian Identity*, Kuala Lumpur: Oxford University Press, pp. 209–226.

Maurer, Jean-Luc and François Raillon (1994) 'The Ideology of Social Change in Indonesian Politics: a Comparative analysis of Sukarno's and Suharto's discourses', in Wolfgang Marschall (ed.), *Texts from the Islands*, Bern: Institute of Ethnology, University of Bern, pp. 97–118.

McIntyre, Angus (1996) 'Soeharto's Composure: Considering the Biographical and Autobiographical Accounts', Working Paper; no. 97, Clayton (Victoria): Centre of Southeast Asian Studies, Monash University

—— (1997) 'In Search of Megawati Soekarnoputri', Working Paper; no. 103, Clayton (Victoria): Monash Asia Institute, Centre of Southeast Asian Studies, Monash University.

McKendrick, David (1992) 'Obstacles to "Catch-up": The Case of the Indonesian Aircraft Industry', *Bulletin of Indonesian Economic Studies*, vol. 28, no. 1, pp. 39–66.

McLeod, Ross H. (1997) 'Postscript to the survey of recent developments: on causes and cures for the rupiah crisis', *Bulletin of Indonesian Economic Studies*, vol. 33, no. 3, pp. 35–52.

—— (1998) 'Indonesia', in Ross H. McLeod and Ross Garnaut (eds), *East Asia in Crisis: From Being a Miracle to Needing One?*, London and New York: Routledge, pp. 31-48.

McLeod, Ross H. and Ross Garnaut (eds) (1998) *East Asia in Crisis: From being a miracle to needing one?*, London and New York: Routledge.

McVey, Ruth and Benedict R.O'G. Anderson (1971) *A Preliminary Analysis of the October 1 1965 Coup in Indonesia*, Interim Report

Series, Modern Indonesia Project; no. 52, Ithaca (New York): Modern Indonesia Project, Southeast Asia Program, Cornell University.

Mietzner, Marcus (1998*a*) 'Godly men in green', *Inside Indonesia*, no. 53, pp. 8–9.

—— (1998b) 'Between *pesantran* [*sic*] and palace: Nahdlatul Ulama and its role in the transition', in Geoff Forrester and R.J. May (eds), *The Fall of Soeharto*, Bathurst (New South Wales): Crawford House Publishing, pp. 179-199.

Moertopo, Ali (1982) *Strategi Pembangunan Nasional*, Jakarta: Yayasan Proklamasi and CSIS.

Morfit, Michael (1986) 'Pancasila Orthodoxy', in Colin MacAndrews (ed.), *Central Government and Local Development in Indonesia*, Singapore: Oxford University Press, pp. 42–54.

Mugianto (1998) 'Sebuah Kesaksian' [A testimony], Jakarta (8 June 1998): Kontras documentation, (unpublished).

Muhamed, Khadijah (1998) 'Malaysia's migrant labour and the Asian crisis: What next?', *Asia-Pacific Magazine*, no. 13, pp. 25–26.

Muhammad, Mar'ie (1998) 'Indonesian Drama' (Paper presented at the Asia Research Centre, Murdoch University 20 August 1998), Perth (Western Australia): Murdoch University (unpublished).

Mulder, Niels (1978) *Mysticism and Everyday Life in Contemporary Java*, Singapore: Singapore University Press.

—— (1996) *Inside Indonesian Society. Cultural Change in Java*, Amsterdam and Kuala Lumpur: Pepin Press.

Naisbitt, John (1996) *Megatrends Asia. Eight Asian Megatrends That Are Reshaping Our World*, New York: Simon and Schuster.

Noegroho, Anggit and Bambang Harsri Irawan (eds), (1998) *Rekaman Lensa Peristiwa Mei 1998 di Solo* [Lens recording of the May 1998 event in Solo], Solo: Aksara Solopos.

Nusantara, A. Ariobimo, R. Masri Sareb Putra and Y.B. Sudarmanto (1998) *Aksi Mahasiswa Menuju Gerbang Reformasi* [Student actions towards the gates of reform], Jakarta: Gramedia Widiasarana Indonesia.

Pemberton, John (1986) 'Notes on the 1982 General Election in Solo', *Indonesia*, no. 41, pp. 1–22.

Polomka, Peter (1971) *Indonesia Since Sukarno*, Harmondsworth: Penguin Books.

Pour, Julius (1998) *Jakarta Semasa Lengser Keprabon (100 hari menjelang peralihan kekuasaan)* [Jakarta in the time of abdication (100 days leading up to a shift in power)], Jakarta: Penerbit Elex Media Komputindo, Kelompok Gramedia.

PSPI (Pusat Studi dan Pengembangan Informasi [Study Center and Information Development]) and Partai Bulan Bintang [Moon and Crescent Party] (1998) *TANJUNG PRIOK BERDARAH, Tanggung Jawab Siapa?* [Tanjung Priok bleeding, whose responsibility?], Jakarta: Gema Insani Press.

Quarles van Ufford, Philip (1987) 'Contradictions in the Study of Legitimate Authority in Indonesia', *Bijdragen tot de Taal-, Land-, en Volkenkunde*, vol. 143, afl. 1, pp. 141–158.

Radelet, Steven and Jeffrey Sachs (1998) 'The Onset of the East Asian Financial Crisis', Paper presented at a seminar at USAID (29 January 1998) and at the National Bureau of Economic Research (NBER) Currency Crisis Conference (6/7 February 1998), internet WWW page, at the URL <http://www.hiid.harvard.edu/pub/other/eaonset.pdf> (version current at 8 June 1998).

Ramadhan, K.H. (1996) *Soemitro. Former Commander of Indonesian Security Apparatus*, Jakarta: Pustaka Sinar Harapan.

Ramage, Douglas Edward (1995) *Politics in Indonesia. Democracy, Islam and the Ideology of Tolerance*, London and New York: Routledge.

Randall, Jesse (1998) 'Political Gangsters', *Inside Indonesia*, no. 53, pp. 4–5.

Rani, Markus, Anthon P. Sinaga and Ronald Ngantung (eds), (1997) *Rekaman Peristiwa 1996* [Recording of events in 1996], Jakarta: Suara Pembaruan and Sinar Harapan.

Riza, Faisol (1998) 'Kesaksian Korban Penculikan Faisol Riza' [Witness of kidnapping victim Faisol Riza], Jakarta (20 June 1998): Kontras documentation, (unpublished).

Robison, Richard (1986) *Indonesia: The Rise of Capital*, Sydney: Allen and Unwin.

—— (1990) *Power and Economy in Suharto's Indonesia*, Manila and Wollongong: Journal of Contemporary Asia Publishers.

—— (1993) 'Indonesia: Tensions in state and regime', in Kevin Hewison, Richard Robison and Gerry Rodan (eds), *Southeast Asia in the 1990s: Authoritarianism, democracy and capitalism*, Sydney: Allen and Unwin, pp. 41–74.

—— (1995a) 'Organising the transition: Indonesian politics in 1993/94', in Ross H. McLeod (ed.), *Indonesia Assessment 1994: Finance as a*

Key Sector in Indonesia's Development, Canberra: Research School for Pacific and Asian Studies, Australian National University and Singapore: Institute of Southeast Asian Studies (ISEAS), pp. 49–74.

—— (1995b) 'Economic and Political Liberalisation in Southeast Asia: Inexorable Force or Red Herring' (Working Paper no. 56), Murdoch (Western Australia): Asia Research Centre, Special Research Centre on Social, Political and Economic Change in Asia, Murdoch University.

—— (1997) 'Politics and Markets in Indonesia's Post-Oil Era', in Gerry Rodan, Kevin Hewison and Richard Robison (eds), *The Political Economy of South-East Asia*, Melbourne: Oxford University Press, pp. 29–63.

Romano, Angela (1996) 'The Open Wound: Keterbukaan and Press Freedom in Indonesia', *Australian Journal of International Affairs*, vol. 50, no. 2, pp. 157–169.

Said, Salim (1998) 'Suharto's Armed Forces: Building a Power Base in New Order Indonesia, 1966–1998', *Asian Survey* vol. 38, no. 6, pp. 535-552.

Salim Hairus H.S. and Andi Achidian (1997) *Amuk Banjarmasin* [The amok of Banjarmasin], Jakarta: Yayasan Lembaga Bantuan Hukum Indonesia (YLBHI).

Samego, Indria (1996) 'Penelitian Peran Sosial Politik ABRI' [Investigation of the socio-political role of ABRI], *Studia Politika*, no. 1, pp. 159–161.

Schulte Nordholt, N. G. (1980) 'The Indonesian Elections: A National Ritual', in R. Schefold and J. W. Schoorl (eds), *Man, Meaning and History*, The Hague: Martinus Nijhoff, pp. 179–203.

Schwarz, Adam (1994) *A Nation in Waiting. Indonesia in the 1990s*, Boulder and San Francisco: Westview Press.

Seagrave, Sterling (1996) *Lords of the Rim*, London: Corgi Press.

Shiraishi, Takashi (1996) 'Rewiring the Indonesian State', in Daniel S. Lev and Ruth McVey (eds), *Making Indonesia: Essays on Modern Indonesia in Honor of George McT. Kahin*, Ithaca (New York): Cornell University Press, pp. 164–179.

Siegel, James (1993) 'I was not there, but...', *Archipel*, no. 46, pp. 59–65.

Silaban, Sintong, Antoni Antra Pardosi, Aldentua Siringgoringo, Bernard Nainggolan and Tumpal Sihite (1997) *Sabam Sirait: Untuk Demokrasi Indonesia* [Sabam Sirait: For Indonesian democracy], Jakarta: Pustaka Forum Adil Sejahtera.

Simanjuntak, Togi (ed.) (1996) *ABRI Punya Golkar?* [Does ABRI own Golkar?], Jakarta: Institut Studi Arus Informasi (ISAI).

Sjahrir (1993) 'The Indonesian economy: the case of macro success and micro challenge', in Chris Manning and Joan Hardjono (eds), *Indonesia Assessment 1993. Labour: Sharing in the Benefits of Growth?*, Canberra: Department of Political and Social Change, Research School of Pacific and Asian Studies, Australian National University.

Smith, Heather (1998) 'Korea', in Ross H. McLeod and Ross Garnaut (eds), *East Asia in Crisis: From being a miracle to needing one?*, London and New York: Routledge, pp. 66–84.

Soeharto (1989) *Pikiran, Ucapan, dan Tindakan Saya. Otobiografi* [My thoughts, words and deeds. Autobiography], Jakarta: Citra Lamtoro Gung Persada.

Soekarnoputri, Megawati (1996a) *Pidato Politik Ketua Umum Partai Demokrasi Indonesia Megawati Soekarnoputri. Acara Penutupan Hari Ulang Tahun ke 23 PDI, 26 Mei 1996* [Political Speech of the general chairman of the Indonesian Democratic Party Megawati Soekarnoputri. Closing of the twenty-third anniversary of the PDI, 26 May 1996], Jakarta: DPP/PDI.

Soekarnoputri, Megawati (1996b) 'Seruan Megawati Soekarnoputri, Jakarta 29 Juli 1996' [Press release of Megawati Soekarnoputri, Jakarta 29 July 1996], (unpublished).

Soesastro, Hadi and Chatib M. Basri (1998) 'Survey of Recent Developments', *Bulletin of Indonesian Economic Studies*, vol. 34, no. 1, pp. 3–54.

Soesilo (1998) *Monopoli Bisnis Kroni and KKN Keluarga Cendana: Asal Usul - Kiprah Akhir Kejatuhannya* [The business monopolies, cronyism, corruption, collusion and nepotism of the Cendana family: causes of its eventual and natural fall], Depok: Penerbit PERMATA – AD.

Southwood, Julie and Patrick Flanagan (1983) *Indonesia: Law, Propaganda and Terror*, London: Zed Press.

Stanley (1996) 'Alternative press challenges information blockade', *Inside Indonesia*, no. 48, pp. 17–18.

Sumardi, Sandyawan (1998) 'Rape is rape', *Inside Indonesia*, no. 56, pp. 19–20.

Suryadinata, Leo (1997a) 'Golkar of Indonesia: Recent Developments', *Contemporary Southeast Asia*, vol. 19, no. 2, pp. 190–204.

—— (1997b) *The Culture of the Chinese Minority in Indonesia*, Singapore and Kuala Lumpur: Times Books International.

—— (1998) *Interpreting Indonesian Politics*, Singapore: Times Academic Press.

Swantoro, F.S. (1997) 'The Political Dynamics in the Face of the 1998 General Assembly Session', *The Indonesian Quarterly*, vol. 25, no. 4, pp. 356–361.

Syamsuddin, M. Din (1993) 'Political Stability and Leadership Succession in Indonesia', *Contemporary Southeast Asia*, vol. 15, no. 1, pp. 12–23.

Tanter, Richard (1990) 'The Totalitarian Ambition: Intelligence Organisations in the Indonesian State', in Arief Budiman (ed.), *State and Civil Society in Indonesia*, Monash Papers on Southeast Asia; no. 22, Clayton (Victoria): Centre of Southeast Asian Studies, Monash University, pp. 213–288.

TGPF (*Tim Gabungan Pencari Fakta* [Joint Fact Finding Team]) (1998) 'Laporan Akhir Peristiwa Kerusuhan tanggal 13–15 Mei Jakarta, Solo, Palembang, Lampung, Surabaya, dan Medan' [Final report on the riots of 13–15 May in Jakarta, Solo, Palembang, Lampung, Surabaya and Medan] seri 1–6 [series 1–6], Jakarta: TGPF (unpublished).

Thee Kian Wie (1998) 'Indonesia's Economic Performance Under the New Order. The Effects of Liberalisation and Globalisation', *The Indonesian Quarterly*, vol. 26, no. 2, pp. 123–142.

Thoolen, Hans (ed.), (1987) *Indonesia and the Rule of Law. Twenty Years of 'New Order' Government*, London: Pinter.

Tim Peneliti Sistem Pemilu [Election system research team] (1998) *Sistem Pemilihan Umum di Indonesia: Sebuah Laporan Penelitian* [The general election system in Indonesia: A research report], Jakarta: Lembaga Ilmu Pengetahuan Indonesia (LIPI) and Pustaka Sinar Harapan.

Tjiptoherijanto, Prijono (1997) 'Poverty and Inequality in Indonesia at the End of the 20th Century', *The Indonesian Quarterly*, vol. 25, no. 3, pp. 251–275.

Uhlin, Anders (1997) *Indonesia and the 'Third Wave of Democratization': The Indonesian Pro-Democracy Movement in a Changing World*, Richmond (Surrey): Curzon Press.

UUD 1945. Undang-Undang Dasar Republik Indonesia Dan P.4 Pedoman Penghayatan dan Pengalaman Pancasila (n.d.) [The 1945 constitution of the Republic of Indonesia and the P 4 Guidelines for the realisation and implementation of the Pancasila], Surabaya: Penerbit Apollo.

van Bruinessen, Martin (1998) *Rakyat Kecil, Islam dan Politik* [The small people, Islam and politics], Yogyakarta: Yayasan Bentang Budaya.

van de Kok, Jean and Robert Cribb (1987) 'Survey of Political Developments', *Review of Indonesian and Malaysian Affairs*, vol. 21, no. 2, pp. 143–172.

Van Dijk, Cees (1992a) 'Verkiezingen in Indonesië: middenweg als democratie?', *Internationale spectator*, vol. 46, no. 5, pp. 246–250.

—— (1992b) 'The Indonesian General Elections 1971–92', *Indonesia Circle*, no. 58, pp. 54–63.

—— (1994) 'Recent Developments in Indonesian Politics: the Year 1993: 1998 casts its shadow', *Bijdragen tot de Taal-, Land-, en Volkenkunde*, vol. 150, afl. 2, pp. 386–413.

—— (1996) 'Recent Developments in Indonesian Politics: Ulama and Politics', *Bijdragen tot de Taal-, Land- en Volkenkunde*, vol. 152, afl. 1, pp. 109–143.

—— (1997) 'Recent Developments in Indonesian Politics: The Partai Demokrasi Indonesia', *Bijdragen tot de Taal-, Land- en Volkenkunde*, vol. 153, afl. 3, pp. 397–430.

van Klinken, Gerry (1994) 'Sukarno's daughter takes over Indonesia's Democrats', *Inside Indonesia*, no. 38, pp. 2–4.

—— (1998) 'Taking on the timber tycoons', *Inside Indonesia*, no. 53, p. 25.

Vatikiotis, Michael R.J. (1993) *Indonesian Politics under Suharto. Order, Development and Pressure for Change*, London and New York: Routledge.

Vatikiotis, Michael R.J. (1998) 'Romancing the dual function: Indonesia's Armed Forces and the fall of Soeharto', in Geoff Forrester and R.J. May (eds), *The Fall of Soeharto*, Bathurst (New South Wales): Crawford House Publishing, pp. 154-166.

Waluyo, Joko (1998) 'Smoking gun', *Inside Indonesia*, no. 53, p. 24.

Wardhana. Veven S.P. (1997) *Kemelut PDI di Layar Televisi: Survei Pemberitaan PDI di lima Stasiun TV* [The PDI crisis in television broadcast. A survey of the news about the PDI on five TV stations], Jakarta: Institut Studi Arus Informasi (ISAI).

Warr, Peter G. (1998) 'Thailand' in Ross H. McLeod and Ross Garnaut (eds), *East Asia in Crisis: From being a miracle to needing one?*, London and New York: Routledge, pp. 49–65.

Wenban, Gayle (1993) 'Golkar's election victory: neither smooth nor fair', *Inside Indonesia*, no. 37, pp. 12–14.

Wertheim, W.F. (1989) *Hebben mensen rechten in Suharto's Indonesië?*, Amsterdam: Komitee Indonesië.

Wessel, Ingrid (1996) *State and Islam in Indonesia: On the Interpretation of ICMI*, Südostasien, Working Papers; no. III, Berlin: Humboldt-Universität zu Berlin, Philosophische Fakultät III, Institut für Asien- und Afrikawissenschaften.

Wibisono, Christianto (1995) 'The Economic Role of the Indonesian Chinese', in Leo Suryadinata (ed.), *Southeast Asian Chinese and China: The Politico-Economic Dimension*, Singapore: Times Academic Press, pp. 87–99.

Winters, Jeffrey (1996) *Power in Motion: Capital Mobility and the Indonesian State*. Ithaca (New York): Cornell University Press.

Wiratma, I Made Leo and Nanda Hasibuan (1997) 'Review of Political Development: Post-Election Political Developments', *The Indonesian Quarterly*, vol. 25, no. 3, pp. 224–232.

World Bank (1997) *Indonesia Sustaining High Growth with Equity*, Washington DC: World Bank.

—— (1998) *East Asia: The Road to Recovery*, Washington DC: World Bank.

Yanuarti, Sri (1996) 'Panwaslak dan KIPP: Dilema Pengawas Pemilu di Indonesia' [Panwaslak and the Independent Election Monitoring Committee (KIPP): the dilemma of election monitoring in Indonesia], *Studia Politika*, no. 1, pp. 36–47.

YLBHI (Yayasan Lembaga Bantuan Hukum Indonesia [Indonesian Legal Aid Foundation]) (1997) *1996: Tahun Kekerasan: Potret Pelanggaran HAM di Indonesia* [1996: The year of violence: Portrait of human rights violations in Indonesia], Jakarta: YLBHI.

Young, Ken (1998) 'The crisis: contexts and prospects', in Geoff Forrester and R.J. May (eds), *The Fall of Soeharto*, Bathurst (New South Wales): Crawford House Publishing, pp. 104-129.

Zaidun, Mohamad and Aribowo (1996) 'Kasus Jawa Timur: Sebuah Potret Pemilu' [An East Java case study: a portrait of the election], in Ifdhal Kasim (ed.), *Mendemokratiskan PEMILU*, Jakarta: Lembaga Studi dan Advokasi Masyarakat (ELSAM) , pp. 113–134.

Zulkifli, Arief (1996) *PDI di Mata Golongan Menengah Indonesia* [PDI in the eyes of the Indonesian middle class], Jakarta: Grafiti.

Print Media

The Age (Melbourne, daily)
Aksi (Jakarta, weekly)
Asiaweek (Hong Kong, weekly)
The Australian (Sydney, daily)
Australian Financial Review (Canberra, daily)
Berita Kontras (Jakarta, irregular)
Bisnis Indonesia (Jakarta, daily)
Bulletin Ringkas BPS (*Biro Pusat Statistik*) (Jakarta, monthly)
Detektif & Romantika (Jakarta, weekly)
The Economist (London, weekly)
EIU (Economist Intelligence Unit) *Country Report Indonesia* (London, quarterly)
Far Eastern Economic Review (Hong Kong, weekly)
Forbes (New York, bi-weekly)
Forum Keadilan (Jakarta, bi-weekly)
Gatra (Jakarta, weekly)
IMF Survey (Washington DC, bi-weekly)
International Herald Tribune (Paris and Singapore, daily)
Jakarta Post (Jakarta, daily)
Jawa Pos (Surabaya, daily)
Kompas (Jakarta, daily)
Media Dakwah (Jakarta, monthly)
Media Indonesia (Jakarta, daily)
Merdeka (Jakarta, daily)
Mutiara (Jakarta, weekly)
Panji Masyarakat (Jakarta, weekly)
Pikiran Rakyat (Bandung, daily)
Republika (Jakarta, daily)

Sinar (Jakarta, weekly)
Solopos (Solo, daily)
South China Morning Post (Hong Kong, daily)
Suara Independen (Jakarta, monthly)
Suara Karya (Jakarta, daily)
Suara Merdeka (Semarang, daily)
Suara Pembaruan (Jakarta, daily)
Surabaya Post (Surabaya, daily)
Sydney Morning Herald (Sydney, daily)
Tajuk (Jakarta, bi-weekly)
Tapol Bulletin (London, quarterly)
Tempo (Jakarta, weekly)
Time (Asian edition) (Hong Kong, weekly)
Ummat (Jakarta, weekly)
Warta Ekonomi (Jakarta, weekly)
Weekend Australian (Sydney, weekly)
Washington Post (Washington DC, daily)

On-line media and news services

American Reporter [internet WWW page at the URL: <http://www.american-reporter.com> (version current at 9 April 1999)].

Antara [internet WWW page at the URL: <http://www.antara.co.id> (version current at 19 February 1999)].

Associated Press [internet WWW page at the URL: <http://www.ap.org> (version current at 19 February 1999)].

Digest [internet WWW page at the URL: <http://www.pactok.net.au/docs/inside/digest/digindex.htm> (version current at 19 February 1999)].

Dow Jones Newswires [internet WWW page at the URL: <http://www.dowjones.com/newswires> (version current at 5 July 1998)].

Kabar dari PIJAR [internet WWW page at the URL: <http://www.findmail.com/list/kdpnet> (version current at 19 February 1999)].

PPP Online [internet WWW page at the URL: <http://www.ppp.or.id/pemilu> (version current at 29 June 1997)].

Reuters [internet WWW page at the URL: <http://www.reuters.com> (version current at 19 February 1999)].

SiaR [internet WWW page at the URL: http://law.murdoch.edu.au/minihub/siarlist (version current at 19 January 1999]

Tempo Interaktif [internet WWW page at the URL: <http://www.tempo.co.id> (version current at 19 February 1999)].

Wall Street Journal Interactive Edition [internet WWW page at the URL: <http://www.wsj.com> (version current at 19 February 1999)].

Audio-visual Material

Kerusuhan Mei '98/Solo [The May 1998 riots in Solo] (1998) amateur video film, Jakarta: YLBHI collection (unpublished).

Index

27 July riot, 41–48, 49, 50, 61, 76, 83, 112

abductions of activists, 148, 151, 164, 165–170, 174, 229, 233
Aberson Marle Sihaloho, 29 n. 15
ABRI. *See* military
Abu Bakar, 42, 43
Aceh, 85, 234
Al-Azhar Mosque, 135–136, 199
Albright, Madeleine, 210
Ali Yafie, K. H., 203
alumni, 171
Alwi Dahlan, 173, 199
Ancol, 151
Anderson, Benedict, 32
Ansor Youth Movement, 59
Antara, 135
Ari Harjo Wibowo. *See* Ari Sigit
Ari Sigit, 10, 145
Arief, Andi, 166, 168
Arifin, K. H. R. As'ad Syamsul, 51–52
army, 2, 5, 13, 14. *see also* Kopassus; Kostrad; military
Army's Staff and Command School, 217

Army's Strategic Reserve. *See* Kostrad
Arismunandar, Wiranto, 163
ASEAN, 111, 116
Ashari, K. H. Hasyim, 56
Asiaweek, 189, 196, 213
Association of Indonesian Muslim Intellectuals. *See* ICMI
Association of Southeast Asian Nations. *See* ASEAN
Atmajaya University, 217
Australia, 137, 143, 167

Bakorstanas, 137
Bakrie, Aburizal, 136, 143
Bali, 81, 87, 171
Bambang Trihatmojo, 9, 98, 108, 144, 156
Bandar Lampung, 161, 166, 189
Bandung, 62, 70 n. 37, 158, 161, 162, 174, 199, 217
Bandung Technological Institute, 163
Banjarmasin, 83, 167, 225
Bank Central Asia, 185
Bank of Indonesia, 100–101, 107, 144–145
Bank Utama, 108
banks, 10, 44, 107–110, 117, 128, 185, 187, 192, 226

Banyumas, 92
Banyuwangi, 140
Bawazier, Faud, 156
BCA, 185
Bekasi, 185, 188
Bendungan Hilir, 184
Bengkulu, 93, 162
Bimantara group, 9
Bimo Petrus, 166
BMG, 114
Bogor, 168, 179, 181
Brimob, 179
broadcasting bill, 97–99, 102
Brunei, 113
Buddhism, 1, 12
budget, state, 100, 105, 122–123, 125, 127–128, 129, 227
Bukit Sion Church, 52
bureaucracy, 6, 8, 18, 60, 89–91
Buttu Hutapea, 94

Camdessus, Michael, 125, 126
capital flight, 102, 225
Catholicism, Catholics, 1, 12, 109, 138–139
central bank. *See* Bank of Indonesia
Centre for Strategic and International Studies. *See* CSIS
Central Java, 25, 79, 83, 87, 92, 141
Che Guevara, 39
Chinese Indonesians, 11–12, 122, 147, 155
    resentment and violence against, 12, 53, 61 109, 129, 134–143 *passim*, 152, 178, 180, 184–189 *passim*, 191, 196, 223, 227–228, 230–231, 237. *See also* ethnic conflicts; racism
Christians, 5–6, 53, 57–58,
    violence against, 52–53, 61, 66–67, 149
    see also Catholicism; churches, attacks on; Protestantism
churches, attacks on 50, 52–53, 54, 57, 62, 64, 141
CIA, 109
Cirebon, 141
Citraland shopping mall, 184
Clinton, Bill, 124, 145
cold war, 5, 14
collusion, 13, 39, 40, 81, 103 n. 15, 150, 181, 234. *See also* KKN
Commission for the Disappeared and Victims of Violence. *See* Kontras
Committee for the Supervision of Election Implementation, 93
Communication Forum of the Jakarta Student Senats, 201
Communist Party. *See* PKI
Communism, 88. *See also* PKI
conglomerates, 9, 11, 90. *See also* Bimantara group; Chinese Indonesians; Salim group
constitution, 7, 31, 34, 37, 146, 202, 213, 214
Coordinating Agency for the Maintenance of National Stability, 137
corruption, 9, 13, 39, 40, 81, 84, 102, 103 n. 15, 120,

132, 150, 181, 214, 222, 225, 234. *See also* KKN
Council of the People's Mandate, 198
crony cabinet, 154–157, 174, 228
CSIS, 109, 134–140 *passim*, 143
currency board system, 144–146, 156, 157
currency fluctuations, 99–101, 103, 104, 106, 111, 116–117, 123–124, 127, 128, 144, 180, 225–226, 227

dalang, 70
dangdut, 83
Darusman, Marzuki, 177 n. 3
Dayaks, 65–67, 223
debt, private-sector off-shore, 100, 102, 106, 117, 126, 128, 144, 145, 157, 225
democracy. *See* New Order, democracy and
Democratic People's Party. *See* PRD
demonstrations, 5, 131, 137, 140–141, 147–148, 151, 153, 200, 202, 208–209. *See also* opposition; riots; students
Denpasar, 171
Depok, 147, 158, 185
deregulation, 101, 225. *See also* structural reform
Detektif & Romantika, 51 n. 2, 137
devaluation. *See* currency fluctuations
development. *See* economic development

Dili massacre, 5, 47
Diponegoro University, 112
Donggala, 141
DPR. *See* parliament
drought, 114, 118–119. *See also* El Niño
dual function, 4, 18
dwifungsi, 4, 18

East Germany, 20
East Java, 55, 68, 86, 87–88
East Kalimantan, 114
East Nusatenggara, 141
East Timor, 84, 234. *See also* Dili massacre
economic crisis, 13, 95, 96, 99–111, 116–121, 225–226, 234
economic development, 1–2, 3, 11, 14, 81, 84, 234
economic disparity, 48, 50, 67, 68–70, 81, 84, 223
Economic and Financial Resilience Council, 126, 128
economic growth, 1, 3, 88, 99, 100, 123
economic policy, 8, 10, 110. *See also* political economy; Suharto, economic policy
The Economist, 102
education, 3, 236
Egypt, 182, 197, 198, 199, 230, 231
El Niño, 114–115, 118
elections, 6–7, 25, 75–95, 204, 224–225. *See also* Golkar; PDI; PPP
emergency powers, 103, 150, 195, 199
environment, 113–116, 120

ethnic conflicts, 50–74 *passim*, 88, 109–110, 122, 223, 236–237. *See also* Chinese Indonesians, resentment and violence against
ethnic groups, 1
EU, 167
exports, 8, 100, 117

Fadli Zon, 216
Faisol Riza, 165–166
Farid, Mahmud, 61–63
Fathia, Berar, 151
Fatimah Achmad, 36, 87
Feisal Tanjung, 20, 23, 39, 40, 45 n. 47, 68, 104, 135, 137, 148, 149, 156, 157, 180, 197, 215
FKSMJ, 201
forest fires, 113–116, 226
Forkot, 161, 200, 201, 214
Functional Groups. *See* Golkar

Gadjah Mada University, 112, 163, 166
Gajah Mada, 15
Gambir incident, 38
Gatra, 59
GDP growth. *See* economic growth
General Election Committee, 92
generation of '45, 160, 198
Genggong, 58
Germany, 111, 127
Getar, 124, 138
Ginanjar Kartasasmita, 157, 204, 211

Gini ratio, 69 n. 34. *See also* economic disparity
Giri Suseno, 211
Glodok, 189
Golkar, 6, 7, 25, 26, 92, 104, 121 127, 131–133, 156, 179, 207, 210, 221, 224, 225
  1997 election and, 38, 55, 58–59, 65, 72, 75–95 *passim*,
Golput, 85, 86
Grafiti Pers, 51 n. 2
Greater Jakarta Students Communication Forum. *See* Forkot
green dragon operation, 63–64, 71–73
Grogol, 184
Guruh Sukarnoputra, 30

Habibie, Bacharuddin Yusuf, 4, 18–21 *passim*, 56, 58, 97 n. 2, 107 n. 23, 157, 181, 182, 203, 211, 231, 233, 236
  vice-president, 127, 132, 138, 142, 147, 151, 152, 153, 227, 228
  president, 202–206 *passim*, 213–219 *passim*, 232, 235
Hamengkubuwono X, Sultan, 132, 209
Hanke, Steve, 144
Harmoko, 92, 97, 103, 132, 172, 192, 199–202 *passim*, 210, 231
  Golkar and, 26, 56, 79, 82, 88–89, 92, 104, 131, 156
Hartono, 20, 58, 63, 65, 68, 72, 73 n. 43, 90, 97, 98, 156, 157, 164, 171, 173

Harun, Lukman, 59
Hasan, Bob (Mohammad), 115, 125, 145, 155, 163
Hatta, Mohammad, 31 n. 19
high school students, 44, 173, 178, 180, 185, 191
Hinduism, 1
Human Rights, 84, 167, 170
  abuses of, 5, 60, 61, 142, 234
  see also abductions of activists; Komnas HAM
Humanika Foundation, 65
Hutomo Mandala Putra. *See* Tommy Suharto

ICMI, 18–21, 56–64 *passim*, 72–74, 113, 129, 130, 157, 181, 198–199, 202, 206, 208, 218, 224, 232, 235
Idul Fitri, 141
IKIP, 176
ILO, 117, 120
Imam Prawoto, 54
Imam Utomo, 60
IMF, 99–111 *passim*, 117, 120–127 *passim*, 132, 143–147 *passim*, 152–158 *passim*, 174, 176, 225–227 *passim*
Imron, K. H. Amin, 68
Independent Election Monitoring Committee, 86
Indonesian Academy of Sciences. *See* LIPI
Indonesian Chamber of Commerce and Industry. *See* Kadin
Indonesian Christian University, 163
Indonesian Civil Servants' Corps, 89
Indonesian Communist Party. *See* PKI
Indonesian Democratic Party. *See* PDI
Indonesian Legal Aid Foundation, 165
Indonesian People's Assembly. *See* MARI
Indonesian Committee for Solidarity with the Islamic World. *See* KISDI
Indonesian Solidarity for Amien and Mega. *See* SIAGA
Indonesian Students' Solidarity for Democracy. *See* SMID
Indonesia's Meteorological and Geophysical Agency, 114
Indosiar Visual Mandiri, 98
inequality. *See* economic disparity
inflation, 100, 117, 119, 123
International Labour Organisation, 117, 120
International Monetary Fund. *See* IMF
Internet, 160
investment, investors 10, 49, 101
IPTN, 107, 125, 127
Irama, Rhoma, 83
Irian Jaya, 119
Irwan, Alexander, 92
Islam, 1, 4, 5, 12, 18–19, 51–52, 53, 63, 77, 79, 80, 88, 109–113 *passim*, 121, 134–143 *passim*, 149, 152, 208, 216, 223, 227, 231, 237. *See also* ICMI; NU; PPP; religion
Isman, Zainuddin, 68

Jamaludin Suryohadikusumo, 115
Jakarta, 69 n. 34. 85, 86, 87, 116, 117, 124, 127, 134, 150, 158, 171, 180, 182–189
Jakarta Post, 92, 98
Jami Mosque, 62
Japan, 167
Jawa Pos, 54, 65
Jember, 140
Joint-Fact-Finding Team. *See* TGPF
Jordan, 194 n. 31

Kadin, 117, 136
Kalimantan, 113–114, 119
Kartasura, 191
kejawen. See mysticism
keterbukaan, 17, 20
Kia, 9
KIPP, 86
KISDI, 136, 137, 216
KKN, 103 n. 15, 159. *See also* corruption; collusion; nepotism
Klender, 186
KNIL, 13
Komnas HAM, 5, 36, 43, 45 n. 47, 59, 91 n. 33, 168–169, 177 n. 3, 187 n. 19. *See also* human rights
Kompas, 64
Kontras, 167, 169 n. 29, 170
Kopassus, 21, 45 n. 47, 135, 149, 169, 179, 189, 190, 192, 194, 208, 215, 217, 229, 230
Korpri, 89
Kosgoro, 198

Kostrad, 14, 21, 141, 148–149, 193, 195–196, 200, 207, 208, 214, 217, 229, 232, 233
Kragan, 141
Kristiadi, J., 138
kuningisasi, 79
Kuntoro Mangkusubroto, 211
Kwik Kian Gie, 35 n. 28, 144 n. 35

Laksono, Agung, 156, 162
Lampung, 141
land disputes, 69 n. 35
legitimacy. *See* New Order, legitimacy of
Leksono, Karlina, 209
Liem Bian Koen. *See* Wanandi, Sofyan
Liem Sioe Liong 115, 125, 145, 185, 187. *See also* Salim group
LIPI, 77, 130
logging, 114–116
Lombok, 141
Love the rupiah movement, 124, 138
LPU, 92

MacIntyre, Andrew, 13
Madura, Madurese, 51 n. 2, 53, 65–67, 84, 223
Majapahit, 15
Majid, Nurcholish, 132, 203, 205, 206, 210
Mahesa, Desmond, 148, 167
Malang, 171
malaria, 119
Malaysia, 66, 101, 113–114, 118

Marcos, 197
MAR, 198
MARI, 39–41, 76
marines, 207
Matraman, 189
Medan, 23, 39, 171, 172, 176–180, 189
media, 36, 37, 50, 80, 85, 135, 142, 159, 164, 170, 183, 212. *See also* press
Media Dakwah, 135
Mega-Bintang (Mega-star), 82
Megawati Sukarnoputri, 23–39 *passim*, 42, 48, 49, 57, 63–64, 71, 76, 77–78, 85, 86, 94, 129, 130, 131, 134, 152, 168, 169, 184, 199, 210, 221, 227
Menteng, 38
Metareum, Ismael Hasan, 68, 78, 94
middle-class, 113, 118, 170, 174, 209, 230
migrant labour, 117–118
military, 4, 6, 8, 17–26 *passim*, 35–38 *passim*, 41–42, 45, 48, 77, 90–91, 103, 104, 122, 135–143 *passim*, 148–149, 153, 205–206, 214, 218, 227, 229, 232 233, 237
  riots and, 47, 53, 58–60 *passim*, 62, 67, 68, 71–72, 74, 140, 141, 142, 175–180 *passim*, 188, 189–197, 224
  students and, 150–151, 154–174 *passim*, 182–183, 206–208, 228–229
  see also army; police
molotov cocktails, 54, 171, 186
Mossad, 109

MPR, 7, 20, 22, 30–31, 97, 103, 104, 129–130, 133, 147–151, 153, 169, 170, 181, 198, 199, 204, 210, 214, 228, 229, 231
Muchdi Purwopranjono, 193, 194, 215, 217
Mugianto, 166
Muhammad (prophet), 51
Muhammad, Mar'ie, 103 n. 15, 105 n. 20, 107–109, 126 n. 8, 144–145, 155, 226
Muhammadiyah, 73, 200, 203, 227
Munir, 167, 169 n. 29
Murdani, Benny (Leonardus Benyamin), 17, 20, 109, 134, 138, 143, 168
Murdiono, 55, 111
Murtopo, Ali, 138
Muslims. *See* Islam
mysticism, 14–15, 18, 32–34. *See also wahyu*

Nahdlatul Ulama. See NU
Nasution, Abdul Haris, 104
national car project. *See* Timor car project
National Commission for Human Rights. *See* Komnas HAM
navy, 20
nepotism, 9–10, 99, 109, 110, 120, 181, 222, 225, 234. *See also* KKN; Suharto, family's business interests
Netherlands, 168
New Order, 1–22, 26, 220, 233, 235

New Order (*continued*)
  democracy and, 33–34, 48, 94, 95, 224, 236, 237
  legitimacy of, 2, 3, 48–49, 221, 224, 234
Nezar Patria, 166
NGOs, 22, 36, 76–77, 165, 167, 177, 193, 199, 209, 220, 221–222
non-government organisations. *See* NGOs
North Sumatra, 23, 87, 141
North Sumatra University, 171
NU, 19, 37, 55–60, 63–64, 75, 76, 83, 198, 203, 206, 218, 224, 232. *See also pesantren*
Nuraiana, H. R., 63

Old Order, 27, 104
openness, 17, 20
opposition, 12, 21–22, 38–40 *passim*, 48, 76–77, 112, 133, 154, 221. *See also* students, opposition; Suharto, opposition against
Opsus, 138

Pahuaman, 67
Pakpahan, Muchtar, 39, 76
Palembang, 167, 168, 189
palm oil, 114
Pancasila, 6, 18–19, 54, 57, 77
Pancasila Youth, 179, 191, 207–208
Panwaslak, 93
parliament, 4, 6–7, 77, 97–98, 102, 103, 172, 199, 200–201, 206–217 *passim*, 229, 231
parties, political. *See* political parties
PDI, 5–6, 23–49 passim, 55, 75–95 *passim*, 132, 150, 151, 221, 224
Pemuda Pancasila. *See* Pancasila Youth
people power, 37, 48, 160, 208, 209, 217, 218
People Summit, 151
People's Consultative Assembly. *See* MPR
People's Representative Council. *See* parliament
perestrojka, 17
Permadi, 168
pesantren, 55–65 *passim*, 76, 80
Philippines, 37, 113, 197
Pius Lustrilanang, 148, 167, 229
PKI, 2, 14, 40, 41, 172, 185, 229
plantations, 113–116 *passim*
PNI, 27
police, 40, 48, 60, 64, 66, 134, 137, 168, 176, 179, 182–183, 208
  riot control, 38, 42–44, 53, 141, 142
  violence against, 44, 61–62, 177, 184–187 *passim*
political economy, 8–13, 110, 173. *See also* corruption; economic policy; nepotism; Suharto, economic policy; Suharto, family's business interests
political parties, 5–6, 24 n. 4, 221. *See also* Golkar; PDI; PKI; PNI; PPP; PRD
Pontianak, 67
poverty, 3, 117, 120, 234
PPP, 5, 55, 75–95 *passim*, 132, 150, 225

Prabowo Subianto, 21, 45 n. 47, 101, 135, 148–149, 169 n. 29, 193–196, 199, 208, 213, 214–217, 219, 229, 230, 232–233
PRD, 39, 41 n. 39, 76, 83–84, 109, 134, 148, 166, 169, 222
preman. See thugs
president, 7, 22, 29–34. *See also* Habibie; Suharto; Sukarno
press, 10, 20, 36, 51 n. 2, 54, 58, 65 n. 30, 135, 182, 200
Probosutejo, 10, 108
Protestantism, 1
provocateurs, 178–179, 185–186, 191
P. T. Timor Putra Nasional. *See* Timor car project

Ramelan, Rahardi, 157, 211
racism, 12, 50. *See also* Chinese Indonesians, resentment and violence against; ethnic conflicts
Raharja Waluya Jati, 165–166
Rais, Amien, 59, 73–74, 103, 112–113 129, 130, 131, 136 n. 24, 142, 152, 154, 160, 184, 198–210 *passim*, 227
Raja Inal Siregar, 23
Ramadan, 56, 79, 135, 141
rape, 187–188, 191–192, 196, 231
RCTI, 98
red dragon operation, 63–64, 71
religion, 1, 52. *See also* Buddhism; Catholicism; Christians; Hinduism; Islam; Protestantism

Rengasdengklok, 64
riots, 46, 47, 50–74 *passim*, 78–79, 84, 119, 139–142, 152, 175–180, 184–197, 219, 222, 223–224, 228, 230, 233, 236. *See also* 27 July riot; demonstrations; military, riots and; police, riot control; Situbondo; Tasikmalaya; violence
rupiah. *See* currency fluctuations; economic crisis
Rusdianto, 166

Saadilah Mursyid, 205, 210
Sabam Sirait, 35 n. 28
Sachs, Jeffrey, 144 n. 35
Saleh, 51–52
Salemba, 158–159, 165, 172
Salim, Emil, 132–133, 160, 184, 199, 204
Salim group, 11, 107
Sambuaga, Theo, 156
Sanggau Ledo, 50, 66
santri, 53, 63
Santri Communication Forum, 62
Sarawak, 113–114
Sarumpaet, Ratna, 130, 151
Sarwono Kusumaatmaja, 115, 116, 132, 160, 184
Sasono, Adi, 59, 64, 181, 199, 224
Satelindo, 156
Satrio Budiarjo Yodono, 97 n. 2
Sawito Kartowibowo, 31 n. 19
Schal, Abdullah, 68
Schwartz, Adam, 57
SCTV, 98

Seagrave, Sterling, 135
Semarang, 112
Sembiring Meliala, 26
Seno Bella Emyus, 46–47
Seskoad, 217
sexual assault, 187–188, 192, 196, 231. *See also* rape
SIAGA, 130–131, 148, 168
Siantan, 67
Sigit Harjoyudanto, 10
Simalungan, 179
Singapore, 113, 114
Siti Hardiyanti Rukmana. *See* Tutut
Siti Hediati Hariyadi, 10, 101, 108
Siti Hutami Endang Adiningsih, 10
Situbondo, 50, 51–60, 63, 67, 70, 72, 224
Slipi, 188
SMID, 148, 167, 169
Solo, 79, 189–193, 230
South Korea, 9, 48, 99, 111, 121
South Sulawesi, 141
South Sumatra, 88, 141
Southeast Sulawesi, 141
Special Forces Command. *See* Kopassus
special powers. *See* emergency powers
spiritual power. *See wahyu*
starvation, 119
structural reforms, 105–106, 110, 123, 125–126, 128, 145–146, 226. *See also* deregulation; economic policy; Suharto, economic policy

students, 4, 7, 39, 109
  opposition, 22, 30, 48, 121, 130, 150–153, 154, 158–165, 176, 180–184 *passim*, 190, 199–201, 204, 206–207, 209, 214–220 *passim*, 226, 228–231 *passim*. *See also* opposition; Suharto, opposition against *see also* high school students
Suara Independen, 71
Suara Pembaruan, 54
Subagyo Hadisiswoyo, 215
subsidies, 123, 125, 157, 175, 176
Sudi Silalahi, 217
Sudirman (general), 104
Sudirman, Basofi, 55, 83
Sudrajad Jiwandono, 145
Suharto, 1–4 *passim*, 13–18, 20–21, 26, 29–34 *passim*, 40, 54–58 *passim*, 71–77 *passim*, 92, 97, 103, 104, 110, 111, 115–116, 121, 136, 149, 154–155, 182, 195, 215, 220, 224, 236
  economic policy, 3, 101, 107–108, 120–121, 122–128 *passim*, 143–147, 151–152, 157–158, 226
  family's business interests, 9–10, 18, 98–99, 109–110, 145, 156, 185, 226. *See also* Bambang Trihatmojo; nepotism; Probosutejo; Siti Hediati Hariyadi; Timor car project; Tommy Suharto; Tutut
  opposition against, 75–76, 96, 110–113, 121, 129–131, 150–152, 154–174

passim, 198–201, 226, 228–229
   re-election, 29–34 *passim*, 37–38, 49, 104, 110, 121, 122, 131, 147–151, 153
   resignation, 197, 203–206, 211, 213–214, 218–219, 231–232, 235
Suherman, 62
Sujatmiko, Budiman, 39, 76
Sukarno, 2, 6 n. 6, 14, 15, 25, 27–28, 33, 82 n. 14, 168, 230
Sukmawati, 39
Sukowaluyo, 35 n. 28
Sumargono, Achmad, 136, 216
Sumatra, 101, 113, 114
Sumitro Jojohadikusumo, 132
Surabaya, 50, 63, 81, 86, 158, 161, 162, 168, 189
Surabaya Post, 54, 60
Surakarta Muhammadiyah University, 190
Suryadi, 23–28 *passim*, 36, 38–41 *passim*, 45–47, 78, 81, 86–87, 93–94, 95, 184, 221
Sutejo, 98
Sutiyoso, 38
Sutrisno, Try, 20, 132, 138, 139
Syafrie Syamsuddin, 135, 189, 193, 194, 209
Syamsuddin, Din, 59
Syarwan Hamid, 24, 45 n. 47, 136, 164, 200, 201, 202, 231
Taher, Tarmizi, 55
Tambunan, R. O., 46 n. 49
Tanah Abang, 70 n. 37, 184
Tangerang, 184, 185
Tanjung Priok, 5, 139

Tanter, Richard, 72
Tarmadi, Tayo, 62–63
Tarumanegara University, 182–183
Tasikmalaya, 50, 60–63, 67, 70, 72, 224
Tasikmalaya Islamic Young Generation, 62
Taslam, Haryanto, 151, 165, 167–168
Taufik Kiemas, 36
technocrats, 101, 110, 132, 155
Tempo, 20, 51 n. 2
TGPF, 176, 177 n. 3, 178, 185, 188–196 *passim*
Thailand, 99–100, 101, 105, 113, 128, 225
thugs, 45–46, 59–60, 178–179, 196, 207, 222
Tiananmen, 209
Tien Suharto, 12
Timor car project, 9–10, 99, 101, 106, 125, 146, 156, 172
Tirtosudiro, Achmad, 181, 199, 204
Tommy Suharto, 9–10, 125, 146. See also Timor car project
TPI, 98
Trisakti shootings, Trisakti University, 182–184, 193, 198, 230
TRuK, 187 n. 19, 188 n. 21
Tuban, 141
Tutut, 9, 20, 98, 107, 124, 144, 146, 155–156, 163, 228
   Golkar and, 58, 65, 72, 79–80, 82–83, 157, 224
TVRI, 90, 98, 199

UGM. *See* Gadjah Mada University
UI. *See* University of Indonesia
Ujung Pandang, 70 n. 37, 180
ulama, 55, 58, 204
Ummat, 112–113
UMS, 190
unemployment, 117–118, 121, 123
United Development Party. *See* PPP
United States, 14, 109, 124, 144, 167, 181, 195
universities, 77, 112, 148. *See also* students
University of Indonesia, 147, 150, 158–159, 163

Vatican, 109
vice-president, 7, 132–133. *See also* Habibie, Bacharuddin Yusuf; Sutrisno, Try
violence, 2–3, 4, 14, 16, 34, 46, 83–85, 131, 140, 161–162, 171, 181, 225, 230, 236–237. *See also* Chinese Indonesians, resentment and violence against; Christians, violence against; churches, attacks on; ethnic conflicts; riots
Voice of the Concerned Mothers, 209
Volunteers for Humanity, 187 n. 19, 188 n. 21

Wahid, Abdurrahman, 19, 57–59, 63–76 *passim*, 80, 82–83, 103, 129–131 *passim*, 199, 203–204, 206, 210, 224, 227, 232

wahyu, 15, 32, 34. *See also* mysticism
Wanandi, Sofyan, 109, 134–140 *passim*, 142, 152, 196, 227
Wanandi, Yusuf, 109, 134
Washington Post, 123
West Java, 88
West Kalimantan, 50, 65–68, 87, 114, 223
Wijoyo Nitisastro, 126 n. 8
Wiranto, 21, 148, 149, 156, 157, 162–164, 169, 170, 172, 177 n. 3, 194 n. 31, 195, 202–219 *passim*, 229, 230, 232–233
women, 7, 173, 178, 209
workers, 7, 39, 117–118, 173, 180

yayasan, 12–13
yellowisation, 79
YLBHI, 165
Yogie S. M., 23, 24, 39
Yogya Department Store, 186
Yogyakarta, 86, 112, 150, 158, 161, 162, 180, 181, 209
youth, 25, 53, 66, 83 178. *See also* high school students; Pancasila Youth; students; thugs
Yudhoyono, Susilo Bambang, 162–163, 203
Yusril Ihza Mahendra, 210
Yusuf Merukh, 28

Zaini, K. H. Achmad, 51–52, 60
Zul Effendi, 42 n. 42

The Nordic Institute of Asian Studies (NIAS) is funded by the governments of Denmark, Finland, Iceland, Norway and Sweden via the Nordic Council of Ministers, and works to encourage and support Asian studies in the Nordic countries. In so doing, NIAS has published well in excess of one hundred books in the last three decades.

Nordic Council of Ministers